W.F. VELTMAN was born 1923. He discovered anthro Nazi occupation, and late for 41 years where he taug Humanities. He was also responsible for directing many theatrical productions at the school. Mr Veltman gave many lectures in the Netherlands and abroad and published books on cultural and historical subjects including Dante, Shakespeare, Goethe and Victor Hugo and hundreds of articles in the educational magazine *Vrije Opvoedkunst* ('Free Education'). He died in 2018.

THE TEMPLE AND THE GRAIL

*The Mysteries of the Order of the Templars and
the Grail and their Significance for Our Time*

Willem Frederik Veltman

TEMPLE LODGE

Translated from Dutch by Philip Mees

Temple Lodge Publishing Ltd.
Hillside House, The Square
Forest Row, RH18 5ES

www.templelodge.com

Published in English by Temple Lodge in 2021

Originally published in Dutch under the title *Tempel en Graal, Over de mysteriën van tempelorde en graal en hun betekenis voor onze tijd* by Hesperia, Rotterdam, Netherlands, 2nd revised edition in 1992

Quotations from the New Testament were taken from *The New Testament, A Rendering by Jon Madsen*, Floris Books 1994; Old Testament quotations are from the Revised Standard Version (RSV)

A CIP catalogue record for this book is available from the British Library

ISBN 978 1 912230 76 1

Cover by Morgan Creative featuring 'The Temple of the Grail' (Pach Brothers) from *The Victrola Book of the Opera* (1917)
Typeset by Symbiosys Technologies, Vishakapatnam, India
Printed and bound by 4Edge Ltd., Essex

CONTENTS

1. Introduction

In 1928 Walter Johannes Stein published his book the English title of which is *The Ninth Century*. It has the intriguing subtitle *World History in the Light of the Holy Grail*.[1] Stein was a history and literature teacher at the first Waldorf School in Stuttgart, Germany. In his voluminous book he traces the historical background of the medieval Parsifal saga as related principally in the epic by Wolfram von Eschenbach. It leads him to surprising results to which, by the way, literary historians have so far hardly paid any attention.

A most important conclusion of this study, however, is that behind the legendary figures in the epic, real historical personages are hidden who were related to each other by blood. The era in which the 'adventures' took place was the ninth century. Unfortunately, a sequel to this book, which would have dealt with the tenth century and the founding of cities in Europe in relation to the figure of Lohengrin, Parsifal's son, never went beyond some initial studies and one article.[2]

Walter Johannes Stein died in 1957. Nine years later his masterly book was reprinted with a biographical sketch written by Herbert Hahn and a brief but most interesting article by Johannes Tautz about the author and his work. In the Prologue to his biography of Stein published in 1989, without using the words reincarnation and karma, Tautz hints at the relationship between Walter Johannes Stein and the figure of the hermit Trevrezent, brother of the unhappy Grail King Amfortas. I will come back to this point later in this book.

World History in the Light of the Holy Grail is a title that raises questions. Is it possible to write world history in the light of a legendary symbol that suddenly pops up in the medieval literature of the Christian Occident, and the origin and significance of which is already interpreted in different ways by the first Grail poets? Did Stein choose this title because he was visualizing a contemplation of history that would encompass in a wide arc the old pre-Christian cultures, the Middle Ages, and modern times, with the Grail as its *Leitmotiv*? In that case, the concept of the Grail would have to have a much richer content and farther-reaching significance for him than is usually attributed to it. Indeed, this clearly shows in his book. And when we make ourselves familiar with the greater reach of this concept which, by the way, Stein owed to his teacher Rudolf Steiner, the title he chose becomes a challenge. It is a challenge particularly for the historian who attempts to show that history is more than what is brought to light by documents, and that this 'more' is to be found in spiritual motives, the only factors that can reveal meaningful connections between documented facts. These spiritual causes are accessible as ideas to human knowledge.

On the one hand, Walter Johannes Stein's Grail book grew out of a practical situation, namely an important literary-historical course in the eleventh grade of the first Waldorf School for which, as he says in his book, he had to gather material. On the other hand, it came from an inner urge to immerse himself in this subject, an urge so strong that it bordered on a holy passion. It is indeed credible that there existed a deep personal destiny connection between Stein and the Grail theme.

Now, something remarkable occurred. Because of the personal destiny of Walter Johannes Stein the 'Parsifal block' became an essential part of the eleventh grade curriculum of all the Waldorf Schools that developed after the first one in Stuttgart. The first block of literary history that Stein gave in the first eleventh grade in 1923 became more or less a model for that block in all Waldorf High Schools in the whole world.[3] Every student experiences something exceptionally important from this material. It is undoubtedly one of the central themes of Waldorf education. You could say that the Parsifal block in the eleventh grade is a test that shows whether a Waldorf School is a real Waldorf School.

Isn't this a good example of how all historical events develop? History is no blind natural process, but neither is it a process caused by abstract ideas floating around in the air. Even if there were such things as ideas freely floating around, they would still have to be taken hold of by a human being; otherwise they remain ineffective. In most cases by far, streams in history arise because one human being has a spiritual impulse and, wrestling with it and suffering through it, makes it effective, with the result that it is then joined or taken over by others. We need only think of people like Martin Luther or, in more distant historical periods Alexander the Great and the patriarch Abraham.

Although since 1928 an impressive number of books have been published by Waldorf teachers, in my view *The Ninth Century* remains *the* quintessential book of the Waldorf School. The book is actually not at all easy to read, because of its huge chunks of study material, long quotations, contemplations that are not really worked through, and flashes of astonishing insight and genius. But whatever the shortcomings may be—and Stein himself was well aware of them—it breathes the living spirit of the Waldorf School, and by its content touches the essence of the historic stream which includes the entire work of Rudolf Steiner.

Because of this, someone who works in the Waldorf movement might well feel an obligation to continue Walter Johannes Stein's work in some way. I don't mean someone should try to write the sequel to his book but, for example, to take the challenge of its imposing title; to teach, and perhaps describe, world history 'in the light of the Holy Grail'. In the Introduction to his book Stein writes:

> All the important ideas which will be found in it emanate either directly from Dr. Steiner himself, or have been gained by further research based upon them, in harmony with his intentions. Not that the work has not been done independently. Experience has taught us that Dr. Steiner's ideas have life in them, which has not yet been exhausted in all that he was able himself to bring to fruition. The world of his ideas will never be contained in any book, for it is inexhaustible. There can be no completed work, for his Thought is *Life*, striding onward from resurrection to resurrection—a Spirit Being, showering light. We can become independent and creative when with sacred ardor we grasp the unspoken and unprinted products of Rudolf Steiner's spirit.

A courageous word that defies all criticism, in the first place from those who take exception to anything that deviates from the *fable convenue*, the conventional view of history, and further from those who view Rudolf Steiner's books as dogmatic documents and cannot accept the idea that someone can build on them with his own independent thoughts. Also important as addressed to authors who, on the one hand, derive their important ideas from Rudolf Steiner but, on the other hand, do not acknowledge this because they are afraid not to be accepted as equals by the scientific community.

In the following chapters I will, just as Stein did, make extensive use of material derived from Rudolf Steiner's spiritual research. I do not use this material as proof for any headstrong views of my own, but as fruitful points of departure, ideas that throw light on historical relationships.

This book deals with two subjects that will be brought into a mutual relationship with each other: the Grail and the Order of the Templars. The first seems to belong entirely to the realm of poetic imagination; despite the extensive historical documentation, the second also shows legendary elements, something enigmatic that fascinates and at the same time disappoints every researcher because plausible explanations of the so-called mystery of the Templars are nowhere to be found in the immense literature on the subject.

I don't pretend to come up with satisfying solutions to those riddles in this book, but I do think that, by putting the relationship between Grail and Templars in the foreground, I can bring a number of new points of view that throw light on facts that were hard to explain until now. On the one hand we shall see that the 'poetic imagination' of the Grail mystery has its origin in a concrete historical stream, albeit a hidden one; on the other hand, that the totally real history of the Knights Templar is in reality of an esoteric nature. The latter is presumed to be true by most researchers in this field, but there are many mutually contradictory views of the nature and origin of this esoteric element.

In addition, I will attempt to sketch the continuation or metamorphosis of the Grail- and Temple impulses in the further course of history to today and into the future. In this way, the content of this book is a direct continuation of my previous publication about Goethe and Europe; its subtitle is *A Contemplation on the Current World Situation*. Here also, but along completely different tracks than in the book about Goethe, I will try to approach the essence of our current world problems.

At first sight, it may seem as if the subject of the Grail and the Order of the Templars has no relationship to this. However, the view I will share here will clearly demonstrate the current relevance of this subject, as well as its relationship to *Goethe and Europe*. In the process a picture will grow of the specific function of Europe, which is to take a middle position between East and West and thus to connect these human polarities with each other. This beneficial, connecting task of the European middle, which is not yet there or is continually being thwarted, must first be taken up in human consciousness as an idea in the realm of thought.

The reader will notice that the chapters are composed in such a way that there are repetitions or overlaps here and there. Apart from the fact that in these repetitions the material always appears in a different context, because of which it gains in depth, the incredible compass and complexity of the subject make it necessary to introduce points of rest through repetition in order to facilitate the study of the work.

2. THE MYSTERIES

1. The Castle in Burgenland

A real work of art contains more truth than so-called reality. The Greek philosopher Aristotle said about drama that it shows more truth than a simple description of an historical event. For the latter only represents what happened to take place by chance in the course of time, whereas a work of art pictures the acts and statements of human beings such as they must be in accordance with inner necessity. With Aristotle's statement in mind, which is indisputably correct, may the reader permit me to take at the beginning of my contemplations a few scenes from Rudolf Steiner's second Mystery Drama *The Soul's Probation*. [4]

Three principal characters in the drama have achieved the inner maturity that permits them to be able to look back on their previous life on earth. As Steiner indicates in his introductory words about 'persons, figures and events' of the play, the pictures of this retrospect back to the fourteenth century are intended as the results of imaginative—meaning spiritual—knowledge. They do not represent actual historical events, but form an idealized portrayal of them.

Although no allusion to the Order of the Templars is made in the play, it is perfectly clear that in the Order of knights it introduces we should recognize an idealized picture of the Templars, specifically at the time of their demise. It is also known that, when he was writing these scenes, Rudolf Steiner had a particular Templars' castle in mind situated in Burgenland, the area where he had lived as a child.[5]

The retrospect to the fourteenth century, which a few persons in the drama experience inwardly, but is played on the stage as a series of dramatic scenes, takes place in the sixth, seventh, eighth and ninth scenes of *The Soul's Probation*. When we read these scenes, we may note particulars of this Order of knights, some of which sound like well-known facts from the history of the Templars, whereas others are not based on any demonstrable historical report. We can dismiss the latter to the realm of fantasy of course or, in the sense of Aristotle, we can expect to find 'more truth' precisely in those places. What are these particulars?

From the context it is clear that the knights exercise an important social influence on their environment. In scene 6 peasants speak about the 'lords of the castle' who provide them with work and bread. There is also talk about a mine that is operated by the knights; the leader of these works is in the service of the knights.[6] Their influence therefore reaches into economic life—a universally known historical fact.

Another thing that is mentioned, however, are the teachings spread by the knights, which generate strong opposition from the abbot of the neighbouring—clearly Dominican—monastery. From conversations the knights have with each other it is clear that their teachings are not about a Christendom rooted in the dogmas of the Church, but in revelations received by spiritually enlightened masters directly from the divine world. This can be called an esoteric Christianity, as distinct from the exoteric Christianity of Rome.

We are struck by two things. First, the spiritual impulse that is manifested here is completely future oriented—the knights know that their Order will be destroyed, that their Grand Master has already been put to death, and that it will be their personal destiny to perish while fighting for a good cause. They are resigned to this, albeit with difficulty for some. The second surprising element in the teachings of the knights is the manner in which they speak of the future, namely in the most concrete sense. The conviction of a personal return, in other words, reincarnation, is openly expressed:

Grand Master: Our enemies are spying out the means
By which they can take hold of our possessions.
These we've surely not acquired for profit,
But as a means to gather round us people
Into whose souls we can implant
Seeds for the future.
These seeds will ripen in their souls
When out of spirit realms they find their way
Into a later life on earth.

And a little later:

What we have planted in their souls
Indeed may for the present die.
But those who breathed our spirit light
Will come again, and then bestow
Upon the world what we intended in our work.

In the trial to which the Templars were subjected by the King of France the knights were accused of heresy. Why is there never any mention in the trial reports of any teaching of reincarnation, which certainly was considered a serious heresy by the Church of Rome? Is it because the Templars did not have ideas of reincarnation? If we would come to this conclusion, we would overlook the nature of the machinations of the French king. Even if the king had heard about such teachings, other things were much more important to him which could produce 'confessions' gained under the most hellish torture, confessions that would not be easy to recant—as the course of the trial indeed demonstrated. I will come back to this in Chapter 5. The fact that the teaching of reincarnation does not figure in the trial documents is most certainly no proof that it was not widespread among the Templars, at any rate among the initiated knights.

Another aspect of the teachings that were spread from the castle in *The Soul's Probation* might surprise us even more. In scene 9 the daughter of the mine supervisor asks her mother to tell her one of the fairytales:

> Which our dear father brings us from the knights.
> Indeed, there's surely no one
> Who does not love to hear them.

This also seems rather strange and may hardly sound credible to many people. And yet, it is not so incredible if we consider that initiated Cathars also told fairytales to the faithful. All true folk- and fairytales were originally given to the people by initiates; the same is true for the myths and sagas of all peoples. But which fairytale does the mother tell her daughter? The history of good and evil.

Dame Kean: Once upon a time there lived a man
Who pondered much about the world.
His brain was tortured most of all
By his desire to know the origin of evil;
But he could give himself on this no answer.
'The whole world comes from God,' so argued he,
'And God can only have the good within Himself.
Then how do evil men come from the good?'
Time and again he pondered, all in vain.
The answer could not be discovered.
One day it came to pass, this gloomy thinker
Upon his way beheld a tree,
Which was in conversation with an axe.
And mark! The axe was saying to the tree:
'What is impossible for you to do, that I can do.

> I can fell you; but not you me.'
> The tree then gave this answer to the haughty axe:
> 'A year ago a man cut out the wood
> From which he made your handle
> Out of my body, with another axe.'
> And when the man had heard this speech
> A thought arose within his soul
> He could not clearly put in words.
> It gave, however, answer to his question
> How evil can derive from good.

It is obvious that Steiner did not just by chance put this fairytale about the origin of evil in the mouth of a woman who had received it as teaching from the castle of the knights. In a poetic form, he gives a clear answer to a question that has occupied many authors about the Templars, namely whether the 'hidden' aspects of the Order were related to Manichaeism.[7]

The fairytale contains in the form of a simple picture the fundamental idea of Manichaeism, which differs from the way it is usually represented. Mani's teaching is often described as an absolute dualism. Good and evil are principles that are in all eternity present in the world as irreconcilable opposites; evil has no beginning and no end. This view, however, was brought into the world by the opponents of Manichaeism and in no way reflects the original teaching of Mani. The creation myth of Manichaeism contains the following (very briefly rendered):

> The spirits of darkness wanted to take the light realm by storm. They came to the border of the divine realm and wanted to conquer it. However, they were unable to do this. The gods of the light realm now wanted to punish the demons of the darkness, but they found in their realm only the good, the beneficial. They then took a part of the light realm and mingled it into the material realm of the darkness. This brought the latter into a crisis, a kind of fermentation process, a chaotically whirling movement from which something new arose, namely self-destruction and death.
>
> In a process of gigantic conflict and creation the human race then came into being. The primeval human being was sent out of the light realm into the darkness, in order that by vanquishing death in the realm of the darkness evil may be overcome.

The core of this myth is most characteristic. The realm of the darkness is not punished; it is not overpowered by force, but by mildness, by love. Because the light realm offers its most noble being, which mingles with the darkness, evil can be redeemed in the future.

What is the fundamental idea underlying this view of evil? None other than what was said in the fairytale. Good and evil are originally indistinguishable; the wood of the axe was, at first, part of the body of the tree. In this sense, good and evil are both present in all eternity! But when out of original good something separates itself, or is deliberately taken out, initially perhaps to fulfil a good purpose, at that point evil can also come into existence, when the good function is applied to a bad purpose. If the extremely useful instrument of the axe were out of vanity to assume an activity of its own that goes against the appropriate order of things, this same excellent instrument would then become malignant.

Manichaeism, which had spread far into East Asia, and also into the regions where Christianity was spreading, was fought tooth and nail by the Roman Catholic Church, notably by Church Father Augustine who, before he converted to Christianity, was a follower of Mani for nine years. Just like so many opponents, both past and present, they fight against views they themselves, out of a lack of understanding, put into the statements they dispute, although these views are often the exact opposite of what was meant by those statements.

The same happened here. The fiercely denounced dualism of Mani's teaching is in reality something entirely different. When we study the Manichaean texts we find nowhere that the realm of darkness is considered equal to the divine light realm. It is a realm of counter-images, in which the principle of resistance is working. By viewing the element of evil as a principle of resistance it is possible to recognize good and evil as belonging together in the plan of creation. In this sense, Goethe's *Faust* is permeated by the Manichaean principle.

Out of this insight, human beings, in lieu of wanting to escape from evil, may want to undergo evil as a test of their capacity to resist. When we then succeed in not losing the inner power of light—which in reality is Christ—and when we practise purity and mildness as we undergo evil, we help make it possible that some time in the future the realm of counter-images may return to the light realm. In other words, we contribute to the redemption of evil.

It is this Manichaean disposition that strikes us and deeply moves us in many of the historical descriptions of the downfall of the Templars. This disposition enabled these men, who had fought the Muslims like lions to defend the Holy Land, to completely subject themselves to the power of evil that had turned against their own lives. Nowhere do we find a curse or a counter-accusation of their persecutors.

Rudolf Steiner's 'Templar scenes' show us an ideal picture of this. The words of the Grand Master at the beginning of scene 7 emanate this superhuman mildness and resignation, which are not based on weakness but on strength. The fact that the knights themselves continually have to wrestle inwardly to understand this and act accordingly is demonstrated in the dialogue between the first and second masters of ceremony (scene 8).

There are two additional particulars I want to mention, which agree more with known historical facts than the ones discussed above. With some emphasis the tolerance of the knights is sketched regarding the Jew Simon, who practises his exceptional medical knowledge in the area around the castle but, because of that, also has the reputation with some peasants of being an evil wizard.

The 'idealized picture' of such life circumstances points in this case to the well-known fact that even though the Templars were the most fervent defenders of Christendom, yet they were tolerant of faithful Muslims and Jews. From their own esoteric knowledge they knew that the Semitic peoples of the Near East—and the Jews living in the Diaspora may be included in this—often possessed profound spiritual wisdom and practical knowledge of nature, which was still completely lacking in the peoples of Europe at the time.

The second point also indicates known facts. In several places in the extensive literature about the Order it is reported that the Templars did not hesitate to accept someone into their midst who, by the standards of the world, bore some serious guilt. In the Order here described this is also the case. It comes up in scene 7 when the first master of ceremonies asks:

Master of Ceremonies.:	Then does our Order tolerate within itself
	Men also, lacking purity of soul,
	Who consecrate themselves to its high goals?
Grand Master:	The one who works devotedly for lofty aims,
	He weighs the good alone in souls of men
	And he allows the bad to find atonement
	Within the course of cosmic justice.

Here again we have a statement of the Grand Master of a notably future character.

In the Middle Ages, people's sense of justice was still completely based on the principle of an eye for an eye and a tooth for a tooth. In our time this has still not changed all that much. The Christian sense of justice of the future lies in the Bible passage of the adulterous woman. Christ does not deny Moses' law of old that condemned the woman to be stoned, but he first draws the accusers' attention to their own sinfulness. When these withdraw in shame, he writes in the sand, which means that the injustice committed by the woman needs to be compensated by the justice of the world. In other words, the earth preserves the guilt of the woman until she can set it right in a subsequent life by her karma, her destiny. But Jesus makes an appeal to her free I-being; He says: 'I do not condemn you either. Go, and from now on do not sin anymore.' (John.8:11)

This is also the basis of the words of the Grand Master; they are only understandable in the light of reincarnation and karma. These two concepts will in the future be viewed as central concepts of Christianity, even if many people today have doubts about it and disagree with it.

When we now review the thoughts I have expressed on the scenes from *The Soul's Probation*, we come to the following provisional conclusion. Let us assume that Rudolf Steiner's picture of the Order of Knights from the beginning of the fourteenth century represents an idealized picture of the Order of the Templars, and that, true enough, in this representation no historical situation is expressed, but rather something that is spiritually true. On that basis we would have to recognize as a most characteristic feature of the Templars an initiation impulse that points to a future Christian culture. This impulse encompasses unmistakable Manichaean elements of our relationship to evil.

In Chapter 5 we will try to present many facts so that this conclusion will be fully supported. But first we have to go more deeply into subjects that were here only mentioned in passing. We have to gain an impression of what is to be understood by the term initiation impulse.

2. The Pre-Christian Mysteries

An unprejudiced contemplation of the great cultures of the pre-Christian past may suggest the idea to us that there have been essential streams in humanity that converged upon the central event when the Turning Point in Time becomes visible in the Mystery of Golgotha. From there, clearly visible as well as hidden streams of development move on toward the future.

Doesn't it look as if Christianity came to renew all the old? Doesn't it work in the evolution of the earth and humanity like the all-renewing, alchemical process that St. John called the Apocalypse, the Revelation— the revelation of the Christ Being Himself? Christianity is not so much a teaching or a religion; it is the living reality of an all-encompassing, all-permeating Being.

In His physical appearance Jesus Christ worked on earth during the Greco-Roman cultural epoch.[8] The cultures that are to be considered as the most important ones in the preparation for Christ's appearance developed in India, Iran, Egypt and Mesopotamia. Anthroposophy speaks in this connection of the first three post-Atlantean cultures. This means a prehistoric primeval culture in India from which the later Hindu culture arose, a very old Iranian (Persian) culture which, just like the Indian, did not leave any records until much later, and finally the known old cultures of the Nile and Mesopotamia.

Each of these cultures embraces periods of growth, flourishing, and decline totalling somewhat over 2000 years. They succeed each other, beginning with ancient India, after the enormous changes in the surface of the earth known to geology as floods, ice ages, land sinking in the sea, and other such catastrophes. What existed previous to this time has the name of Atlantis in occult science.

At the time of Atlantis the earth, which then looked very different from today, was also inhabited. Then too there were human cultures, and these were guided from initiation centres, mystery places or oracles. In these mystery places it was possible for individuals, who by their birth and disposition were found suited to it, to receive what is called an initiation. This meant not only that wisdom from time immemorial was entrusted to them, but also that they learned to behold spiritual worlds directly that for other people of those ancient times were accessible only to a minor extent. Later these worlds became completely closed to ordinary observation. These individuals learned to communicate with higher beings, gods.

Such initiations demanded much from the ones who underwent them, in the form of great physical deprivation and the most intense trials of the soul. No one was permitted to cross the boundaries of spirit land without purification or if afflicted with selfishness. And they were required to preserve total secrecy regarding the mysteries so that the enormous power that the mysteries conveyed to a person would not come into the hands of unpurified, therefore unworthy people.

The initiates were the kings and priests of their peoples. They were the ones who issued directives in all areas of social life according to which people had to live and work. This was the case not only in religion, art, medicine and law, but they similarly regulated agriculture and cattle breeding, yes, originally even human procreation was regulated by initiated leaders.

Such leaders were viewed and revered as gods or demigods by the people, and in the far distant past it indeed happened that higher beings incorporated themselves into such initiates. Indian tradition speaks in this regard of an avatar, which is something different from an incarnated being. In an incarnation a spiritual being descends all the way down into the material substance of a human body; in the case of an avatar there is a partial penetration. For example, divine Krishna was an avatar of Vishnu, not an incarnation.

The mysteries continued to exist in post-Atlantean cultures, and in a number of initiation centres the candidates learned the secret that the highest Creator Being, the Sun Spirit or Logos, the World Word, would one day descend to the earth and become flesh in a human figure.

There were great differences, as well as unmistakable similarities, among the various pre-Christian mysteries. This diversity is connected with the differences among peoples and cultures, and therefore with the special task each people had to fulfil in the whole of human development.

However, if one studies similar characteristics in the various mystery forms and contents, one will find two clearly different types, each of which is connected with a particular group of people who left Atlantis, which was situated between the present continents of Africa, Europe and America, when it went under, and moved eastward. One group moved along a northern path, the other along a southern path.[9] For both groups the point of departure was current Ireland, the most eastern part of the old Atlantean continent, the part that did not sink into the ocean.

The Old Testament reflects this, but does not speak of two streams; rather it shows three streams represented by the sons of Noah: Shem, Ham and Japheth. The Japhetic or Indo-European race went the northern way across Scandinavia and northern Russia into the heart of Asia. Later this movement reversed itself and in successive migrations the Indo-European tribes travelled back to Europe, where some tribes had already remained behind on their way East. The Hamites went the southern way through southern France, Spain, North Africa, Egypt and Arabia. The Semites took a middle way that in a certain sense may be included in the southern way. Both streams met in India where the first of the post-Atlantean cultures arose.

It is self-evident that such movements of peoples across the surface of the earth were led by initiates. The biblical names from Seth to Noah indicate the great initiates of the Atlantean era; the sons of Noah are the leaders or patriarchs of post-Atlantean cultures. In the figure of Noah worked the great initiate of the central mysteries of Atlantis, the sun mysteries. In India he was called Manu. He prepared the post-Atlantean era. All pre-Christian cultures that converged on the Mystery of

Golgotha were, in a certain sense, inspired by Manu. We can find extensive descriptions of this in Steiner's work.[10]

It can be clearly observed from the religions of the above-mentioned peoples what the different characteristics of their mysteries were, for the religions of the people were no other than popularized mystery content. In the initiates this lived as knowledge gained from actual beholding, while in the people it lived as a religious sense.

The northern mysteries brought the initiation candidate to the divine in nature, in stars and planets—it was the macrocosmic path. The southern mysteries led the candidate into the divine realm along the inward path—the microcosmic or mystical path. This latter path is often depicted as a descent into the underworld; we see such pictures in fairytales. The idea here is a mystical sinking down into one's own being in order to penetrate to the divine creative powers 'behind one's own soul'. By contrast, the macrocosmic way aimed to lead the candidate through the veil of the sensory world.

The inward path is most clearly demonstrated by the Egyptian mysteries; through the Isis initiation one reached Osiris inwardly as the Sun at midnight. The great initiate of the northern stream, Zarathustra, pointed his disciples to the Sun Spirit outside in the cosmos.

Given that both streams came from the same place, and met again in the distant eastern land of India, one might expect that at the beginning there was a certain unity and at the point of meeting again a confluence of the two paths of initiation. That was indeed the case. Yoga, the mystery path of the ancient Arian Indians, recognizes the outer-inner of the divine world as a unity.

In the West the unity is more difficult to find, because the mysteries remained more deeply hidden there than in the Asian world. Rudolf Steiner's spiritual research, however, gives us penetrating descriptions of the very secret Hibernian (Irish) mysteries that went back to Atlantean times and were still working in the world into the first centuries after Christ.[11] Although we find here the duality of a masculine Sun principle and a feminine Moon principle in the form of two mysterious statues in the hidden temple, in the experiences of the candidate for initiation this duality grew into a higher unity. In addition, the coming Christ was pointed out who bears the higher unity of the divine spirit being in Himself.

The duality of the northern and southern mystery paths is very clearly present in the Greeks. The two paths are represented there by Apollo and Dionysus, respectively. Apollo, the bright sun god of the super-earthly spheres was viewed as the god of the North. According to tradition, in winter time he dwelt with his beloved northern people, the

Hyperboreans, who are sometimes identified with the Celts. Dionysus, the god whose true being one had to seek among the frightful chthonic gods of the underworld, was at the same time the hero who lived on earth in a far distant past and made a journey South to India, accompanied by his throng of bacchants, satyrs.

It is not difficult to recognize a correspondence with the Manu-Noah stream, the more so as it is said of both Dionysus and Noah that they planted the vine. And yet, we should be very careful with such similarities. Similar does not at all mean identical. The migration of the southern Manu stream took place thousands of years before Dionysus' journey which, according to the researchers who are willing to accept that this myth has a historical core, should be dated around 1400 BC. Another thousand years later Alexander the Great undertook the same expedition to the East, inspired by the divine hero from mythical history.

In the middle between Ireland in the West and India in the East, in ancient Greece, the northern and southern streams also connected with each other. Orpheus, son of Apollo, renewed the Dionysian mysteries of Eleusis, thus forging a unity out of duality. For the highest initiates of Greece the god of light Apollo and the mystical god Dionysus were two aspects of the same divine spirit. They knew that the macrocosmic and microcosmic paths came together in a higher degree of initiation.

We need not be surprised by the fact that in early Christian times the Christ was still viewed in direct relationship with Apollo-Orpheus as well as with Dionysus. Pictures in the catacombs show Christ as Orpheus or as the Good Shepherd with the lamb, just as Apollo was pictured with the bull calf on his shoulders. It is known that the Dionysian mystery cult formed the basis for the Christian ritual.[12] For the Greek initiate who, not coincidentally, had the name Dionysius, St. Paul's speech on the Areopagus in Athens (Acts 17) opened the door to the Christ mystery, because the 'Dionysian' character of the 'Unknown God' was recognizable for a person like him.

Many more pages could be written about characteristics of the pre-Christian mysteries, but to avoid making the picture too confusing, we have to limit ourselves. However, the following is of great importance. The crucial aspect of every form of initiation was the fact that the one who underwent it, had to go through experiences during life already, that corresponded with dying and dwelling in the world of the dead. Both of the paths that led a person above the normal sphere of consciousness had something sinister. Torments like intense fear, agony of soul had to be lived through. When ancient tales tell of superhuman courage of heroes it always indicates strength born from initiation.

Dionysus, head on coin (drachma) c. 520 BC.

In the end, the candidate for initiation could acquire his 'divinity' only outside his body which, through the observations of his senses, also bestowed on him his earthly I-awareness. However, this earthly aspect had to be completely sacrificed so as to be able to become part of the realm of the gods. For this reason, in many places the initiation was sealed by a procedure that put the candidate into a condition that corresponded with having died. But death did not fully occur.

The leading priest or hierophant artificially brought the candidate into a kind of death-like condition in which he remained for three and a half days, enclosed in a kind of sarcophagus or chamber that was used for such initiations in temples. During this time, not only was the spiritual-psychic being of the candidate outside his body, also the life- or etheric body, the body that contains the life forces, was partly loosened from the material physical body. In this condition the person, who had been trained for this during the period of preparation, retained full consciousness, which means that he did not forget the experiences he went through outside his body.

The supersensible organs through which the spiritual realm could be perceived were 'imprinted' onto the etheric body, and the result was a permanent clairvoyance that enabled the initiate to obtain experiences on a higher level of consciousness also after his return to the physical body. His 'raising from death' was at the same time the birth of his higher being. Henceforth he went through life as one reborn, and usually also received a new name.

The advent of Christ on earth radically changed all this. The Gospels leave no doubt in this regard. The Kingdom of Heaven comes to humanity; the connection with the divine realm need no longer take place outside the body with total sacrifice of the earthly I-consciousness, but can henceforth be realized within the normal earthly situation. For this reason the Christ Being fulfils the initiation first of all on Himself, in Jesus of Nazareth, before the physical eyes of human beings.

What used to take place in symbolic-cultic form in the secrecy of temples and oracles, and was shown to the people in ritual acts on specific occasions—such as the death and resurrection symbolism of the Adonis festivals—this now occurred not symbolically but in actual fact: the preparation, death, burial, and resurrection. Deeds of the highest spiritual significance, therefore, were enacted in the open.

Apollo, head on coin (four drachmas) c. 415 BC.

When it is said in the Gospels: 'And see, the curtain in the temple was torn in two, from top to bottom' (Mt.27:51; Mk.15:38; Lk.23:45), this is at the same time a real fact and a spiritual-symbolic event. When the curtain is torn, the Holy of Holies becomes visible to everyone. Christ comes to fulfil and complete the holy mysteries. Through Him they become public. Ever since His coming human beings can gain access to the divine realm through Him, without the old initiation procedure. Because of His sacrifice, anyone who believes in Him has part in the divine realm.

The fact that believing, faith, in the Pauline-Christian sense, is not an essential opposite of knowing, cannot be discussed here. But a question does arise in this connection that needs to have our attention in the next section.

3. The Christian Mysteries

If the mysteries were fulfilled by Christianity, why did secret paths of initiation continue to exist after Golgotha? Why did a hidden, esoteric form of Christianity arise side by side with the Christianity of the Church?

The deed of Christ brought about a new world evolution for all of humanity, irrespective of the fact that this deed could not right away be taken in by the consciousness of humanity as a whole. Also in Palestine, even among those who believed in Him as the Messiah, there were big differences in degrees of spiritual maturity. Among the twelve disciples there were advanced and less advanced individuals, if I may use this trivial expression. Understandably, the various degrees of spiritual development expressed themselves also in degrees of comprehension.

The fact that Jesus Christ appeared as a brother of humanity, as a friend of sinners and tax collectors, as a teacher of the people to whom he proclaimed the coming of the Kingdom of God in parables, does not obviate the fact that he also came as the highest divine-human hierophant of a renewed mystery. It is also evident that he let those who were ripe for it be the first to undergo a Christian initiation. But he did this by following the form of the previous initiations. In this sense Rudolf Steiner describes the raising of Lazarus as an old initiation procedure which, however, was performed before the uninitiated eyes of the bystanders.[13] Jesus expressed with this that the old temple secret had to come into the open.

Lazarus was the 'disciple whom Jesus loved', and who after his initiation received the name John. The indication 'whom He (Jesus) loved' means in connection with the mysteries: the one who is most mature, the one who may receive the deepest secrets. It is therefore understandable that in Christian times the figure of John with his Gospel and Revelation became the origin of an esoteric stream. Those who in the Middle Ages sought the true, inner Christianity called themselves Johannine Christians.

In lectures Rudolf Steiner gave in Paris in 1906, he mentioned brotherhoods that considered themselves as Johannine Christians, specifically the Brothers of St. John, the Albigenses, the Cathars, Templars and Rosicrucians. He said of these groups:

> All engaged in practical esotericism and looked to this Gospel as to their Bible. It may be said in a sense that the legend of the Grail, Parsifal, and Lohengrin emanated from these brotherhoods, and that it was the popular expression of the secret doctrines.[14]

The seven steps on the way of the Johannine-Christian path of initiation were no other than the seven stages described in the Gospel of St. John: the washing of the feet, the scourging, the crowning with thorns, the carrying of the cross, the mystical death, the laying in the grave, and the resurrection.[15] The candidate for the Johannine initiation had to withdraw entirely from social life. For long periods of time he had to completely dedicate himself to meditation on the images evoked by the seven steps. On this path, which was based on the feeling life, the Christian initiates were able to achieve union with the being of Christ, with the result that they also received revelations of the deepest secrets of the human being, the earth and the cosmos.

In pre-Christian initiations, the candidate had to completely surrender himself to the leader of the mystery temple. The Johannine candidate, however, found his initiator in Christ Himself. The Christian initiation did take place 'far from the world', but was no longer bound to a specific temple or oracle, just as the Christ being is not bound to any particular place. As preparation for the actual stages of initiation the candidate immersed himself meditatively in the Gospel of St. John. Its beginning verses (1-14) were of special importance; they emanated, and continue to emanate, the greatest spiritual power.

With these beginning verses St. John placed his initiation book in the tradition of the Logos mysteries (mysteries of the Word) that had their principal centre in the Temple of Artemis in Ephesus, and which led in a more worldly sense in the philosophy of Heraclitus, the Stoa and other, both Jewish and Christian schools of thought to the so-called Logos doctrine. The Egyptian mysteries of Osiris and Isis were also Word mysteries in which the initiate penetrated to the source of creation of the world. With the crucial phrase: 'And the Word became flesh...,' John said nothing less than that the Creator Being Himself, the highest being to which initiation could lead, indeed incarnated in Jesus of Nazareth. In the first fourteen verses of his Gospel, therefore, he not only points to the primeval wisdom of Asia, Egypt, and Greece, but he states its fulfilment: God has truly become a human being.

In connection with our subject we want to bring forward two additional elements from the Gospel of St. John that belong to the essence of the Christian initiation. Both are connected with well-known, but often insufficiently understood moments in the passion scenes of Golgotha. Jesus spoke from the cross to His mother and to 'the disciple whom he loved': 'Woman, see that is your son' and to the disciple: 'See, that is your mother.' And the Gospel says then: 'And from that hour the disciple took her to himself.' (John.19:27)[16]

John took the mother of Jesus into his own being. What does this mean, and why does he not (and never) use the name Mary? By using the description 'mother of Jesus' he veils the secret that was still known in Christian Gnosis and, more generally, in the first beginnings of Christianity, that the *mater dolorosa* who stood under the cross of Golgotha bore in her being the maidenly, cosmic soul force that was called Sophia, wisdom. Mary is her exoteric, Sophia her esoteric name. John has to take this Sophia being, the purified astral body, to himself. It means that Christ gave him the task to show people the way to the purified, undefiled soul forces. What in the pre-Christian mysteries was called catharsis, purification, is for a Christian the path to the Virgin Sophia. A person who strove to strip his lower soul parts of earthly contamination, who transformed his soul into a pure Virgin, could receive the spirit principle that was called the Holy Spirit into himself, which could fructify him and awaken him to eternal life.

The worship of Mary, which played such an important role in the Middle Ages, originates in the Christian initiation and still had this esoteric significance for the knights of the Order of the Templars.

John was the only disciple from the intimate circle of twelve around Jesus who witnessed the crucifixion. He is also the only evangelist who reports that a Roman soldier drove his lance into the right side of Jesus, which caused blood and water to flow out of the body. Everything that in later Grail legends relates to the mystery of the blood and the lance has been derived from this place in the Gospel of St. John. This shows us that the esotericism of the Grail is part of the essence of Johannine

Christianity. Although legends that arose later made a connection between the Grail tradition and Joseph of Arimathea and not with John, which might create the impression of two separate esoteric streams in Christianity, it is in my view more correct to put the emphasis more on unity than on diversity. The same is true for those aspects of Christian esotericism that are related to the apostle Paul, the Gnostics, and Mani.

The advent of Christ on earth brings a new initiation stream, originating from Him and flowing into Him. He is the summation and the goal of all spiritual striving. This is why, in its essence, esoteric Christianity can only be one and undivided. But when Christ is the fulfilment of the old initiations, these have to be taken up and made part of the new stream. The pre-Christian mystery cultures disappear, but their essence has to be rejuvenated and resurrected, in a certain sense, in the light of the new Mystery.

For this reason, there is also diversity in Christian esotericism. There are different persons, mighty individualities—one may call them teachers of humanity—who have the task to lead the old over to the new. We can see how the apostles, or persons who were directly connected with their circle, went to the places where the old mysteries had flourished; John went to Ephesus, Paul and Dionysius the Areopagite together founded an esoteric school in Athens close to the old mystery centre of Eleusis; Joseph of Arimathea went West and brought esoteric Christianity to the Celtic mystery culture.

Even the fact that Peter went to Rome is related to a mystery. For many centuries the Palladium, a small statue of Pallas Athena, which at one time had been the spiritual centre of Troy, had lain buried under the Vesta Temple in the heart of the city of Rome. This statue was connected with the mystery of the sun. The Christian initiates knew that Rome was a central place of the hidden sun symbol.[17] Constantine the Great also knew about the spiritual power of the Palladium, for when he moved the capital of the Roman Empire to Byzantium, he secretly took the Palladium with him from Rome and had it buried again in Byzantium, which he renamed Constantinopolis.

Until the fourth century Christianity was still able to find connections with the old mysteries. We have mentioned already that the Mass was a metamorphosis of an old, pre-Christian mystery ritual.

In Alexandria (Egypt) and Antioch (Syria), centres of Hellenistic culture, lived the great teachers of earliest Christianity: Origen, Clement, Lucian, and Arius, who connected their teachings, directly or indirectly via the philosophies of Plato and Aristotle, with the old mysteries.

All of Christian Gnosis, with its sometimes dubious but always grandiose conceptions about the human being and the cosmos, was really nothing other than dying mystery knowledge that needed to be renewed and rejuvenated. There was therefore great diversity, but these thinkers were looking for the reality of Christ, the unity in this diversity.

We see how the following happens. The old mysteries die off; after the fourth century they have definitively disappeared. The once flourishing sanctuaries of Eleusis, Ephesus and Samothrace lapse into oblivion. Concurrently, out of the Christian Church in Rome comes a distinct tendency to destroy all mystery tradition and all connection with ancient wisdom.[18] Enmity reigns against all esotericism, and it has persisted down to our time, not only in the Church, but especially in science and public opinion.

St. Augustine, the greatest Church Father of the West, stands in the foreground as the declared enemy of Manichaeism, the most important esoteric stream in Gnosticism. Origen and Clement of Alexandria are declared heretics by Roman Christianity, and so is Arius. The East-Roman Emperor Justinian does build a church dedicated to Holy Sophia, but closes the academies in his realm where the old wisdom was taught.[19]

Also western and central Europe where Irish Christianity, which was still deeply connected with the old Celtic and Germanic mysteries, continued to have much influence until the sixth and seventh centuries, were gradually Romanized. The old mystery element was destroyed or was assimilated, which entailed externalization and thereby a weakening, and eventual replacement by dogmas. The last little remnant of spiritual wisdom became, to put it abstractly, mandatory faith.

From the fourth century on, souls seeking spiritual depth no longer found fulfilment in Roman Christianity with its legal and power orientation. The so-called apostate Emperor Julian was deeply disappointed when his Christian priests could not give him answers to his questions about the sun secret of Christ. Esotericism had to be practised more and more in secret. Thus it became a virtually unknown chapter in the history of Europe—unknown and hidden, but of the greatest importance for the development of European culture.

A characteristic of this esoteric Christianity is certainly that it appears at certain times and disappears again, then emerges in a new form in order seemingly to perish again.

4. Spiritual Guidance

It is not really possible to approach the enigmas of Temple and Grail without considering the hidden aspects of human development. In spiritual science as developed in the beginning of the twentieth century under the name Anthroposophy by Rudolf Steiner, we find a treasure of material about the spiritual guidance of humanity, which in earlier times was known only in esoteric brotherhoods. Rudolf Steiner brought part of this 'secret science' into the open on his own responsibility. He did this out of his insight that it is necessary at the present time; he could and was permitted to do this because he had not learned the 'secret knowing' from others, but had penetrated it on his own. The fact that this opening of occult knowledge to public access often evokes misunderstanding and even malicious attacks is evident.

Rudolf Steiner entrusted the most esoteric contents to the limited circle of the members of the Anthroposophical Society. The lecture cycles for the members, however, did also end up in the hands of opponents who, partly out of a lack of understanding, partly out of maliciousness, mocked them or fiercely contested this esotericism. To face this, complete openness was called for. Therefore, since the refounding of the Anthroposophical Society in 1923 all the printed lectures, also those which had been restricted to members, have been available to anyone. In my opinion, this is desirable despite continued misunderstandings and enmity, because there is today a superabundance of dubious occultism on the market, which causes serious confusion and distortions of the truth. It is therefore more than ever necessary to make the results of exact clairvoyance, as brought by Rudolf Steiner, better known.

If we may view the raising of Lazarus as an initiation performed by Christ Himself on the disciple He loved, how do we then consider the other instances of raising from death reported by the evangelists: the daughter of Jairus (Mt.9; Mk.5; Lk.8) and the youth of Nain (Lk.7)? Were these also initiations and did esoteric streams originate from them as was the case with Lazarus-John? Rudolf Steiner throws some light on this question in his lectures on the Gospel of St. Luke,[20] but especially in extremely interesting statements in a lecture of which, however, only notes exist that, as far as I know, have never been published. Emil Bock mentions these things in his book *The Three Years* but without giving any details.[21]

Rudolf Steiner first mentions the Three Wise Men from the East who went to Bethlehem to honour the Jesus child. He calls them representatives of the three pre-Christian post-Atlantean cultural epochs, the old Indian, Persian, and Egyptian/Chaldean epochs. The gifts they bring to the child are symbols of the spiritual fruits of these cultures. Then he says that for the future Christ had to raise three individualities from death who also represent these three cultural epochs, but they have to make the Christianized wisdom gifts of those epochs fruitful for later times. Their future working mirrors that of the past. The first post-Atlantean cultural epoch is reflected in the seventh, the second in the sixth, and the third in the fifth, our time.

In the daughter of Jairus, the leader of the synagogue of Capernaum, a representative of the old Indian culture comes to life again. It is clearly a mystery act that was performed there, for only the three most mature disciples were present, Peter, John and James, the same ones who later were present at the Transfiguration on Mount Tabor. They were told to keep silence about the event in Jairus' house. About the individuality of the twelve-year-old girl we know nothing; Rudolf Steiner does not divulge anything about her. He does point to the karmic connection between the woman who had suffered from an issue of blood for twelve years and the daughter of Jairus. The three disciples received a teaching in karma in a certain sense. According to a legendary tradition contained in countless apocryphal documents that date back to the time of the events in Palestine, the woman who is healed of her bleeding is none other than Veronica who later, when Jesus is bearing the cross, wipes the sweat off Jesus' face with a cloth. In the 'Veil of Veronica' an image of the face of Christ remains visible.

The raising of Lazarus was related to the second, the old Iranian, cultural epoch. The great teacher of this epoch was Zarathustra. His individuality reincarnated in the Jesus boy in the royal lineage from David. At the beginning of our age two descendants of David were born.[22] The one child was descended in the royal line from Solomon. He was the one described by Matthew, and to him came the Wise Men from the East with their gifts. This child was taken to Egypt by his parents when they heard that Herod wanted to kill him. His genealogy forms the beginning of the first chapter of Matthew's Gospel. The parents, who were both descendants of David, were called Joseph and Mary by the evangelist. This royal mother of Jesus was the later *mater dolorosa*.

Some months after the events described by Matthew, another couple, also called Joseph and Mary, and likewise descendants of David but through his other son Nathan, travelled from Galilee to Bethlehem for the great census ordered by emperor Augustus for his whole empire.

In Bethlehem the 'Nathan Jesus child' was born who was described by Luke. In him no great teacher of humanity was reborn as was the case with the other Jesus child, but an angelic being who had never before been incarnated in a human body. In the Jewish and original Christian tradition this being was called the 'sister soul of Adam', the pure paradisial part of the first human being, the part that was held back in the spiritual world at the time of the fall into sin. Indian tradition knows this being as Vishnu who revealed himself in many avatars, including Krishna. In the Nathan Jesus the so-called *nirmanakaya* of Buddha also revealed itself, the spiritual form in which the Enlightened One continues to work after his death. This spiritual form no longer incarnates on earth, but can shine through a human being.

Until their twelfth year both boys lived in each other's vicinity in Nazareth where the 'Solomon family' settled after their return from Egypt. Then these two beings became one when the I of the Solomon boy—the Zarathustra-I—moved over into the soul of the Nathan boy. Luke reports this in a hidden way in the story of the visit to the Temple at the end of the second chapter of his Gospel.

The Solomon boy, who sacrificed his I to the other, died soon thereafter. The Zarathustra-I then lived for eighteen years in the Nathan Jesus, from his twelfth to his thirtieth year. Shortly before the Baptism in the Jordan it left him in order to allow the Christ-I to descend into the human being Jesus.

Not much later the Zarathustra-I reincarnated as the teacher of Arius (probably Lucian of Antioch), and since then he has been known in occult science as a spiritual leader under the name of Master Jesus. He inspired Arianism, the later mysticism of the Middle Ages, and the so-called Friend of God. Zarathustra, therefore, could not be raised by Jesus Christ. Lazarus-John took his place, the individuality who helped Solomon build his Temple in a prior life, namely the Phoenician master builder Hiram Abiff, one of the most important descendants of Cain. Rudolf Steiner says that his development in a certain way paralleled that of the individuality of Zarathustra.

We see here the connection of the Johannine element with the Temple of Solomon. During His crucifixion Jesus points to John as the son of His mother. This woman was the mother of the Solomon child, the reborn Zarathustra therefore. The substitution mentioned above is confirmed by this.

In the course of time the two messianic families became one. The Mary of the Luke Gospel died soon after the event in the Temple in

Jerusalem; the elderly Solomon Joseph had already died earlier. The
Nathan Joseph then married the Solomon Mary. The Nathan child thus
came into a stepfamily as regards the physical aspect, but the Zarathustra-I that had lived in him since his twelfth year came back to his original mother, brothers and sisters.

The significance of these complicated relationships is not easy to
explain. Emil Bock has convincingly discussed this messianic mystery
in his book *The Childhood of Jesus*,[23] making use not only of Rudolf Steiner's spiritual knowledge, but also of legends, Gnostic documents and
other traditions. It must also be recognized that the secret of the two
messianic families must have been known to artists until the sixteenth
century; witness the countless pictures that show this subject, either
openly or veiled.

As regards the individuality of Lazarus-John, according to Rudolf
Steiner, he received a new initiation toward the end of the Middle Ages
and became the inaugurator of the esoteric stream that may be regarded
as a metamorphosis of the Johannine stream, namely the Rosicrucians.
The leader of this stream is not called by the name of John, but Christian
Rosenkreutz.[24]

The third raising from death relates to a representative of the third,
the Egyptian-Chaldean, post-Atlantean cultural epoch—the youth of
Nain (Lk.7:11-17). It was said of him that he was 'the son of a widow'.
This is a technical term from the mysteries. The Egyptian initiates called
themselves 'sons of Isis', the sorrowful widow whose spouse Osiris had
been killed. In a previous life the youth of Nain had been a young man
who removed the veil from the statue of Isis in Sais, Egypt. No mortal,
said the local tradition, was permitted to lift that veil, meaning that no
one was allowed to do this without preparation for immortality (initiation). Due to his deed he had to die.

Virtually nothing is known about his life as the youth of Nain. The
people who were around him when he was carried to his burial on a bier
say after his raising: 'A great prophet has risen among us.' Rudolf Steiner
notes that these words do not refer to Jesus but to the youth. The large
number of bystanders indicates that he was highly regarded.

This individuality was reborn in the third century in order to bring
the fruit of his raising by Christ to realization in a mighty esoteric-gnos-
tic movement. As Mani, or Manes, he was again called a son of a widow.
In his teaching, Manichaeism, everything is recapitulated which had
lived in old religions as mystery wisdom, but now in the light of Christian Gnosis. Mani's teaching enabled followers of the old Egyptian and

Chaldean star wisdom, Persian adherents of the Zoroastrian religion, and Buddhists to develop understanding of the Christ being. As Mani this powerful individuality, who stood under the influence of the Paraclete, the Comforter or Holy Spirit, worked in preparation for his later task of truly bringing all religions together.[25]

For that, he had to be born again in an exceptional incarnation in which, to begin with, all the wisdom he had gained and every conscious connection with Christ had to be submerged into complete ignorance and forgetfulness. As a 'pure fool' he had to go into the world: Parsifal, the son of Herzeleide. After long wanderings he is then chosen as the Grail King. The saga says that in the end the Holy Grail is brought from the West to the East again. Parsifal himself also goes East. In this movement is expressed that this individuality, as a new teacher of Christianity, will one day make the connection between East and West in the light of the Holy Grail. The teaching of reincarnation and karma will play an ever more important role in this.

In a certain sense, Parsifal can be viewed as the representative of our time, the fifth post-Atlantean cultural epoch in which the third (Egypto-Chaldean) epoch is mirrored. The youth of Nain is the one who has to carry the positive fruit of Egypto-Chaldean wisdom into our time in Christianized form (the Grail). For that task Christ Himself raised him from death. In the total ignorance of Parsifal we recognize a character trait of humanity of our time. In our time we have to find our way out of ignorance and doubt back to the light of the spirit.

When we now wonder whether there is also a representative of Jewish mystery wisdom who went through death and resurrection, we should cast our eyes on St. Paul. The initiated Pharisee Saul becomes the Christian initiate Paul by his experience before Damascus. He does not go through a process of dying comparable to that of the youth of Nain, the daughter of Jairus, and Lazarus, but he is blind for three days, and neither eats nor drinks. He is not a representative of a prior cultural epoch that died off. Through him, however, the redemption of the law of Moses through Christian love has to be most deeply experienced. His 'conversion' is truly a new initiation. On his great apostolic travels he is led by the Resurrected One Himself, as can clearly be concluded from some of the statements in his letters (Gal.1:16; 2:20).

He can build directly on the foundation of Greek mystery knowledge; the school in Athens that he founded and that was led by Dionysius the Areopagite was a true mystery school. Out of an esoteric Christian inspiration, the great painter Raphael pictured the meeting of Paul and Dionysius in his famous fresco *The School of Athens* in the Stanza della Segnatura in the Vatican. The notion that the two central figures represent Plato and Aristotle is due to a mistake or falsification.

In this Athenian mystery school esoteric Gnosis was taught. Knowledge of the higher hierarchies and their connection with the divine Trinity will undoubtedly have formed the core of this teaching, in view of the important document about the heavenly hierarchies that came into being a few centuries later out of Pauline-Dionysian esotericism. However, we may assume that all that St. Paul wrote in more exoteric form in his letters to the Christian congregations, was taught in Athens as initiation knowledge. Think, for instance, in the first place of the teaching of the Christian virtues of faith, hope and love, which are a metamorphosis of the Platonic virtues of wisdom, temperance and courage.

In the Middle Ages, people viewed as the representatives of these virtues Peter (faith), James (hope), and John (love). We find this in the *Divina Commedia* by Dante, where the poet describes how he has to pass a heavenly test in these virtues administered to him by these three apostles (Paradiso, cantos 24, 25, 26). And the Templars had three degrees of initiation that were also related to the three virtues and their representatives Peter, James and John. I will return to this in more detail in Chapter 5.

In this connection the following is of great importance. The influence of Pauline-Dionysian esotericism into western Europe is known. One expression of this is the legend of Saint Denis, who goes to Paris where he is martyred.[26] Whether this is historically correct is doubtful, but it is a certainty that his Greek text about the heavenly hierarchies was translated into Latin by the Irish monk John Scotus Eriugena in Paris.

Less well-known is the connection of Pauline esotericism with the influence of a mystery centre by the Black Sea. Rudolf Steiner also mentions it but sparingly. We find the following in a short cycle of three lectures given in 1912.[27] In Colchis on the northeastern coast of the Black Sea, a mystery school was founded in antiquity that existed far into Christian times. Teachers worked there who were inspired by the Buddha who, after his incarnation as Gautama, no longer reveals himself on earth, but from the spiritual world. In these mysteries, the teaching of equality and brotherhood that is characteristic of Buddhism was connected with Christianity. The candidates in these mysteries were guided in such a way that they could absorb Christianity in an intensive manner. They were also able to develop a clairvoyance in such a way that they became special initiates who, in St. Paul's footsteps, received the

Christ impulse into their lives without the intermediary of a religious sacrament.

Rudolf Steiner then describes that Francis of Assisi had been initiated in these mysteries in Colchis in a previous life, and how his profound morality, which he did not preach, but which radiated out from him as a healing power, had received its foundation in his Colchis initiation. At that time, the three impulses of faith, hope, and love had been imprinted into his soul as all-permeating forces.

Before we turn to northwestern Europe to see which mystery stream from there entered into a relationship with Christianity, we have to take a look at the role Aristotle played in world events around the Turning Point of Time. We are staying within the theme of spiritual guidance and, even though it may seem as if we are moving away from the main subject of Temple and Grail, it will become clear that the Aristotelian stream is as important for this subject as the raising from death described above.

5. Wisdom and Knowledge

Greek philosophy, which reached its apex in the teachings of Plato and Aristotle, was a child of the mysteries. In the rich images of the dialogues of Plato the mystery background still seems to make itself visible right through the philosophical concepts, whereas in his great student Aristotle this background is much more hidden. This hiding of the background was something Aristotle did very consciously; we might just as well call it a revelation of the background, but then in an abstract, logical form.

What in ancient times was the hidden wisdom of the mysteries was made known by poets in the form of images, and later by philosophers as thoughts. The wisdom of the few (initiated) individuals became knowledge for future, mature humanity. In a certain sense, the work of Plato and Aristotle was the culmination of Greek culture which, in all its facets, demonstrated the humanization and growing earthliness of the divine—in the arts, literature and philosophy, as also in society. The Greek world was therefore a direct preparation for the coming of Christ to the earth; a different preparation, of course, from that of the Jewish culture, but a no less important one.

In Christian theology, which is the mother of all Western knowledge, Platonism as well as Aristotelianism were to play important roles, because of the efforts that were made to bring the truths communicated by the Gospels into agreement with Greek philosophy. In this process the views of both great philosophers were changed and cut, with the result that the mystery character was pushed more and more into the background. This happened not only due to the changes that were developing in the soul disposition of humanity, but also because of a purposeful striving within the orthodox Church of Rome to ban all mystery elements from Christianity and eradicate these pagan remnants root and branch.[28]

As regards the bastardization of Aristotle, this is at first more an Arabic development and only later became an influence in Christianity and Western philosophy. It is of particular importance for our subject to study these developments, because we can see that through the centuries all esoteric Christian streams, on the one hand had to find a relationship to Rome, the Roman orthodox element, and on the other hand also to Arabism. This is true for the Grail knights as much as for the Temple knights and the Rosicrucians.

In this connection we might go so far as to consider pure Platonism and pure Aristotelianism, which do not in essence contradict each other, as belonging to esoteric Christianity. This insight is in complete agreement with the theme 'world history in the light of the Holy Grail'. Here I do not want to follow the Platonic line, because in Neoplatonism its character changed to some extent; via Plotinus it came to St. Augustine, the founder of Roman orthodoxy. I will follow the Aristotelian line of development.

We know that Aristotle, besides the usual subjects he taught in his Lyceum, imparted a secret knowledge to intimate pupils who had been thoroughly prepared for it, knowledge that was called acroamatic.* We can be quite sure that this acroamatic knowledge was still directly connected with the cosmic nature wisdom of the Eleusinian mysteries, wisdom Aristotle had received through Plato.

Plutarch reports in his biography of Alexander the Great that Alexander wrote a letter to his teacher, reproaching him for the fact that certain contents of his secret teaching were made public in his writings. Aristotle's matter-of-fact reply is characteristic:

> You should realize that these things have been made public and at the same time not made public. After all, they can only be comprehended by those who are able to hear them from ourselves.

There is no doubt that the knowledge referred to here has to do with the natural scientific work of the master. But on close examination, his

---

* Acroamatic is derived from Greek *akroaomai*, to listen to.

Metaphysics is also a direct mystery revelation in the form of abstract concepts; for the background behind this we have to look more to the mysteries of Samothrace (Kabiri) and Ephesus (Logos).

On the basis of his spiritual research, Rudolf Steiner has a different interpretation of the discussion which, according to tradition, Plato and Aristotle had in the Academy, and which supposedly led to a distancing between the two philosophers. According to Rudolf Steiner, Aristotle there received the task to clothe the primeval wisdom of the mysteries, which in Plato's philosophy could still be found in the form of imagery, into abstract imageless concepts. Their so-called distancing should therefore be regarded in a positive sense.[29]

By giving and, respectively, executing this task, Plato and Aristotle put themselves in service of the coming Christ mystery. While the Christ being in the heights of the sun prepared Himself, as it were, for His descent to the earth, in order to appear in Jesus of Nazareth some three hundred years later, Aristotle forged the 'vessel' of logic out of cosmic star wisdom. The Word, the Logos, becomes flesh; it comes to humanity and brings the 'Kingdom of Heaven' with it out of the heights into the depths.

Through Aristotle the human soul has acquired the instrument to receive the spirit of Christianity in as much as logical thinking can still feel akin to the sun spirit. However, if it loses this kinship, logic can become the instrument of anti-Christianity. Aristotle's logic was not the only instrument intended to serve humanity in the great Turning Point of Time. His grandiose contemplations on the soul, on ethics, on the nature of heaven and earth, were in the first place destined to renew the degenerated mysteries of Asia and Egypt, and subsequently to form the metaphysical-ethical garment in which young Christianity could clothe itself.

The words 'intended' and 'destined' are quite deliberately used here. We may assume that Aristotle and his royal student, Alexander, were very consciously future-oriented, and that they stood under the immediate inspiration of the Time Spirit of those centuries, the sun archangel Michael, the countenance of Christ. Especially Alexander had in his appearance and actions the overwhelming surety of a sun hero, the initiated son of the gods. He accomplished in twelve years the superhuman task of bringing Aristotelianism into the declining world of the old mystery cultures; thanks to this impulse, which caused the rise of Hellenism across western Asia and Egypt, the demise of the old world could be arrested for a long time.

The Greek language became the world language. Greek philosophy and knowledge fructified oriental and Egyptian wisdom; a world *culture* followed upon Alexander's world *empire*, the political unity of which fell apart immediately after his death. In this spiritual-cosmopolitan element, by which even the originally barbaric Romans let themselves be influenced, Christianity was able to be taken up. Greek is the language of the Gospel writers, of the letters of St. Paul, of the Apocalypse, but also of all Gnostic documents, Christian, Jewish or pagan. Greek was the first language of the Christian liturgy; the altar sacrament was called the *mysterion*.

What was now the destiny of Aristotelian philosophy and knowledge, and how did they find their way westward and eastward? Through Aristotle's student, Theophrastus, and also via other channels, the writings that relate to logic came to the West; there they formed the foundation of philosophy and science in the Middle Ages, but just as much for our time too. Through the influence of Alexander, however, Aristotle's natural science went in the first instance to the East, and did not come to Europe until many centuries later, and then in a strongly filtered form and intellectualized by the Arabs.

It is not easy to follow the traces of Aristotle's work in the Near East. When this work was discovered by the Arabs in the Academy of Gondishapur in 640 AD, it had already travelled a long way from Athens via Antioch, Edessa and Nisibis, where Aristotle was studied in Nestorian Christian academies.[30]

However, in the thousand (!) years that had passed since Aristotle and Alexander, what had perhaps been intended by the spiritual guidance of humanity did not take place, namely an amalgamation of Greek mystery wisdom in Aristotelian form with a new Persia. This amalgamation could have happened in the light of the Christ mystery. The place of encounter could have been Gondishapur. Such an amalgamation would have been completely in line with the preparation of the Mystery of Golgotha. After all, the great teacher of ancient Persia, Zarathustra, had thousands of years earlier already prophesied the coming of the Sun Spirit, who was to descend into a human being.

The Three Wise Men from the East, three of the last followers of Zarathustra who lived in the land of Saba (Yemen), knew that the individuality of Zarathustra himself would incarnate in this Messiah. They beheld his descending I-being as the golden star (Zoro-aster, as Zarathustra was later called) and went on their way to bring him their offerings. In a certain sense, Persians were destined to understand the human side of Jesus, whereas Greek wisdom was able to penetrate into the secret of the Resurrection, the divine side of Jesus Christ. Comprehension of this secret had been prepared in the Mystery of Eleusis. Dionysius the Areopagite, the Greek initiate, listening to the words of St. Paul, recognized the Risen One as the 'Unknown God' of the mysteries.

The amalgamation mentioned above was thwarted from two sides, by Constantine's orthodox Christianity, and by Sassanid neo-Persia. The East Roman Empire, which encompassed the Near East to the borders of Iran—until the Arabs conquered that part in the seventh century—was, despite its Hellenistic culture, in religious matters still dependent on Rome. The state religion, which was closely controlled by Constantine, took on a distinctly Roman-legalistic character that did not agree with the true spirit of Christianity.

The various Councils, beginning with that of Nicaea in 325 AD when the teaching of Arius was condemned, are like many footsteps of the progressing orthodoxy that meant the fall of original Christianity. Nestorian Christianity, which was closely connected with Aristotle's philosophy, was also declared to be heresy and had to leave the East Roman Empire. To the East of Mesopotamia the neo-Persian, or Sassanid Empire (224-651 AD) came into being under its first king, Ardashir I. The ancient religion of Zarathustra was revived in an outer sense; the holy fire service was extensively celebrated again, but the inner fire spirit was lacking.

The only movement that was able to light this inner fire again was Manichaeism. Mani, a Persian by birth, brought the true renewal of Persia with his powerful teaching of the light realm and the realm of darkness, but now permeated by the mystical power of the Christ sacrifice. After an initial success in the neo-Persian Empire he was condemned to death by King Bahran I in 276 AD. He died in prison and his corpse was brutally mutilated and shamefully exhibited at the city gate of Gondishapur. Although Manichaeism was mercilessly persecuted in the neo-Persian Empire, a memory of this spiritual movement still existed in the time of the caliphs, as demonstrated by the fact that the names of Mani's direct successors, the leaders of the Manichaean community, were listed in the *Fihrist*, a kind of historical catalogue dating back to the year 987.

A lasting connection of Greek-Aristotelian philosophy with the Persian-Manichaean religion never came into being, let alone an amalgamation of the two. In a certain way, the 'apostate' Emperor Julian, who was initiated in the Eleusinian mystery, also sought this connection. His campaign to the East was not a regular expedition of conquest; by the way, neither was that of Alexander the Great. Julian wanted to penetrate into those regions where the Persian sun secret could be found. One might also say: he sought the sun mysteries of Persia as these had been renewed by Mani. But Mani had been executed, and Julian was struck by the hand of a murderer not far from Gondishapur.

Two hundred years later an emperor of a very different calibre than the noble and tragic Julian was sitting on the throne of Constantine, who had transformed Greek Byzantium into an eastern Rome. The fanatically orthodox Justinian closed the 'pagan' schools of philosophy in Athens in 529. The honourable, almost 1000-year-old Academy of Plato had to disappear. The expelled philosophers made their way to the court of the Sassanid King Chosrau I. This migration of Greek scholars who, by the way, spent only a short time in Persia, had been preceded by similar expulsions in earlier centuries, as a result of which Aristotelian philosophy and science came to Persia.

In the seventh century a new connection grew, namely of 'Aristotle' with the Islamic Arabs. These equally militant and studious sons of the desert conquered large parts of the East Roman and neo-Persian empires in an incredibly short time. They eagerly and astutely absorbed the Hellenistic and neo-Zoroastrian cultures there. Aristotle's works were translated into Arabic, and the Academy of Gondishapur became a centre of brilliant scholarship, excelling above all in a medical science that encompassed the secrets of the human being and nature.

In the eighth century the newly founded city of Baghdad also became a centre of scholarship and refined culture. Greed for conquest drove the Arabs through Egypt and North Africa to Spain where the so-called western caliphate developed the same brilliant culture and scholarship as Baghdad in the East. Along this path Aristotle arrived in the West disguised as an Arab.

His natural-scientific works were translated in the East, some first into Syriac, later all of them into Arabic. Al-Mamun, son of Harun-al-Rashid and a Persian woman, ordered these translations after Aristotle had appeared to him in a dream. Al-Mamun saw a very beautiful masculine figure and asked him: 'Who are you?' The answer was: 'Aristotle'. Al-Mamun asked him how he had become so beautiful. Aristotle replied that this came from the beauty of the spiritual laws of thinking. This more Persian-oriented caliph, Al-Mamun, who had conquered the power of the caliphate from his Arab half-brother, then ordered that all of Aristotle's works be translated.

The struggle for dominance between the Arabic and Persian elements in the eastern caliphate, which during the reign of Harun-al-Rashid was won by the Arabic side, actually signified an action by a one-sided moon principle (Islam) that rebelled against the sun principle in lieu of carrying it lovingly.

Here we touch on the heart of our contemplation: *The Grail motif reveals itself in world history*. The Sun Being descends step by step (*gradalis*) to the earth. His coming has to be prepared there, He has to be received and carried. This is a service function that has a connection with the essential being of the moon. Moon forces work in procreation, heredity, in all wisdom of natural laws, and in the instinctive love that is connected with blood relationships. In a certain sense, the primeval wisdom of the mysteries is a moon gift, reflected harmonies of star and sun worlds.

The connection of sun and moon is an important aspect of the Grail secret. We see it already in pre-Christian times in the image of the moon sickle that contains the sun and at the same time carries it. The Sun Spirit Christ descends into the moon vessel Jesus. Jesus of Nazareth is the most noble 'extract' of the moon stream (Israel), which wants to serve the sun. His human I is the I of the highest Sun initiate of the ancient Persian culture, Zarathustra, who cedes his place to the I of Christ at the Baptism in the Jordan.

Greek wisdom was the 'moon extract' of the mysteries, which originated in Asia. The spiritual laws of thinking (logic) of Aristotle were a moon vessel formed to comprehend the Sun Being. Aristotle and Alexander were Sun servants, servants of Michael; they brought a spiritual Ephesus (where the mystery temple of the moon goddess stood), a Moon impulse therefore, back to Asia in order to prepare the way for the Christ Sun.

However, when the moon impulse rebels against the sun, the anti-Grail comes into being. The half-moon that rejects Christ comes within the immediate reach of the evil one. Harun-al-Rashid had his Persian grand vizier beheaded and received his head on a platter—a world historic picture of the anti-Grail.

In the Persian element combined with pure Aristotelianism the moon treasure of primeval wisdom lies concealed. A wonderful medieval saga expresses this in the picture of the white lily, Blanchefleur, who is locked up in the tower of the Emir of Babylon, from which she is rescued by the youth of the rose, Flor. Magnificent and also touching is the description of the impression Blanchefleur's beauty makes on the Emir and his courtiers. Just as in the dream of Al-Mamun, therefore, here also it is the radiant beauty of wisdom that moves the hearts and spirits of these people of the East.

The Arabic cultural impulse continually alternated between the positive and the negative aspects of the moon principle. *And this alternation had a direct impact on the destiny of Aristotelianism.* The positive aspect, the mystery wisdom, albeit strongly diluted and intellectualized but yet recognizable to those who knew it, was brought to Europe. Thus also the Grail message came as *star wisdom* from Provence to the knight Wolfram von Eschenbach via Kyot, who had found the book of the mysterious Flegetanis in Moorish Toledo.

Aristotle's most esoteric book, his work about *alchemy*, reached the West also through the Arabs (see Chapter 4). It came into the hands of a Portuguese knight and in the end reached Basilius Valentinus, the famous alchemist. Alchemists and Rosicrucians were the ones with whom nature wisdom lived on with a mystery character. The *Fama Fraternitatis* by Valentin Andreae describes how Christian Rosenkreutz absorbed the wisdom of the East and of Spain, and connected it with the Christ mystery.[31]

Because of the negative effect of the moon impulse in Arabism, the mystery wisdom was detached from the sun element. It became intellectual knowledge and erudition, but it bore in itself the death forces of materialism. Via the Western European universities such as Paris and Oxford, this kind of Arabism influenced the Christian culture of Europe in a decisive manner.

In the Scholasticism of the thirteenth century the great Dominicans Albertus Magnus and Thomas Aquinas acted against this negative effect of the moon impulse. They fought the Arabized Aristotle in the name of the pure Aristotle. Their Christian sun intelligence gave again to thinking its sensible task of being the bearer of revelation, and the explorer of the supersensible—a Grail impulse of the highest and purest nature.

But the negative side won out. European science was arabized. With the victory of nominalism (Roger Bacon) over realism (Thomas and Albertus) Christian Europe capitulated to the Half Moon. The Christian knights of Charles Martel had halted the surge of the Arabic horsemen at Poitiers in 732, but the Christian thinkers lost the battle against the intellectual power of Cordoba.

Are we surprised when we hear from Rudolf Steiner that Francis Bacon, the figure who in modern times founded natural-scientific materialism as the continuation of Scholastic nominalism, was a reincarnation of Harun-al-Rashid?[32] When we read his work, we run into his anti-Aristotelianism everywhere. His *Novum Organum* is the materialist's answer to the star wisdom of the Greek master. His *Nova Atlantis* is a brilliant science-fiction story in which a kind of super-academy of Gondishapur is described, the house of Solomon (!) on the mysterious island of Bensalem.

In the East positive Arabism succumbed to the Turks whose influence grew ever stronger in the eastern caliphate. The battles by the Templars to defend the Holy Land in the twelfth and thirteenth centuries were battles against the *Turkish* Muslims, not against the highly developed Arabs! At that time the spirit of the old mystery wisdom had not yet totally disappeared from the Near East. The last radiance of this wisdom still flowed through many channels to Europe, carried by Crusaders, Templars, traders and Jews. But the source dried up and degenerated in the barbarism of Osman and Timur.[33] The negative moon aspect likes to connect itself with the aggressiveness of Mars.

And what about Aristotle himself? Where do we find his individuality (what he called entelechy) in this drama of Grail and anti-Grail? As Rudolf Steiner tells us, his individuality had a brief life in the ninth century as the noble young man Schionatulander. The Grail poets relate how for his beloved Sigune he tries to catch a mysterious dog wearing a collar on which twelve virtues were inscribed; he is thus characterized as a seeker for star secrets. He is killed by Orilus who actually had wanted to kill Parsifal. Parsifal finds the dead young man in the arms of Sigune who is holding her beloved on her lap. Here again, therefore, no direct connection grows between Aristotle and Mani, but the connection is formed in a much deeper sense because Schionatulander sacrificed his life for Parsifal.

In the thirteenth century the individuality of Aristotle was born again as Thomas Aquinas. Then he could, as the greatest Christian wise man, bring the Aristotelian stream in the direction of the sun again.[34]

To our time, European science has followed the negative moon impulse. Goetheanism and Rudolf Steiner's Anthroposophy bring an impulse of renewed mystery wisdom in the light of Christ, in other words, a new Grail awareness is beginning to manifest itself in our current culture.

6. The Mysteries of Northern and Western Europe

When the message of Christ's coming to the earth was spread among people this 'good news' moved from East to West. This East-West stream contained a southern (Egyptian) component, while the receiving

West carried a northern component. In a certain sense, the spread of Christianity to the West was a reversal of the Manu-Noah stream out of old Atlantis to Europe and Asia. When we examine it more closely we can in the westward stream of Christianity also recognize a northern and a southern movement. The stream of Christianity was met by something from the North and West that was waiting there, living in expectation.

This comes to expression in a beautiful way in the legends that exist around the sanctuary in Chartres, France. It is said that in pre-Christian times a divine virgin was worshipped there who was to give birth to a child, the world saviour. The wise priests of the place, says the legend, every year sent messengers to Palestine in order to hear whether their expectation had been fulfilled. When the news finally reached them the wise Druids rejoiced, and the people of Chartres rejoiced with them. The later missionaries were surprised by this story and gave the priests and the people the holy baptism.

Of course, about such a somewhat apocryphal legend one can say that there also lived an expectation of a Messiah in the East, in Persia, Egypt, Palestine and Greece; in the people of Israel this was explicitly spoken about by the prophets, whereas in the other peoples it was more hidden in the mysteries. But there is a distinct difference. The great 'Advent cultures' of the East developed over successive epochs of time. This was not the case in northern and western Europe. The Celtic and Germanic civilizations of ancient Europe were still very primitive in an outer sense when in Egypt, Babylon and Greece the mightiest and loftiest works of art and the most beautiful literary and profound philosophical writings already existed.

One could say that the Celtic and Germanic peoples were saving their strength; their unfolding in outer forms of civilization was held back. They had to wait for their time. On the one hand this had its cause in the past, on the other hand it had to do with the future task of the Germanic peoples. For it was only in modern times, meaning since the beginning of the fifteenth century, that they became the bearers of a new cultural epoch (the fifth post-Atlantean epoch). This demanded preparation that emanated from the mystery centres in Europe.

Earlier in this chapter we spoke about movements of groups of people out of old Atlantis to the East. We distinguished two principal streams, a northern and a southern one. The leaders of the northern stream encountered on their way East populations in a state of degeneration that was caused by the moral demise that ultimately caused the downfall of Atlantis. Rudolf Steiner speaks in this connection of *mystery treason*, because of which occult forces had come within reach of unpurified human souls who were therefore able to misuse unheard of magical powers for egoistic purposes. This caused a disastrous moral deterioration in the majority of humanity in old Atlantis. This deterioration, which also affected people's corporeality, ultimately also caused catastrophes in nature.[35] The book of Genesis, the Gilgamesh epic and all the stories of the Great Flood of many different peoples and races agree with the spiritual insights mentioned here regarding the downfall of Atlantis.

The initiated leaders of the northern Manu stream had to see to it that the after-effects of this mystery treason could gradually be neutralized in the course of time. A refinement, an ennoblement of the old population of Europe had to develop. A Germanic myth describes this process in the story of the sons of Heimdall, the divine watchman on the bridge Bifrost. Heimdall, here named Rigr, successively visits three couples: great-grandparents, grandparents and parents. He is extremely poorly treated by the first couple, but after Rigr's stay the great-grandmother gives birth to a child of his; it is pitch black, has wrinkled skin, a bent back, crude limbs and a distorted face. Slave (Träl) becomes the child's name. Better treated by the second couple Rigr also fathers a child; when it is born nine months later, it is a strong son with rosy cheeks and merry eyes. His name is Karl and he becomes a sturdy peasant and handworker. Rigr travels on and arrives at a noble couple who treat him like royalty. Here he also stays three days and nights and fathers a radiant child, with shining cheeks, sparkling eyes and blond hair. Jarl is the boy's name. Later Rigr brings him up himself. Jarl wins land and estates, marries a beautiful woman named Erna, and from them the first kings are descended. They receive the rune script and may call themselves Rigr.[36]

The myth clearly shows a process of ennoblement of humanity guided by a lofty spiritual being who works through a eugenic 'upbringing' of tribes, progressing through thousands of years, from which the Celtic and Germanic peoples gradually developed. When not long before the beginning of our era the Romans made contact with the Germanic peoples, these had no impressive outer culture that expressed itself in architecture or other works of art, nor did they have complex social institutions. However, they had powerfully built, beautiful bodies and a highly developed sense of morality that was demonstrated especially clearly in their respectful attitude toward women, and in their courage, faithfulness and selflessness. (As we know, these positive characteristics that the Romans admired so much have not always been preserved in the later development of the European peoples.)

The Nerthus or Njord mysteries of Jutland (Denmark) also had a eugenic task. Procreation was kept outside egoistic arbitrariness of the people by the leading priests. Unconsciously conducted conceptions took place in spring, and births happened at the time we now call Christmas. Such children were well-born, nobly born, whereas the children who were born at different times, were children of sexual passion, of shame. The guidance by the initiates remained completely in the background. The mysteries were guarded and kept secret with even greater strictness than elsewhere, to see to it that spiritual forces would not be misused again.

The Germanic and Celtic tribes preserved remnants of clairvoyance much longer than the culturally more advanced peoples of Asia, Egypt and southern Europe. This is expressed in the incredible wealth of sagas and fairytales among these peoples. The immense variety among these stories is as astounding as the striking similarities that can be found in the motifs of these popular tales. The great sagas of gods and heroes, however, such as were conserved in the Edda from Iceland, did not proceed from the clairvoyance of common people, but they were images of supersensible experiences the initiates had during their initiation.

In Scandinavia and northern Russia there were originally the mysteries of the Drotten, later better known as the Druids. They were founded in the far distant past by the initiate Sig, Sieg or Sigge. In the form of a higher being of the rank of an archangel, the god Odin worked in him, who was later called Wotan or Wodan by the Germanic tribes. The content of these Drotten or Druid mysteries consisted of the resurrection of the sun god Baldur, who had been killed. This indicates the development of a consciously schooled clairvoyance that was able to penetrate into higher spiritual realms, which was possible because in this initiation a circle of twelve people collaborated, each with a special soul power or spiritual capacity which they placed in service of the whole. In this way the thirteenth could experience the revelation of the god who manifested himself in the circle of the twelve. This thirteenth, central figure was also viewed as the representative of the Holy Trinity.

In the myths of the Edda all initiation experiences are represented by spiritual beings—a twelvefold pantheon of the gods, and the powers of evil who have to be conquered.

However, a tragic mood characterized all that relates to the old European mysteries. This was reflected in the myth of the Twilight of the Gods. The initiates of ancient Europe lived very consciously toward a downfall. Even though they knew themselves united by their initiation with Baldur or Hu, the representatives of the human being in his original cosmic form, they also knew that these gods were mortal and that above the 'Asen' and 'Vanen' a higher reality, a more powerful godhead had to reign.

For Germanic souls, therefore, the Christ revelation was an even much more powerful fulfilment than for the peoples in the South-East. In this regard the following is of great importance. The original mystery impulses of post-Atlantean Europe emanated from the North. From there, a spiritual influence radiated to the centre, the West and also the South of Europe.

Greek tradition speaks here of the Hyperboreans, a mysterious priest folk or priest order that sent messengers to Dodona and Delos every year. It was the true sun folk of Apollo, with whom heroes of Greece were also permitted to participate in the meal of immortality (Perseus). Some historians want to identify the Hyperboreans with the Celts, but that can't be right because the Celts did not distinguish themselves in the general Indo-European population as a separate, independent group of tribes until late, and the tradition of the Hyperboreans goes back to a much earlier past.

In this tradition lives a memory of a paradisial sun aeon, in which primeval divine wisdom streamed into the still immaterial, etheric earthly world. The beings who carried this out later withdrew from the earth, but the North of Europe still preserved some of their workings around the pure, almost timeless area of the North Pole. The Scandinavian, and especially the Finnish sagas testify to this.[37]

The Drotten mysteries, therefore, carried a Hyperborean impulse. The leading hierarchical spirit, however, whose task it was to prepare the future, Odin, moved the centre of the European mysteries to northern Germany. There are sufficient indications for us to regard the so-called *Externsteine* in the vicinity of Paderborn as this mystery centre.

But Odin's influence also reached to the area of the Black Sea. We have already seen that there was a mystery centre in this region until deep into Christian times. A Greek saga names Colchis as the place where the Argonauts went to fetch the Golden Fleece, a clear indication that this was also an initiation centre that existed already around 1400 BC.

Colchis is situated at the foot of the Caucasus mountains, the cradle of the Indo-European race.

Also by the coast of the Black Sea, but farther to the West, around the Sea of Azov, lived the Cimmerians who were probably—and there is much scientific proof for this —proto-Germanic tribes from Scandinavia, Finland and Russia who went South. From there, a later stream moved back to central and western Europe. This Germanic stream brought the Wotan culture as a last inspiration of the Odin being. At that time the rune script was developed as a very first *intellectual* impulse.

The Celtic Druids sharply rejected this impulse. Only from that time, around 1000 BC, do we see a clear distinction between Celts and Germans. The Celts held on to their sun- and moon service, their old clairvoyance that was connected with nature, whereas the Germans were on their way to the Twilight of the Gods, the loss of the sun initiation due to the darkening force of the intellect. They prepared themselves for our time, when the intellect formulates the natural laws and has banned all divinity from nature. In this historical process they first had to absorb the influence of Rome, and later that of Arabism.

The expansion of the Germanic peoples drove the Celtic tribes to the West. There they ran up against populations that had been led by Druids for centuries. In the extreme West, on the island of Ireland, there were deeply hidden mysteries that can be traced back to the original Atlantean sun oracles. There was certainly a connection between the northern European Drotten mysteries and the Hibernian (Irish) mysteries. One of the pre-Celtic tribes that populated Ireland, and which are referred to as divine beings in Irish mythology, the Tuatha De Danaan, certainly came from Scandinavia, perhaps from Jutland.[38]

In section 2 of this chapter the mysteries of Ireland were already briefly mentioned. We have to imagine that behind all that is told of the Celts of the West, who only arrived in the British Isles and Ireland around 500 BC,[39] where they found a megalithic Druid culture, these great sun mysteries stand hidden in the background. This is true not only for the menhirs and dolmen, but also for the tradition of King Arthur with the Round Table and the magician Merlin, and equally for Irish Christianity that from the sixth to the ninth century was brought to the European mainland.

When we immerse ourselves in this original Christianity of the West, some remarkable characteristics will catch our eye.[40] First of all there is the contrast with Roman orthodox Christianity, and further it has the distinct mystery background that we discovered in the Druid initiation, for we find the circle of twelve with the thirteenth in the middle both with Arthur and with the Irish and British monks who travelled to Europe.

Moreover, what particularly strikes us is the cosmic orientation of this Celtic Christianity. Christ was still viewed as the true Baldur, the true Hu, the sun spirit who worked in the world of cosmic life. He was for this reason often called the Lord or King of the Elements. The sign of the cross was shown as the sacred sun symbol, and not as the instrument of torture like the later pictures of the crucifix.

The Irish saints were often scholars and poets, Druids therefore, who honoured especially the *Greek* texts, both of the New Testament and those of the Greek Church Fathers. The translation of Dionysius' book about the hierarchies by the Irish monk John Scotus Eriugena has already been mentioned. The Grail traditions all point to this Celtic western region; according to Robert de Boron, Joseph of Arimathea went with the chalice of the Last Supper to England. His Grail table was emulated by Merlin and appears as the Round Table that was made for Uther Pendragon, King Arthur's father. Chrétien de Troyes and Wolfram von Eschenbach also describe the encounter of Grail knighthood with Arthurian knighthood in their poems. I will come back to these connections in Chapter 4.

When we trace the history of the once so powerful Celts we see that this people—if we may call this composite of very different tribes a people—went under. The Christian Arthurian knights and the Irish and British monks brought a last lustre of mystery wisdom from ancient times, transformed into a deep Christian impulse. However, just as in south-eastern Europe and the Near East, this mystery lustre disappeared when Rome spread its power more and more widely. The Germanic peoples connected themselves in a certain regard with the 'Roman Wolf', and later also with the half moon of Islam, but the Celts did not!

The Celts disappeared as a people because they sacrificed themselves. Rudolf Steiner speaks about this sacrifice in his lecture series about the European folk souls.[41] He says there that the folk soul of the Celts renounced a higher step of development in the rankings of the hierarchical beings, and instead became *the leading spirit of esoteric Christianity.* This means that everything that was described in earlier parts of this chapter as Johannine, Pauline, and Gnostic-Manichaean Christianity, to the extent it has a mystery character, is connected by a common spirit that must be understood as a very concrete entity, namely the same archangel who guided the Celtic tribes in ancient Europe.

While the Germanic tribes experienced the doom of their old gods, but as a people they triumphantly took possession of a Europe that had to prepare itself for our current era, the Celts faded away or were conquered by Germanic invaders. Most of the old Celtic mystery culture was lost because of the destruction the Vikings inflicted especially on Ireland. However, perhaps it was a world historical task of these wild Norsemen and Danes to prevent the remnants of a glorious spiritual past from exercising a negative influence after its time.

It is not without significance that one of the most dreaded leaders of the Norsemen, Rollo, after a failed siege of Chartres in 911, converted to Christianity. He adopted the baptismal name of Robert and became a vassal of Charles the Simple whose daughter he married. His fiefdom received the name of Normandy. From there Duke William conquered England in 1066.

Legend has it that the appearance of the Bishop of Chartres with the holy tunic of Mary flying from a lance on the ramparts of the besieged city frightened the Norsemen so badly that they turned and ran. This was said to be the reason why the defeated Rollo was converted. A modern person takes such a story with a grain of salt, but it is interesting that this event meant the end of the terror of the Vikings, and that Chartres earlier had a clear Celtic mystery character, to which an esoteric Christian element was added, which found its outer expression in the presence of the holy tunic of Mary in the church of Chartres.

The history of ancient Europe is complicated with its countless mass migrations, which for us modern people seem to be rather senseless or poorly motivated. But we have to presume that all these immense movements of thousands of people at a time, all this mutual influence and interpenetration, was brought about by wise spiritual guidance. As a result of all this a strong individual consciousness developed in Europe. This also brought the danger with it that those who received initiation were able to use the forces they thus acquired for their own personal purposes, which could cause abuse of spiritual power. Think only of the horrors of human sacrifices and other such practices that were indeed perpetrated by priests in mystery centres.

But principally, the measures that were taken from the mystery centres for thousands of years had a positive effect. Personal courage, physical strength and virtue were highly regarded. For modern people it is often hard to believe how generous the ancient Germanic person was with his strength and virtue. Medieval knighthood, which was not only a matter of sagas and poems but was actual historical reality, was inherited from the old Germanic world.

The message of Christ's death and resurrection brought immense change in the tragic mood of the expectation of the demise of the old gods, in other words, of the old clairvoyance. Rudolf Steiner says the following about this in a lecture given in 1909 (emphasis by Veltman):

> In the old mysteries, the initiate was not completely victorious over death. However, the great Mystery of Golgotha faced him. Just within the European mysteries, this historical mystery was accepted with the deepest understanding, different from somewhere else. A mood prevailed there which can be expressed possibly as follows. The human beings said to themselves, when we were initiated, it meant an ascent to a divine-spiritual world, but the breath of mortality penetrated it. However, someone who can settle in that which one can experience in the figure of Christ, in this biggest impulse, who finds a relationship to Christ can know: as well as the sun illumines the plant and wakes up life in it, the Christ impulse can flow into the human soul. Thereby it takes up the force that gives the soul knowledge of its eternity and immortality, knowledge of the victory over death. Because the soul gets a right understanding of Christ, it is animated. The human being said to himself, *there is still an inner knowledge except that which can be taught externally about Christ, the search of the soul, Ceridwen, for Hu or Baldur, but for another Baldur, who accomplished the Mystery of Golgotha.* If the soul experiences this, it attains a higher clairvoyance than by the old mysteries. Here in Europe, one soon understood quite deeply, what that means.[42]

This inner knowing, this true search of the soul for the deepest connection with Christ, came to expression in the *secrets* of the Grail. The deeper connection remained a secret, because in general the world was not yet mature enough to take in the true significance of Golgotha, which was experienced in its relation to the blood of the Redeemer. The fact that this Grail secret is the secret of the individual human I in its relationship to the being of Christ will be discussed later. I conclude this section with a brief contemplation meant as a supplement to the theme of spiritual guidance that was discussed in section 4.

When Rudolf Steiner speaks of the great spiritual teachers of humanity he uses a term from ancient Indian wisdom: bodhisattvas. We have to imagine a circle of twelve wise individuals who went through many incarnations in the course of centuries, in which they gained universal knowledge and experience that made them into creative beings. They are permeated down into the life forces of their bodies by a higher hierarchical being of the order of an archangel. They lead epochs and cultures, and bring new impulses into humanity. They have specific tasks in successive times, but together they form a kind of vessel for a much higher being who can make use of them, just as the human I makes use of its soul functions and physical organs. This higher being we indicate with the name Christ.

The ancient European mysteries were inspired by such a bodhisattva being who was called Odin, later Wotan. The human bearer of this bodhisattva spirit had the name Sig, a name we find in countless hero names. The surprising thing is that Rudolf Steiner points out that this highest leader of the Celtic-Germanic peoples, after concluding his task in Europe, incarnated as the Indian prince who rose in his twenty-ninth year to the dignity of Buddhahood, which means that he had reached such a high degree of development that he would no longer need to appear in an earthly incarnation in the future, but could work directly out of the spiritual world.

At first hearing, this communication seems rather absurd: the Germanic god who gloried in physical strength and fighting metamorphosed into the quiet, peace-loving Buddha, the teacher of compassion and release from suffering. But on closer consideration, our surprise is resolved into a reverent comprehension of the enigmatic ways the spiritual leaders of humanity have to use. Odin is most profoundly aware of the abyss of the Twilight of the Gods, the demise of the gods, which will be brought about by all that for which he had to prepare his Germanic peoples, namely the connection with the powers of matter—evil.

In the Orient he brought the fruit of his previous experiences: mildness and compassion with humanity. But as Buddha he would also develop further. At the birth of the Nathan Jesus child Buddha's higher being shone into the soul sheath of the paradisial child. The shepherds in the field outside Bethlehem experienced the glory of light that radiated from Buddha as a host of angels.[43]

Rudolf Steiner mentions a second great 'teacher of the West'. No myths or sagas speak of him; he is the most hidden one, Skythianos. His name is only rarely mentioned in the writings of the first Christian times. In the Middle Ages he was named together with Buddha and Zarathustra as the three spirits people had to abjure when they were taken into certain Christian communities. Rudolf Steiner, however, says that exactly these three great teachers of humanity, these three bodhisattvas—Skythianos, Buddha and Zarathustra, guided by an even greater individuality, Mani or Manes, whom Rudolf Steiner calls a high messenger of Christ—are the spirits who serve true Christianity in modern times and toward the future. In the last lecture of the cycle *The East in the Light of the West* he says the following about this:

> It is said that a few centuries after Christ had lived on the earth, there was held one of the greatest assemblies of the spiritual world connected with the earth that ever took place, and that there Manes gathered around him three mighty personalities of the fourth century after Christ. In this figurative description a most significant fact in connection with spiritual development is expressed. Manes called these persons together to consult with them as to the means of reintroducing the wisdom that had lived throughout the changing time of the post-Atlantean age and of causing it to unfold more and more gloriously in the future.
>
> Who were the personalities brought together in that memorable assembly? (It should be remembered that such an event can only be witnessed by spiritual sight.) He called together the personality in which Skythianos lived at that time, and also the physical reflection of the Buddha who had then appeared again, and the erstwhile Zarathustra who was wearing a physical body at that time. Around Manes was this council; himself in the center and around him Skythianos, Buddha and Zarathustra.
>
> And in that council a plan was agreed upon for causing all the wisdom of the bodhisattvas of the post-Atlantean time to flow more and more strongly into the future of mankind; and the plan of the future evolution of the civilization of the earth then decided upon was adhered to and carried over into the European mysteries of the Rose Cross. These particular mysteries have always been connected with the individualities of Skythianos, of Buddha, and of Zarathustra. They were the teachers in the schools of the Rose Cross; teachers who gave their wisdom to the earth as a gift, in order that through it the Christ being might be understood.[44]

That which happened on earth during the time that elapsed between the Manes Council and the unfolding of the mysteries of the Rose Cross at the beginning of modern times, that which hinted already of the great plan of the reawakening of the old wisdom, will now have our attention. It is the history of the Grail and the Order of the Templars.

3. The Temple and The Grail

1. Current Interest

The theme of the Temple and the Grail has received a lot of interest in the past few decades. In their 'explosively controversial international bestseller' *The Holy Blood and the Holy Grail*, Michael Baigent, Richard Leigh, and Henry Lincoln have reported the results of their research of ten years into the riddles around Rennes-le-Château, France.[45] They made the most shocking discovery of an historical 'conspiracy' that is based on the incredible notion that the Merovingian kings were descended from Jesus of Nazareth! Their deadly serious investigations are most thoroughly documented. They think, or at least they create the impression of thinking, that by collecting factual material they bring the truth to light. But actually, throughout the book it is ideas that lead them in a particular direction, or a lack of ideas that seduces them to certain conclusions. In the meantime, for these three authors it is a foregone conclusion that the Order of the Templars and the Grail are very closely connected.

The success of this work may perhaps lie in the shock-effect of the final conclusion, namely that the entire event on Golgotha was a fraud. Jesus did not die on the cross, let alone rise from the dead. He was married with Mary Magdalene who bore him children who went with their mother to southern France, and the later Merovingian kings are descended from them. There are descendants of this 'holy blood' alive today, and they are preparing for a restoration of the monarchy in France.

It seems to me that it is not necessarily the so-called discoveries that attract readers; rather, it is the general subject of the book that fascinates many people, namely the exploration of the secrets of the Grail, the Order of the Templars, and similar mysterious themes. It is astonishing how much is still being published every year about the mystery of the Templars. There is, for instance, the thesis of Louis Charpentier[46] that the Templars, while searching under the ruins of the Temple of Solomon, found the temple treasures or at least the Ark of the Covenant, and then brought them to France to give Chartres Cathedral a spiritual foundation. He also states as his opinion that the Templars financed the building of the Gothic cathedrals. Things like this are shrewdly concocted and presented in plausible terms, just like the story of the conspiracy around the holy blood. Such tales fascinate many people.

As if this weren't enough, Jacques de Mahieu comes with the thesis that the Templars got their silver from mines in South and Central America. Louis Charpentier also proclaims this 'secret', and how many others simply copy it without really knowing anything about it? Who hasn't read *The Spear of Destiny* by Ravenscroft, also a bestseller about the Grail with 'explosively controversial' statements—clear fabrications in this case, such as the contact he describes between Walter Johannes Stein and Adolf Hitler.

Books about the Holy Grail and the Holy Blood, and about the secret of the Templars, find many readers, often just because of the sensational aspects they seem to have. But apart from this, the subject of Temple and Grail should for us have an attraction that goes deeper than curiosity or sensationalism. The success of these books, especially those by English authors, it seems to me, lies partly in the fact that they connect the history of our time with these themes—the Spear of Destiny with the backgrounds of the Nazi regime, the Holy Blood with the history of France from the beginning of our age to today.

In their own ways the authors put world history in the light of the Holy Grail. They arrive at extremely interesting findings, but also at extremely questionable conclusions. Such authors are often good at finding occult connections, but the keys they use to open the 'secrets' are often startlingly simple and materialistic—trivial or very cleverly invented lies.

Jean Ferniot writes a novel *Saint Judas*. He arrives at the same conclusion as Baigent, Leigh and Lincoln about the Holy Blood and the Holy Grail: the Mystery of Golgotha was a fraud. In Ferniot's book it is the 'noble terrorist' Judas who uses Jesus for his own ambitious plans but, in order to give Jesus the desired prestige, he sacrifices himself by committing 'treason' and even hanging himself, after instructing Peter to spread the myth of the resurrection among people!

We can, of course, call such tales malignant and slanderous, but we can also allow for the possibility that someone like Ferniot really tries to fathom certain deeper problems of the drama on Golgotha. That happens then in a most undogmatic way. Without any hesitation, age-old, proven facts are thrown overboard, or explained in ways diametrically opposed to the conventional. Judas' treason, the most profound evil that yet brought about the highest good—death and resurrection—is indeed an enigmatic event when we want to understand it psychologically. That Judas had political aspirations, that he may have been a revolutionary agitator who viewed the Messiah mostly as the end of the hated Roman occupation, is in itself a plausible hypothesis.

Spiritual Science provides Ferniot's hypothesis with a surprising foundation, by pointing to the karmic connection between Judas Iscariot and Judas Maccabeus who, barely two hundred years earlier, had led a successful revolt against the Syrian oppressor of Judea. Ferniot does not know this occult fact, but he immersed himself so deeply in the figure of Judas that he still arrives at something plausible. But then his intellect tempts him into untruthfulness when he wants to bring his image of Judas into harmony with the Mystery of Golgotha.

Another example: Baigent, Leigh and Lincoln follow the supposition of the English professor Smith that the raising of Lazarus was an initiation. We have already heard that Anthroposophy also describes it in that way—a very important finding that can shake the whole traditional idea of miracles from its foundation. But what do we read a little further on in *The Holy Blood and the Holy Grail*? The poignant mystery of Lazarus' initiation, through which he becomes the initiate John, is changed into a trivial family coterie. It seems as if it is the authors' object to place everything to do with Jesus in the light of blood relationships. For Lazarus is the brother of Mary Magdalene and therefore, in the view of this book, the brother-in-law of Jesus. The explanation of the word Grail is also placed in this light: San Grail = Sang Real, or Sang Royal, Royal Blood. Jesus' blood was the blood of David, King of Israel. The point in both cases is the following.

It is of the greatest significance that in our time we develop a totally new relationship to the truths that the traditional Christian churches have proclaimed for two thousand years, but which seem to have lost their power. This renewed relationship to true Christianity, or to the truth of Christianity, however, is only real if the materialistic-intellectual type of thinking that has eroded and destroyed the faith—also within the Church—is replaced by thinking that is nourished from spiritual sources.

Books like the ones discussed above, however, do not draw their controversial points of view from such spiritual sources at all. Really true esotericism, occultism founded on real spiritual knowledge, cannot be found in them. Does not the current importance of the Temple and Grail theme lie in the fact that—with the means that are adequate in our current phase of consciousness, in other words, with a renewed spiritual thinking—many people in our time would want to undertake a new Grail quest? And wouldn't they want to strive to realize the ideals of the Temple knights and Rosicrucians today in a totally renewed, metamorphosed form?

The future of which the Grand Master of *The Soul's Probation* is speaking is surely our time! Only, what is happening? Human souls may come to earth with the unconscious urge to become 'Grail Knights' or 'Temple Knights' of this time. What do they find? A culture abounding in esotericism, eastern and western, Cabbala, astrology, mysticism, alchemy, magic, mysteries of the Templars, of the Grail, and much more.

But what is the common element in this abundance of spiritual 'food'? In none of these streams, movements, sects, novels, articles and semi-scientific bestsellers do we ever find any reference to the basic fact of the resurrection of Christ as an actual, real event. The fact is either denied or treated symbolically, which also means a denial of its reality. And modern Grail seekers are actually deceived, because all the so-called spirit offered by these sources, all more profound content, all mystery, are but empty husks without the central mystery of the death and resurrection of Jesus Christ. When this central mystery is not recognized, acknowledged, accepted, the intellect will invent things such as that the secret of the Temple of Solomon has to be excavated, or that there is a secret around Jesus' heredity, with the result that all of Christendom, the past history and therefore also the future will undergo a total revolution.

The Temple of Solomon was destroyed not long after it had fulfilled its function from the past, namely to be the place of preparation for the mystery of the resurrection. The heredity of Jesus comes from the past; the blood of Abraham and David flowed in him. With Jesus' death this blood flowed into the earth, but at that time it was the blood in which the highest Sun spirit had worked for three years. A new heredity came into being on Golgotha, but not a physical one! The resurrection body was a spiritual body, even though it revealed itself to the intimate disciples as something physically visible, tangible. From this body emanates a *future* stream. That is the true Grail secret. That is the impulse that fired the Templars. That is the theme of this book.

At this point we first have to find out what the Temple was in reality, what the various aspects of the Grail are, and how these two subjects are related to each other.

2. Phoenix

Spread throughout Rudolf Steiner's work, including his more than six thousand lectures, we can find shorter or longer observations on the theme of the Grail. One of the most remarkable of these is in a lecture given in Berlin in 1904, *Über die Wanderungen der Rassen* (*About the Wanderings of the Races*). Only notes of the listeners exist of this lecture, which were published in the *Gäa-Sophia Yearbook* of 1929.[47]

Speaking about the Templars in this lecture, Steiner calls them 'the original envoys of the Holy Grail' (*die eigentlichen Sendboten vom Heiligen Gral*). He says that on the place where the Temple of Solomon had stood (the place was given to the first nine Templars by King Baldwin II of Jerusalem in 1118 as the home of the Order) the Templars built a 'Place of Wisdom' where the knights were *initiated by the Holy Grail*. It is a great pity that this lecture was not stenographically recorded, because the part I am quoting is a riddle in its brevity. The knights were initiated—we can understand that—but we have no indication of what constituted this initiation. Who initiated them? The Holy Grail! Are we to think of one (spiritual) being, or of a circle of guardians of the Grail? Both are possible. At any rate, the word Grail cannot have been used here in the sense of a thing or a symbol, for neither of these can initiate someone.

And still, a number of thoughts might rise up in us due to this strange statement. In the mysterious first ten years of the Order, during which the number of knights around the founder Hugues de Payens did not increase (with one exception, Hugo de Champagne), no great war-like expeditions were undertaken. They may have been years of preparation and initiation that took place in secrecy, not years of making excavations to look for hidden treasures or documents from the Temple that might have escaped notice when the Temple was destroyed by the Romans in the year 70 AD, or to unearth the holy Ark of the Covenant—which the priests were supposed to have buried during the siege of Jerusalem—in order to give it a consecrated purpose. None of this. It was a time of reflection and learning, meditation and asceticism, leading to a Grail initiation.

After this period, in 1128, the group was able to go to France, and at the Council of Troyes it received its official confirmation as a spiritual Order of knights.

We may further presume that the location in Jerusalem, of the foundation of the Temple of Solomon, was deliberately chosen, and that a Christian initiation centre formed itself there based on what was still working as temple wisdom from the past.

When we try to fathom the wisdom that is connected with the Temple of Solomon we first of all have to consult the texts of the Old Testament. Both passages that describe the building of the Temple mention master builder Hiram. 'He was the son of a widow of the tribe of Naphtali, and his father was a man of Tyre, a worker in bronze; and he was full of wisdom, understanding, and skill, for making any work in bronze' (1 Kings 7:14). And in 2 Chronicles 2:13,14 we read: 'Now I [this is the King of Tyre speaking] have sent a skilled man, endued with understanding, Hiram-Abi, the son of a woman of the daughters of Dan, and his father was a man of Tyre. He is trained to work in gold, silver, bronze, iron, stone and wood, and in purple, blue and crimson fabrics and fine linen, to do all sorts of engraving and design any work of art that may be assigned him, with the help of your craftsmen, the craftsmen of my lord, David your father.'

As appears from this text, this master builder Hiram Abi, or Abiff, was an initiate, since the term 'son of a widow' was used for him. He added to Solomon's Temple design the 'bronze sea' and the two columns Jachin and Boaz. It is not so important that one text describes his mother as a descendant of Naphtali and the other of the daughters of Dan; what counts is that he came from Tyre. He even had the same name as the king of this area, a friend of Solomon who provided him not only with cedar wood and gold from Ophir for the Temple, but also sent him many workers to help with the construction.

The contribution Hiram Abiff made to the building of the Temple of Solomon was of eminent significance. He was an initiate from Tyre, a Phoenician city where there was an important mystery temple. We may presume that his initiation and his contribution to the temple construction in Jerusalem were connected with the mystery wisdom of his hometown. To learn more about this we have to look to other sources than the Bible.

The name Phoenicia is directly related to the Phoenix being that was highly honoured there, and that the Greeks called Heracles (Latin Hercules). Its Phoenician name was *Ar-chal*. Translated into English the name would sound something like *Fire-Light-Being Conquers*. We all know the picture of the Phoenix bird that burns itself in fire and rises alive again from its ashes. What is the meaning of this picture?

In the ancient cultures that preceded the coming of Christ on earth we find the worship of a god who was called by different names but who, in the various aspects under which he revealed himself, is yet recognizable as one and the same being who had a direct relationship to the sun. The Indians called him Vishnu-Krishna, the Greeks, Apollo, the Irish Celts, Lugh. For these peoples the emphasis lay on the triumphant character of this godhead; he was described as the vanquisher of evil, of the powers of the dragon or serpent. The same godhead is meant when mystery tradition speaks of the Phoenix bird. But the Phoenix aspect puts greater emphasis on the motif of voluntary death and victory over death: a *resurrection being*.

The first Christians made a direct connection between this Apollo-Phoenix being and Jesus. Rudolf Steiner confirmed that this is not a symbolic connection but a real one.[48] He explains that the Jesus child described by Luke was the first incarnation of an angelic, still divine human soul who, as sister soul of Adam—one could also say Adam's higher spiritual being—did not become part of the fall into sin. Therefore, it still had the paradisial purity of the first human being, sinless and connected with the leading sun hierarchies.

Before this being, in the figure of Jesus of Nazareth, was permitted to receive the highest Sun-Ego into himself at the Baptism in the Jordan and, because of this, to vanquish death through the fire-light force of Christ, he accomplished three cosmic deeds of sacrifice that may be viewed as three stages leading up to the Mystery of Golgotha. In these three cosmic deeds of sacrifice this Jesus-Phoenix being was permeated by the cosmic Christ, and was able because of this to protect the human being from the excessive, corrupting influences of the serpent- and dragon forces of Lucifer and Satan. These powers tried to invade first the physical body (the senses), then the life forces, and finally the soul forces in such a way that the human race would have been cut off from the goal of its development if these efforts had succeeded.

These sacrificial deeds are reflected in various mythological pictures, such as the battle of Apollo against the Python, or of Lugh against the sinister Fomor powers. Krishna is to be regarded as an avatar of this being, not a true incarnation, because this only took place in Jesus of Nazareth. Jewish occult teaching also knows this being and calls it Nezach, victory.

The Mystery of Golgotha, the fourth sacrifice, took place to protect the fourth principle of the human being, the I, from being overpowered by Lucifer-Satan. The I-principle, which human beings received from the sun hierarchy of the Elohim, physically expresses itself in the blood. Our blood is the instrument, the vehicle of our I. The pure 'vessel' in which the healing power, the fire-light-victory power, was triumphant over the powers of darkness for the fourth time, is Jesus. Through him the Christ, the highest sun spirit, the creative Logos, was able to become the spirit of the earth, so that the earth can be reunited with the sun world in the future.

The Jesus-Phoenix being is one of the twelve bodhisattvas and receives its power out of the constellation of Pisces. But how should we now understand the tradition reported by Wolfram von Eschenbach that the Grail is a *stone*, an emerald from the crown of Lucifer that fell to the earth in a battle with Michael? Wolfram's term *lapsit exillis* is sometimes rendered as 'stone fallen from the heavens', *lapsit ex coelis*.

The crown of Lucifer, the carrier of the cosmic light of wisdom and originally connected with Christ, was the circle of twelve wise star beings. But when Lucifer turned against his cosmic brother a battle in heaven ensued. One of the twelve cosmic 'stones' from the crown of wisdom sacrificed itself and fell with Lucifer to the earth. Wolfram says through the mouth of Trevrezent, the hermit whom Parsifal meets after years of futile wanderings, about the Grail knights:

> They live from a stone of purest kind. If you do not know it, it shall here be named to you. It is called *lapsit exillis*. By the power of that stone the phoenix burns to ashes, but the ashes give him life again. Thus does the phoenix molt and change its plumage, which afterward is bright and shining and as lovely as before. [...] The stone is also called the Grail.[49]

A few lines later he says that every Good Friday a white dove from heaven lays a holy host on the stone. This gives the stone the extraordinary power to nourish people with earthly food that possesses the fullness of Paradise. Thus Wolfram reveals and at the same time veils the character of the Grail.

Another tradition says that there was in the temple of Heracles in Tyre an emerald chalice that radiated a strong light at night. This chalice, which was supposed to be identical to the stone from Lucifer's crown from which a love-offering chalice had thus been made, came into the possession of the Queen of Saba (or Sheba), who gave it to Solomon. Eventually this chalice was present in the house where the Last Supper took place. A Jew brought the chalice to Pilate who gave it to Joseph of Arimathea, who became the first Guardian of the Grail.

Both the emerald chalice of the temple of Heracles and the later Grail chalice should not so much be conceived as a thing, an object, but rather as an imaginative indication of a mystery experience that brings the human being into contact with the Resurrection Being. In the Phoenician mysteries the golden-green shining chalice must have been an imagination of the god Ar-chal, the Jesus-Phoenix Being. For Joseph of Arimathea it was initially Jesus' tangible body and flowing blood that he was able to receive. Later the Resurrected One revealed Himself to him when he was imprisoned in a tower.[50]

Where do the Phoenix mysteries originally come from? In an important work about cultural history, Sigismund von Gleich[51] points to pre-Islamic Arabia, the land of Sheba or Saba. Its culture stretched not only over today's Yemen, but also over the high country where the current capital of Saudi Arabia is situated. This fertile part of the Arabian peninsula produced, in addition to incense and myrrh, also gold—the three gifts with which the Three Wise Men from the East (in this case Saba) honoured the child Jesus. This Arabian gold was shipped through the city of Apira (biblical Ophir) on the Persian Gulf.

A few centuries before Christ, Persian initiates developed these central Arabian gold mines; they were still guardians of Zoroastrian wisdom. Among the people of Saba who lived in the mountains where the gold was mined, we find the worship of the star Sirius, the star of Zarathustra. There were also Phoenix mysteries there. This means that the initiates of these pre-Islamic Arabs of Saba beheld in the spheres of the stars and planets the being who would one day, for the salvation of humanity, bring *the* great sacrifice on earth to overcome death.

We are struck by the old Sabean altars that often bear the image of the sun and moon that we also find in Egypt: the crescent of the moon supporting the sun disc. One might call this the Grail symbol. Rudolf Steiner pointed out that the cosmic Grail image is the silver crescent of the moon showing in it the dark side of the moon, which receives the spiritual working of the sun.[52] In a clear night sky we can often very clearly observe the light crescent with the dark disc in it. In this connection, Von Gleich speaks of a Sabean precious stone on which the Phoenix is engraved as it rises from its ashes; above it this Grail symbol is visible.

That the home country of the Phoenix must have a connection with Paradise is clear. Eduard Glaser, who did trailblazing archeological work in Saba, states that central Arabia has to be the earthly remnant of what was the Garden of Eden according to the Old Testament. Von Gleich, who has the greatest respect for Glaser, refers on this point to Genesis 2:11 and 10:29, where the land of Havilah is mentioned 'where there is gold'.

Tradition tells the same thing about Ireland which, of old, was also regarded as an earthly reflection of Paradise. The stories of the Grail, even the very different renderings of Robert de Boron and Wolfram von Eschenbach, speak with emphasis of a connection between the Grail and the Celtic West. Von Gleich said about this:

> From two places therefore, that both have a relationship with paradisial impulses from prehistoric times, came historical streams

which were then, connected with each other, called to carry the Grail secret, the secret we can only comprehend when we consider the paradisial, divine human being who never went through the Fall. Wolfram had insight into this secret, for he calls the Grail 'the fullness of Paradise.' These are no poetic fantasies.

We might pose a question that, in relation to all of this, is not without interest, namely what is the connection of the Sabean culture in pre-Islamic Arabia with Phoenicia, the land that was originally called Canaan? Sigismund von Gleich gives an interesting, but not perfectly clarifying, answer to this question in his book referred to above. He points to the mysterious figure of Melchizedek, who is called priest of God Most High in Genesis. As great initiate of the Sun mysteries Melchizedek may not only have been the inaugurator of the mysteries of Hebron,[53] but also have brought the Sabean mysteries to Canaan. Von Gleich:

> The connections that are barely indicated here might lead us to surmise that the Phoenician Kabiri mysteries, which Abraham encountered in Hebron, had their origin in the highest Kabir who revealed himself through Melchizedek, and who through mystery traditions was connected with the Sabean Sun-Paradise mysteries of central Arabia. Thus it is possible that already in the days of Abraham the central secret of Arabia, the mystery of the sun being Phoenix, was brought from Saba to Canaan by the mystery stream of Melchizedek. At first it was then guarded in Jerusalem (the Salem of Melchizedek), and later in the Phoenician temples where we find it again in the temple wisdom of Tyre and Sidon.

In this connection there is an interesting passage in a lecture of Rudolf Steiner's cycle *From Jesus to Christ* where, speaking of the Jesus-Phoenix being, he says:

> It was preserved in an important mystery center, as in a tabernacle...

And two pages later:

> There was a transference from a mystery center in western Asia, where this human kernel had been preserved, into the body of the Nathan Jesus child.[54]

Without a doubt the Phoenician temple mysteries must have been meant here. Those who were initiated in these mysteries, as must have been the case with the master builder Hiram, were initiated in the pre-Christian Grail mystery; perhaps we may even say: were *initiated by the Holy Grail*.

In this context the role of the Queen of Saba is quite remarkable. All it says in the Old Testament is that she wanted to become acquainted with

Solomon's wisdom and wanted to test it. He exceeds all her expectations, and after an exchange of the most precious gifts she returns to her country. But legendary tradition gives her a much more important role. In addition to the story of the emerald chalice from the Heracles-Phoenix temple that she is said to have given to Solomon, she also appears in the so-called Temple Legend as a key figure in the drama that unfolds between Hiram and Solomon. She is also mentioned in the legend of the Holy Cross, which we can find in *Golden Legends* by Jacques de Voragine; there she is mentioned as the one who predicts to Solomon the crucifixion of Jesus Christ.

In any case, it is evident that when in Jerusalem the definitive home of the Ark of the Covenant was built, there came both from Phoenicia in the person of Hiram, and from Saba in the person of its Queen Balkis, a spiritual stream to this place and this building, a stream that connects the Grail mystery with the Temple of Solomon.

We now have to consider the construction of the Temple and the place where it was established.

3. Jerusalem, Holy City

The reign of King Solomon was the outer culmination of the history of the twelve tribes of Israel. Prepared by the indefatigable warrior David, an era of rest, prosperity, prestige and power dawned for the descendants of Abraham, Isaac and Jacob, unlike any time before or after. Immediately after Solomon's death the kingdom was divided in two, a rupture that led to an immense series of calamities, trials and strayings by the people of Israel.

Ever since the powerful initiate Moses had led the people out of Egypt through the desert to the promised land, the twelve tribes had arranged themselves around their movable sanctuary, the Tent of Meeting with the Holy of Holies in it, the sign of the covenant between God and His people. When the city of Jerusalem, the mystery place of Melchizedek, had finally come into David's power, a definitive house for the God of Israel could be built. The edifice that was erected by David's son Solomon was not merely an outwardly visible reality; it was also a symbol of far-reaching significance.

To comprehend this significance we have to take the Bible completely literally. Through Nathan as intermediary, Yahweh spoke to David of 'a House for my Name'. Which name? None other than the one revealed to Moses when he stood before the burning bush: 'I AM'. In the course of human evolution the awareness of the I as the most inward perception of our own spiritual being developed only very gradually. It was the destiny of the Jewish people to receive and unfold this I-experience as mystery teaching and religion. This people learned to distinguish what can be experienced as the lower I out of the natural disposition of the human being, from what comes 'from above' as the higher I-being. The latter was felt to be heavily veiled, a most holy secret. It was the sacred Name of God which no one, except the consecrated priest on the Day of Atonement, was allowed to pronounce.

At the time when Solomon became king, the Jewish people had become sufficiently mature that the 'House for God's Name' could be built, in other words, that the higher I-principle had to be given *a dwelling place in the human being*. The Most High, who formerly had His throne in distant cosmic spaces, prepared Himself to live in the sanctuary of the soul of the earthly human being. An outer symbol had to be erected for this: the temple as image of the human body within which, hidden in darkness as in a most secret tabernacle, the I-God could dwell.

Before embarking on a more detailed description of the Temple of Solomon, we have to turn our attention to the city of Jerusalem, because it is no coincidence that it was determined that the Temple of Solomon was to be built there. Before David was forbidden by the Lord to found the Temple himself (2 Sam.7), he had in a certain sense already made preparations for the construction. He had built his palace on Mount Zion, in the western part of the city, and the Ark of the Covenant had been moved there. In a dramatically stern manner, however, an angel of God directed him with a flaming sword to the opposite Mount Moriah in the eastern part of the city. You see, after he had ordered a census of the people he incurred the wrath of God over himself and his people. The pest that then broke out could only be averted by David's building an altar on the threshing floor of Ornan on Mount Moriah. Subsequently, this place was destined to become the place of the Temple (1 Chron. 21,22).

It is the great merit of Emil Bock's masterful studies of the Old and New Testaments that he has shown the primeval polarities of the Holy Land and, in particular, the city of Jerusalem. The contrast between paradisial Galilee and the infernal desert landscape of Judea culminates in a certain respect in the contrast between Zion and Moriah. Zion is a luxuriant sun hill facing the barren moon hill Moriah. Between the two there was originally a deep cleft running north-south that separated the higher Zion part from the lower Mount Moriah. Solomon had the cleft filled in, so that the striking division through the Holy City disappeared.

Mount Zion in the western part must have been a very ancient sun sanctuary. We know that in Abraham's time the mystery place of

Melchizedek, the priest of El-Elyon, God Most High, was there. He brought to the 'Moon priest' Abraham (Abraham was for an extended time in Haran, a Babylonian city where the centre of the Mesopotamian moon religion was situated) the offering gifts of *bread and wine*. Abraham bowed down to this lofty being and offered him a tenth of all he had. This is all the Old Testament says about Melchizedek. The Letter to the Hebrews, however, speaks of him as follows:

> This Melchizedek of whom we are speaking is King of Salem, the priest of the highest God. He went out to meet Abraham who was returning from the war of the kings. He blessed Abraham, and Abraham gave him a tenth of all that he possessed. His name when translated means, firstly, king of righteousness, and then he is also called king of Salem, that means king of peace. He is without father, without mother and without ancestors, without beginning of days or end of life: he is of similar nature as the Son of God and he is a bearer of priesthood forever. Imagine how great he must be that Abraham, our patriarch, sacrificed a tenth of all the spoils of war as a sacrifice to him! (Hebr.7:1-4)

This passage leaves no doubt as to what is happening here. Behind the name of 'King of Righteousness and Peace' hides a high spiritual being, an initiate who has already left the lower stage of humanity behind, and has become 'of similar nature as the Son of God'. Rudolf Steiner points to the connection of Melchizedek with Manu (Noah) of the ancient Indians.[55] He says that this high initiate of the Atlantean Sun Oracle, who was the great preparer for Christ, revealed himself to Abraham in the guise of the forefather of the Semites. Melchizedek bore the etheric body, the formative life forces, of Shem. The legends of the Jews confirm this spiritual fact, because they call the mystery place of Melchizedek the *School of Shem*.

More light is thrown on the figure of Melchizedek in a book by Ephraim the Syrian (306-373 AD)[56] that describes that Adam told his son Seth to balsam his body after his death and lay it in the 'treasury', a cave in the mountain under Paradise. He also had to see to it that all descendants would know that, in case they would leave the place, they had to take Adam's body with them and bring it to the centre of the earth, where he would one day be redeemed. This is done. Noah takes the bodies of Adam and Eve from the treasury into the Ark and lays on them the three offerings of gold, incense and myrrh. When Noah, who lived another 350 years after the great Flood, feels his end approaching he tells his son Shem to take the body of Adam out of the Ark and bring it to the centre of the earth. He has to take bread and wine with him as provisions, and choose Melchizedek as his travelling companion, who has to remain at the grave of Adam as its guardian. Shem then takes the body of Adam out of the Ark and goes on his way with the young Melchizedek. An angel accompanies them and leads them to *Golgotha*, the centre of the earth. When Shem and Melchizedek lay the corpse of Adam there on the earth, the earth opens in the form of a cross. They lay the body in the opening, which then closes again. The name of this place is henceforth 'Place of the Skull'.

> Then Shem spoke to Melchizedek:
> You are the servant of the Most High God,
> For you alone God chose
> That you should serve Him in this place.
> Remain here forever!
> And never in your life remove yourself from this spot!
> Take no woman!
> Do not cut your hair!
> Shed no blood in this place,
> Offer no wild animals or birds,
> But rather bread and wine.
> Build no edifice in this place.
> The angel of the Lord will always come to you
> And take care of you!
> Then Shem embraced Melchizedek,
> Kissed him and blessed him.
> Thereupon he returned to his brothers.

Salem therefore was a place consecrated to El-Elyon, the Most High God. It was the place where the mystery of the primeval human body, which had still been formed in Paradise, was guarded by a being who was king and priest, not by earthly choosing, but by divine decree. And finally, the central substances in the mystery ritual here referred to were *bread and wine*.

Jerusalem is the navel of the earth, where heaven and underworld border on each other, as do life and death: the creative sun world and the hardened constriction of bitter materiality.

The Hill of Atonement, the Place of the Skull, where the cross of the Redeemer was raised over the oldest grave of humanity—where the New Adam rose from the rocky tomb, clothed in the immortal robe of the Resurrection body—is not situated exactly in the middle between Zion and Moriah, between sun and moon, but a little to the left, just as the human heart is not in the middle of the chest, but a little to the left. Still, the forces of the depths that had manifested in frightening forms in the original cleft, must also have been active in the immediate vicinity of Golgotha at the time of the crucifixion.

There are good reasons to assume that Golgotha and the nearby tomb are indeed the place where Constantine later built the Church of the Holy Sepulchre. The spot now lies in the middle of the old city of Jerusalem, but at the time of the crucifixion it was outside the city by the north-western corner of the erstwhile city wall. This part of the western hills was a little removed from the original cleft, but was probably a western side-arm of it. Be that as it may, the gardens with their Zion nature that were situated there (one of them belonged to Joseph of Arimathea, who had prepared his own grave there) bordered directly on the bare top of Golgotha, which had a distinct Moriah character. According to an eyewitness report of the sixth century AD there were still deep clefts in that area. And deep down there were subterranean water streams that were connected with the Siloah spring in the South.

The place where David's castle stood, with the royal palace and the neighbouring provisional chapel for the Ark of the Covenant before this was taken to the Temple on Mount Moriah, is most probably the place where the original Melchizedek sanctuary was located on the south side of Mount Zion, with the standing sun stone (menhir) that gave the hill its name, the cultic symbol of the Most High God.

When Solomon moved the centre of religious and political life—the royal palace and the Temple—to the eastern part of town, the southern part of Zion became a place of silence. David and all Judean kings until Hezekiah were buried there. These tombs were plundered in the course of time, even by King Herod, but otherwise this part of town remained peaceful and quiet.

Here, over David's grave, the Essenes established the house of their Order, where Jesus and His disciples were assembled at the Last Supper. Here the words were spoken over the bread and wine as the body and blood, the offerings of a new covenant. Here the Risen One appeared in the midst of His disciples, and here also the Pentecost event took place, the descent of the Holy Spirit. For the original congregation in Jerusalem the house of the Order of the Essenes, the *coenaculum* as it was later called, remained the place of meeting where the first Christian religious services occurred—the ritual repetition of the sacramental offering of bread and wine.

4. The Temple of Solomon

After these topographical and legendary-historical particulars of the Holy City of Jerusalem, we will place the Temple of Solomon in the above-described context. The actual temple was of an almost unimaginable architectonic simplicity. It was not the sanctuary itself that gave to Solomon's buildings their resplendent aspect, but the royal palace with its pillars and cedar wood beams and large spaces.

For the measurements of the sanctuary Solomon took those of the Tent of Meeting and doubled them; he also added a forecourt. The side structures with rooms at three levels, spaces for the priests and for supplies, at first do not seem to have a function in the symbolism of the building. This symbolism is related to the physical body of the human being, which has to become the Temple of God. However, when we learn what the measurements of the building were, we can in the first instance not understand how this rectangular block of 60x20x30 cubits[*] had anything to do with the human body. This can only become clear when we take into consideration the measurements of the precursors of the Temple of Solomon, namely the Tent or Tabernacle that Moses built following divine instructions, and even Noah's Ark long before it. Before we do this, we will point out the more obvious symbolism of the three parts of the temple structure, and the related symbolism of the cultic arrangement of the interior.

The three elements of the Temple—the forecourt, the Sanctuary and the Holy of Holies—can be viewed as the body, soul and spirit, which makes the Temple an image of the perfect human being. Part of the forecourt are the two columns, Jachin and Boaz. What these columns symbolized will be discussed later. They belong at any rate to the 'bodily' aspect.

The soul part contained the most important ritual objects, the Incense Altar, the seven-armed lamp stands, and the table with the twelve showbreads. The curtain that closed the passage to the Holy of Holies must also be considered part of the Sanctuary. This curtain showed four colours that symbolized the four elements of earth, water, air and fire. The number of the showbreads was related to the twelve signs of the zodiac, while the seven arms of the lamp stands were connected with the seven planets. The human soul, moved by incense to piety and devotion, grew to cosmic heights, but then it had to hold back before the threshold of the actual realm of the spirit.

---

[*] A cubit was approximately equal to 20 inches, or 50 centimetres.

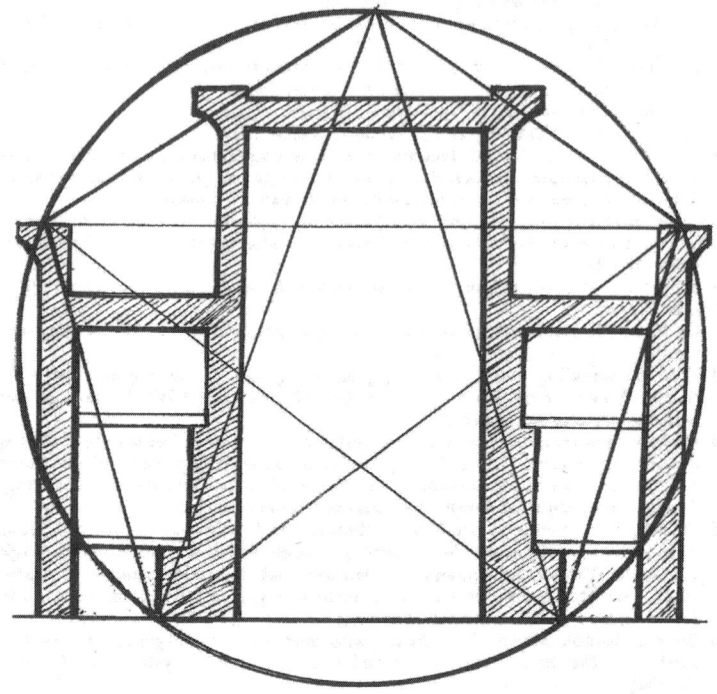

The Temple of Solomon

The veil of the earthly elements covered the divine secret of the Most High. The I-God was imageless; He lived in the perfect cube of 20x20x20 cubits, the Holy of Holies. This part, into which no light could penetrate, was on the west side of the building; the entrance faced East. These three characteristics of the Holy of Holies, its West-facing location, its cubic form, and its darkness, are connected with death. And indeed, standing before the veil of the elements of the senses, the Israelites would bring to consciousness the fact that they had lost the Godhead behind it by their neglect of God's commandments. The answer to their sin was death. Death concealed the countenance of God. Beholding God meant death.

God Himself first had to appear in an earthly human body, had to descend into the realm of death and thus vanquish death as the extinguisher of consciousness, before the curtain hiding the Secret could be opened. The Messiah is the fulfiller of the Temple symbolism.

Legend has it that the bones and skull of Adam were buried in the heart of the city. This means that what was still living in the paradisial original condition, namely the human being as the image and likeness of God dwelling in the Garden of Eden, became mortal by falling away from God. The earth became his home and at the same time his grave. But the grave of the earth, the body that bears death in itself, will one day be a renewed, living sun realm again; the human body will be a renewed, living house of the spirit. For this the Most High wanted to make the sacrifice of penetrating the body and blood of one human being. This body and this blood are indeed descended from Adam, but they are indwelt by the sinless, cosmic, never before incarnated Adam soul, the Jesus-Phoenix being.

The I that worked in the blood of Jesus until His thirtieth year was not yet the Christ I, not yet the 'Name of God', but His pure vessel. At the Baptism in the Jordan, however, the highest I could be received into this vessel, into one human being, so that it may then live in *the* human being. By accepting this higher I, the 'body of Adam' received its spiritual fullness again, the 'fullness of Paradise'; it became the resurrection body of Jesus Christ, the New Adam. This Grail secret is brought to expression in the Temple a thousand years before the mystery of death and resurrection. The wisdom of Solomon, however, was not sufficient to bring this to realization; he had to accept the help of the Phoenician initiate, Hiram.

To understand the measurements of the Temple we first have to know what Noah's Ark actually was. The Ark was not a physical ship. How would all animal pairs have found room in a space of 300x50x30 cubits? This strange oblong box was the 'construction thought' of the human being itself, the way it had to form itself physically in the post-Atlantean era. This was prepared in Atlantean times and had to be saved from the decadence brought about by the moral fall of the Atlanteans (see Chapter 2).

How did the current, post-Atlantean human body come into being in its three-dimensional form? Rudolf Steiner describes this in the following way in *The Temple Legend*. [57] The measurements of our current body originate from the higher aspects of the human being, from our soul being and the complex of life- and formative forces that permeate our physical body. Immediately after death we have the feeling that we are growing in size. We no longer live in the physical sheath we just left behind, but we become aware of our life body in which all images of our life are conserved as in a great memory tableau. We see this tableau concurrently with the awareness that we are living in an enlarged, non-material body.

This enlarged, non-material body, says Rudolf Steiner, had to be awakened as an image in ancient Atlantean times, so that one day the physical body would be able to condense itself to today's dimensions. The etheric or life form we now experience after death first had to arise as idea, at a time when the life body and the physical body did not yet so completely interpenetrate as is the case today during our life. This etheric, formative model was impressed, as it were, upon human beings by the spiritual leaders of mankind in Atlantean times. When we imagine ourselves surrounded by an etheric form from which our current physical body can come into being in the right way, we are surrounded by the form of Noah's Ark with its 300x50x30 cubits.

All of humanity was brought up and educated with the help of active symbols, says Rudolf Steiner. In the dimensions of our physical body we have the measurements of Noah's Ark in us. When human beings stretch their arms above their heads, they portray the relation of length and breadth of 300 to 50: 6 to 1. In ancient Egypt the goddess Nut was often depicted on the inside of a sarcophagus with her arms stretched upward. The temple is the body; the body is the temple!

We see the next important step in the making of the Tent of Meeting. Here we find the dimensions of 30x10x10 cubits for the part of the Temple itself; around it was an open court of 100x50 cubits where the altar and the laver* stood. The tent or Tabernacle itself had two parts, the Sanctuary, 20 cubits long, where the Incense Altar, the seven-armed lamp stand and the table with the twelve showbreads stood, with behind this the Holy of Holies, 10 cubits long, separated from the Sanctuary by a curtain. Here the Ark of the Covenant and the Tablets of the Law were kept.

When we draw into this space a human figure lying down with his arms stretched above his head, the head lies in the Holy of Holies. The dimensions of the Ark, 2.5x1.5x1.5 cubits, then correspond with the dimensions of the skull of the prostrated figure. If this figure sat upright, the crown of the skull would just touch the ceiling of the tent.

In the Temple in Jerusalem the fundamental idea of the Ark and the Tabernacle had to be continued, but a *future element* had to be added to it. Spiritual science tells us that the development of the earth and humanity takes its course in great phases. Occult literature distinguishes seven aeons (great eras), each consisting of seven cultural epochs; we currently live in the fifth cultural epoch of the fifth, or post-Atlantean,

---

* A large wash basin where the officiating priests washed their hands and feet.

aeon. At present what will be realized in the sixth aeon, including a new, different form of the human body, already has to be prepared. Rudolf Steiner says the following about this:

> In the aeon that follows on ours, the sixth aeon, the human body will again be formed entirely differently. Even today, the human being has to bring to life in him those thought forms that can produce the ground on which the human body develops the right proportions in the next aeon; that must be demonstrated to the human being. Today the human being is built with the proportions of 300x50x30. In the future he will be built completely differently. How is the human being given the thought form today that will give him the future human form in the next aeon? [...] This occurs through the proportions of the Temple of Solomon. The measurements of the Temple represent in profound symbolism the entire structure of the physical human form as it will be in the next, the sixth, aeon.
>
> Everything that works in mankind originates from within, not from without. What in one era is thought and feeling, is outer form in the next era. And the individuals who lead the development of mankind have to instill into mankind, many thousands of years ahead of time, the thought forms that must later become physical reality. That is the function of the thought forms that originate in such symbolic pictures as Noah's Ark, the Temple of Solomon, and also the four apocalyptic living creatures, Lion, Bull, Eagle and Human Being. They have a very concrete significance. [58]

Now, the difficulty is that it is not at all easy to discover what is so new in the measurements of the Temple of Solomon as compared with Noah's Ark or the Tabernacle: 60 cubits long and 20 cubits wide, exactly twice those of the Tabernacle. Only the height of 30 cubits deviates from the proportions of the previous sacred spaces. However, is that of essential importance, given the fact that the Holy of Holies clearly preserves the form of a cube: 20x20x20 cubits? And were the additional 10 cubits of the height perhaps necessary for the construction of the roof, which was not needed in the Tent, and therefore was perhaps a purely technical necessity without any symbolic function?

The solution to this riddle is not clearly to be found in the Old Testament books of Kings and Chronicles. And what Rudolf Steiner said about it in another lecture—of which again only listeners' notes are available—is certainly not crystal clear (see note 57). But it does help. The point was that the form of the temple had to express symbolically that a transition needed to be made from the *square* to the *pentagon*. The development of the human being on earth had taken place in such a way that with the birth of the I-consciousness a fourth principle was added to an existing threefoldness. We have already come to know the threefoldness of the physical body, etheric body or body of formative forces, and the soul body that is called astral body. These parts of the human being had already come into being in earlier cosmic developmental phases.

In Atlantean times the birth of the I-consciousness was prepared; we can find a first germ of this in the small group of original Semites around the great leader of humanity, Manu; the Hebrews called him both Noah and Melchizedek. In the people of Israel, later primarily the descendants of Judah, this feeling of I had gradually developed to the point that a higher I-principle could be added to the then existing fourfoldness. The divine self, whose name was I AM, was preparing to descend into this people, into the son of David.

At the time of Solomon, about a thousand years before the coming of Christ, the Lord already instilled into His people the awareness that the human being himself had to become a Temple for God's Name, for the higher I AM. The Godhead no longer revealed Himself by signs in the realm of the elements as He did to a great extent to Moses.

> In the breast of the human being, concealed in the deepest sanctuary of the human self, the Godhead is to be made into a moral God. In this way, the human body became a great symbol of the Holy of Holies.[59]

This fact is then made into an architectural symbol; the human body, which is the house of God, must become a temple. To the sacred square of Pythagoras the pentagon has to be added. Where do we find this? Rudolf Steiner: 'The entrance, the roof and the side walls together form a pentagon.' Then he mentions the two golden cherubim that stood in the space of the Holy of Holies. He says: 'The fifth principle, which has not yet descended, is still guarded by the two higher beings, buddhi and manas. It is the beginning of the manas development of the human being.'

The higher element in the human being reveals itself in the first instance as the spirit self, in theosophical literature called manas. In Christian esotericism this was called the Holy Spirit. The manas development of the human being indicates the future development in which human beings have to unfold the Holy Spirit principle in themselves as their Higher Self. An even higher, sixth principle is indicated with the word buddhi, or life spirit. In Christian esotericism this principle was called the Son.

In the 1905 lecture already referred to, after the passages mentioned here about the building of the Temple, Steiner speaks about the Knights Templar: 'They took up the idea of the Temple of Solomon in order to develop it as a living reality for the future.' That is what the first knights prepared themselves for during ten years on a place that was situated in the immediate vicinity of the old Temple. What this meant will be considered in Chapter 5.

For a complete understanding of the symbolism of the Temple, however, we have to consider the specific contribution made by the Phoenician initiate, Hiram to its construction on Mount Moriah.

5. Hiram and the Temple Legend

The wisdom of Solomon was the ripe fruit of a thousand-year development within the people of Abraham, Isaac and Jacob. In a certain sense it was 'inherited' wisdom, which through destiny appeared concentrated in one exceptional personality. Contemporaries as well as people who lived later experienced in Solomon's personality a messianic prefiguration of the universal human being. Solomon's seven names indicate the seven elements of the human being. It is no coincidence that the name that was most used, 'Solomon, Bearer of Peace', is related to the fifth aspect, spirit self or manas.

All the same, history and legend agree in their depiction of Solomon's weaknesses. In no way was he able, as human individuality, as human I, to fulfil the messianic picture of perfection. It clothed him like a royal mantle; it was his *persona*,* but his individuality could not yet attain to this perfection. The building of the Temple, for instance, which was his most significant deed—he was able to conceive it as an idea, but the technical execution of it had to be done by the wise man from Tyre, Hiram Abiff. By itself, this would have generated an excellent and most fruitful collaboration, if in these two men an age-old dichotomy of the human race had not come to the fore, namely that of Cain and Abel.

The Bible story about the building of the Temple is silent about this, but the Temple Legend is perfectly clear about it. Rudolf Steiner tells us that the legend, which belongs to the esotericism of the Freemasons, goes back to Christian Rosenkreutz.[60] Since the fifteenth century it was told in the brotherhoods of the Rose Cross, and later among the Freemasons. The deeper significance was known only to a few initiates.

---

* The Latin word *persona* means mask.

In Chapter 2 we have already mentioned the relationship between Christian Rosenkreutz and the master builder Hiram.

In Hiram we should not only see the Phoenician initiate who knew the mystery of the sun bird Phoenix and the chalice of the love offering, but also an exceptional representative of the Cain stream in humanity. That profound secrets were connected with the figure of Cain is only vaguely indicated in the book of Genesis, namely with the strange words Eve spoke after giving birth to Cain: 'I have gotten a man with the help of the Lord.' (Gen.4:1) Emil Bock translates this as: 'As husband I have gained Yahweh.' [61] The Temple Legend gives an explanation of this enigmatic saying. Cain was not a son of Adam, but was conceived in Eve because one of the sun spirits (Elohim) united himself with her. Cain was therefore originally a son of a god, a being who did not come from sexual procreation, a human being from before the Fall. The second child, Abel, did indeed come into being through earthly procreation. However, the consequences of the Fall also had their effect on Cain. When his offering was rejected by Yahweh, he erupted in anger and killed his brother.

Then follows another enigmatic passage in the story. God says: 'If anyone slays Cain, vengeance shall be taken on him sevenfold.' (Gen.4:15) What this means is that, in spite of the curse that rested on them, Cain and his descendants may not be persecuted and killed. And then this dynasty of Cain is described as the stream of creative people, builders, inventors, technicians and artists.

In the conventional moral view that grew in later times, Cain is the arch-evil one and Abel the good and innocent one. But Genesis itself, and certainly the later Temple Legend, oblige us to think about these figures in much more nuanced terms. The imaginative picture of the trees in Paradise can help us with this. In Paradise the Tree of Life and the Tree of Knowledge of Good and Evil are still connected with each other; they form a kind of unity. By his eating of the Tree of Knowledge a profound change occurs in the human being; he has to leave Paradise, the Tree of Life is withheld from him. There are therefore clearly two trees in the story.

What do these pictures mean? Under the influence of Lucifer the human being separated himself from the sun guidance of the Elohim. In his *consciousness* he experienced his first autonomy: knowledge of good and evil. The result of this was death. In other words, henceforth a *dying* part of our organism provides us with an autonomous consciousness: our nerve-sense system is the 'withered' Tree of Knowledge in our body.

Now the human being could place himself under the leadership of Yahweh, who as one of the creative sun spirits made the sacrifice of leaving his original sun sphere and connecting himself with the sphere of the moon, so as to oppose Lucifer from there.

Yahweh worked unconsciously in the blood and heredity; He wanted to preserve the human 'freed' consciousness for the divine world through religion, reconnection. Pleasing to him was the stream of Abel (continued after his death by Seth), the *religious* human being. The full consequences of the Fall were experienced not by the Cain person, but by the Abel person in his relationship to the Invisible. He admitted the death force in his consciousness, which opened his physical eyes (Gen.3:7), but veiled God in darkness.

By contrast, the Cain stream in a certain sense kept a connection with the Tree of Life, because Cain's origin lay in the paradisial sun element. He was the magical human being, whose *will* was still filled with cosmic creative power. The death element (knowledge of good and evil) was initially not yet present in his consciousness. However, the Fall worked in him in the will: he committed the *deed* of killing. But his descendants are just as necessary for the development of humanity as those of Seth, Abel's replacement.

This is the reason why Cain may not be killed. He was removed; there was to be enmity between the sons of Cain and the sons of Abel-Seth, until Christ reconciles the two brothers. However, Cain's tragedy has its fruits in art and science. Through these the earth is cultivated, transformed. The fire-forces in the will of the creative human being, which are still sun-related, overcome the death-forces of the Fall, just as religious devotion (the moon force of Yahweh) sanctifies consciousness.

In the construction of the Temple we see the two different streams in the development of humanity represented by Solomon and Hiram distinctly manifested. The religious content, the fullness of bright, lofty wisdom of the ideas that underlie the building come from Solomon; the form, the ultimate realization for which practical wisdom and technical ingenuity were needed, could only come from a son of Cain. It took Hiram's skill as metal worker to fashion the symbolic columns Jachin and Boaz at the entrance to the Temple, as well as the so-called molten sea in the forecourt, a water basin cast in bronze, carried by twelve supports in the form of bulls, three facing each of the four compass points.

After the foregoing, the symbolism of the two columns is sufficiently evident. These two huge structures face anyone who enters the Temple from the East as the two trees of Paradise, the column of life (Jachin) and the column of death (Boaz). As we have seen, the Temple is the body. The columns of death and life, of wisdom (knowledge) and strength are also present in our physical corporeality; we have the life organs and knowledge organs in us as the two withered trees of Paradise.

What was separated by the Fall will in the future be brought together again by the power of Christ. Abel and Cain have to be reconciled. This secret is indicated in the form of imagination by the symbolism of the 'molten sea' and the 'golden triangle', as these can be found in the Temple Legend.

The following is a rendering of the Temple Legend in my own words as Rudolf Steiner tells it in *The Temple Legend* (CW 93).

> One of the Elohim created a human being he called Eve. He united himself with her, and Eve gave birth to Cain. Thereafter Yahweh, another Elohim being, created Adam. Adam united himself with Eve, which resulted in the birth of Abel.
>
> The offerings Abel brought to Yahweh were pleasing to the latter, but the offerings of Cain were not, because Cain had not come into being through him. Because of this Cain committed fratricide by killing Abel. As a result he was barred from all connection with Yahweh. He went away to distant places and became there the patriarch of his own dynasty.
>
> Adam and Eve lived together and, to replace Abel, Seth was born, who is also mentioned in the Bible. Thus two human families grew up, the first descending from Eve and the Elohim being, the line of Cain; the second descending from the human couple that had united themselves with each other by order of Yahweh.
>
> Cain is the patriarch of all those who have created the arts and sciences on earth, such as Methuselah, who invented writing (the *Tau* script), and Tubal-Cain who taught people how to work copper ore and iron. Thus the stream of humanity came into existence which, in direct descent from the Elohim, became proficient in the arts and sciences. Hiram came from this lineage of the sons of Cain. He bore in himself as his hereditary share, all that in the course of many generations had accumulated in the children of Cain as knowledge, art, and technology. Hiram was the most proficient master builder one can imagine.
>
> Solomon came from the stream of Seth; he excelled in all that originated from Yahweh. He possessed a universal wisdom, all that flows forth from the tranquil, lucid, sober wisdom of the sons of Yahweh. This was a wisdom one can express in words, that can deeply move human hearts and inwardly raise a person up, but it did not give one a grip on material things, enable one to construct

something concrete, or to work creatively as an artist or in a scientific-technical way. This wisdom was an inspiration that came directly from God, not one that wells up from human passion or human will and wrestles its way up. This latter kind of wisdom was found in the sons of Cain, those who descended in a straight line from one of the other Elohim. They were the ones who would slave away and want to win everything for themselves through their own effort. Solomon decided to build a Temple, and he sent for a master builder from the lineage of Cain, Hiram.

Around the same time Balkis, Queen of Saba (or Sheba), came to Jerusalem because she had heard of the wise Solomon. And when she arrived she was indeed elated about the lofty, lucid wisdom and beauty of Solomon. He asked for her hand and was accepted. But the Queen then also heard about the construction of the Temple. Now she wanted to meet the master builder Hiram. When she saw him, his gaze alone immediately made a deep impression on her and she fell completely under his charm.

Now envy arose between Hiram and the wise Solomon. The consequence was that Solomon would fain have undertaken something against Hiram, but he had to spare him so that the Temple would be completed. The following then happened. The Temple was finished except for one important part, which was to be Hiram's masterpiece, a bronze water basin. It was to be an image of the sea, cast in bronze, as an adornment of the Temple.

All the metal mixtures had been prepared by Hiram in miraculous ways, and all was ready to begin casting the fiery mass. At the time there were, however, three apprentices whom Hiram had not judged worthy to be admitted to the status of master. They had therefore sworn to be revenged on him, and they wanted to do whatever it took so that the casting of the bronze sea would fail. One of Hiram's friends heard of this plot and told Solomon about it so that he would prevent it. But Solomon let things take their course out of his jealousy of Hiram. He wanted to ruin him.

The result was that Hiram had to watch how the casting of the metal became a catastrophe. The fiery liquid mass exploded and spread because the three apprentices had added water to it which had a disastrous effect. Hiram tried to put out the fire with large quantities of water, but that only made it worse.

While in desperation he had to admit that his masterpiece could not be saved, Tubal-Cain appeared to him, one of his forefathers, and told him to throw himself into the fire without fear, for the fire could not hurt him.

Hiram made the jump and reached the centre of the earth. Tubal-Cain led him to Cain who sat on a throne in the state of his original divinity. Hiram was then given the secret of the creative powers of fire, the secrets of casting metals and many other things. From Tubal-Cain he received a hammer and a golden triangle that he had to wear around his neck. Thereupon he came back and was indeed able to create the bronze sea. He brought the work to a good end.

After this Hiram won the hand of the Queen of Saba. However, he was ambushed by the three apprentices and killed, but before he died he managed to throw the golden triangle into a well. When Hiram was missed, people started looking for him. Solomon himself was anxious and wanted to know what happened. It was feared that the three apprentices might betray the master word, and therefore a new word was agreed upon. The first words spoken when Hiram was found would be the new master word. When Hiram was found he was still able to speak a few words. He said: 'Tubal-Cain has promised me that I will have a son who will have many sons; they will people the earth and complete my work, the building of the Temple.' He then indicated the place where the golden triangle could be found. The triangle was brought to the bronze sea, and both it and the hammer were hidden in a special place in the Holy of Holies. They can only be found by those who comprehend what this Temple Legend of Solomon and his master builder Hiram signifies.

In the next section an effort will be made to throw some light on this significance with the help of Rudolf Steiner's spiritual knowledge.

6. The Invisible Temple

The Temple Legend leads us to a central secret of the development of humanity, a secret which we have, in a certain sense, around us every day, but is yet far removed from our daily consciousness. We have heard that we can distinguish two streams in humanity that have existed from the very beginning of human development on earth, and that work and live like polar opposites to each other. The one stream is represented by Solomon, that of sober wisdom and piety without passion; the other is the stream of the sons of Cain and is characterized by their relationship to fire. Their wisdom is not like cool, clear water, but like blazing fire, impulsive, enthusiastic.

Rudolf Steiner points out that the origin of this difference lies in the contrasting natures of the Elohim who were the creators of the Cain stream and the Abel-Seth stream. Yahweh had progressed further in his development than the Elohim being who had united himself with Eve. The latter being belonged to a group of hierarchical spirits who still bore wisdom and fire—in this connection not physical but astral fire, passion—unseparated in them, whereas Yahweh on a higher level of development had overcome the element of passion.

Both streams work in successive developmental eras. From the fire wisdom of the sons of Cain all arts and sciences have arisen; from the Yahweh wisdom of the sons of Seth arises the sober wisdom and passionless devotion of the religious human being.

With the advent of Christianity, however, the old piety has to become permeated by a new element: a fire that is not passion but pure fire of love. Christ is not only wisdom, he is the incarnation of divine Love itself. The new Christian devotion, which is warm and enthusiastic, arises in the time of the beginnings of Christianity and grows in the Middle Ages, but a connection with the sons of Cain is not yet directly possible. Before the reconciliation of the two inimical brothers in the name of Christ can become reality, the sons of Cain still have to fulfil a very important mission for our time and the near future.

If Christianity were to permeate all people rapidly, the impulse of love would indeed be taken up, but the individual human being, the human heart, would not be able to connect with it in freedom. The human being would then not accept Christ as their brother, but as ruler, as Lord. This is why the sons of Cain, who work with matter, with what are worldly, outer things and measures, have to have centre stage in our cultural epoch. The materialism, which irrevocably results from this, is necessary to the development and schooling of the human individuality.

This brings with it the danger of an ever-increasing egoism, which will ultimately lead to a situation of war in humanity in which each ego will experience each other ego as its enemy. Some of this dark future can already be felt in our time, even in Roman times when the ego already began to push itself strongly to the foreground. In Rome there was the saying *homo homini lupus*, meaning: 'the one human being is a wolf for the other'. Still, the principle of *love* and the principle of *freedom* could never be brought together in another way.

The course of world history clearly shows the growing worldliness and materialism of outer culture. In spite of the negative effects of this materialism in our time, this process as such can be viewed in a positive light, namely as a *continuation of the building impulse of the Temple of Solomon*. Rudolf Steiner calls this the mystery of the Rosicrucians.[62] He refers here to the original movement of the Rose Cross that originated from the same individuality who played such a decisive role in the building of the Temple. How can we understand this?

The Yahweh stream had worked for such a long time and in such a way that the Holy Name of God, I AM, could dwell in the human being; this was indicated in the section about the Temple of Solomon. We could call this the pre-Christian Grail mystery, namely the preparation for the descent of the 'fifth principle', the spirit self, into the physical and soul sheaths of the human being. This is possible because one people placed itself under the guidance of Yahweh, entered into a covenant with that divine-hierarchical being who wants to form a pure mirror of the Most High and, because of that, in a certain sense coincides with Him: Yahweh-Christ.

When the time of David and Solomon had come a house had to be built for the Name of God. This could be accomplished only by the skills of a son of Cain, Hiram, the highest representative of the other stream in humanity. In the symbolism built into the Temple, part is related to the Old Covenant, namely the Holy of Holies and all that is connected with the rituals; but there is also a symbolism of the future hidden in the Temple, in the first place the pentagon that was added to the square. In addition, there are elements that relate to the coming Messiah who will bring the duality that developed in humanity and the world to a higher unity by the resurrection from death. The two columns Jachin and Boaz form a portal that, by its symbolism of Tree of Life and Tree of Death, points to the One who shall regain eternal life out of death—the One who can truly say 'I am the door.' (John.10:7)

The bronze sea may be viewed as a Grail symbol. Heavenly water is caught in a basin in the form of a lily that is made from earthly matter, from metals that were molten in fire and formed into a serving vessel—the image of the descending heavenly being into the vessel of a human body.

This future, however, finds its fulfilment in the events in Palestine at the beginning of our era. The Temple of Solomon—albeit not the original one, because that was destroyed by Nebuchadnezzar, but as it was rebuilt by Zerubbabel (Ezra 3:6) and later rebuilt again by Herod—continued to exist until shortly after the death and resurrection of Christ. In the year 70 the Temple was definitively destroyed by the Roman Emperor Titus and could then no longer be rebuilt. What then is the meaning of Steiner's phrase *a continuation of the building impulse of the Temple of Solomon*?

The temple of the New Covenant is an invisible temple that is no longer the religious centre of one people, but a temple of humanity. The Christ impulse brings the I-principle, which is gradually incorporated in humanity. It will find its expression in social forms that are based on brotherliness and on the feeling that all human beings are equal before God, but besides, all culture has to be nourished from the well of spiritual freedom. For this reason the work on this social temple of humanity still has to be based on the connection with the outer, material world. The people who want to continue to interpret Christianity in an Old Testament form, consider the connection with the material world as wicked. They want to maintain a strict separation between the divine-spiritual, the clear wisdom of religion on the one hand, and the blazing dynamics of material life on the other.

But the secret of the Rosicrucians lies precisely in the fact that they recognize the necessity of the connection with the material world. Only, they want to hallow this connection by ennobling the fire of passion of the sons of Cain into Christian love. That is the deeper meaning of the teaching of Christian Rosenkreutz which, in the form of a legend, a story, moves the souls of those who want to build the temple of the future. At first the water and fire are mixed in an incorrect way by the evil apprentices—unpurified workers. The result is a catastrophe. Hiram, however, is able to combine the elements of 'fire' and 'water', of enthusiasm and sober wisdom, in such a way that the carrying basin comes into being.

The golden triangle is the symbolic expression for the three higher spiritual elements, spirit self, life spirit, and spirit man. This higher, eternal human being can come into existence when the free, self-conscious I begins to transform the lower three members of the human being in the course of its development. These lower three members were bestowed on the human being by divine powers during the great cosmic phases of evolution that preceded that of the earth. They are the three 'vessels' of our earthly being: the physical body, the life body, and the astral or soul body. The fourth principle, the I, works unconsciously at first, but later consciously, to transform these vessels.

The appearance of Christ on earth has given us the possibility that in the I the resurrection power becomes effective that will enable the future higher human being to be born out of the lower human being. This insight implies the idea of reincarnation and karma because, of course, this process cannot be limited to one life. In addition, it is important to remember that this transformation of the lower into the higher human being has to be accomplished on earth, and not in heaven. The earth itself has to be taken along in this great alchemical metamorphosis.

Ever since Egyptian-Babylonian times the sons of Cain have worked on the outer envelope of the human I, the edifice of the social temple.

As regards the gratification of physical desires—this is taken care of by everything that fosters physical wellbeing through technology. Social provisions are all related to the life body of the human being. Moral and ethical rules have their influence on the astral body, which is the carrier of lusts, passions and desires that can be kept within bounds and ennobled by norms of decency.

This building process of the outer social Temple, which has gradually led to our materialistic society from which the lucid, originally divine, wisdom element of Solomon seems to have completely vanished, has yet to be regarded as a prerequisite for further development. Without a connection with the outer world, with spiritless matter, there can be no freedom! But if in our time there is not a sufficient number of people who take in the secret of the bronze sea and the golden triangle, and strive to overcome materialism without turning away from the outer world, the building of the future Temple may fail.

The Queen of Saba, who plays such a crucial role both in the Temple Legend and in that of the Holy Cross (see Chapter 5), represents the human soul. The soul has to choose between Solomon and Hiram, between sober wisdom and piety that leaves the earth untouched, and wisdom that conquers the earth, meaning that it connects with outer earthly culture by overcoming the fire of passion. She chooses Hiram, but this has a tragic consequence in the legend because the master builder becomes the victim of the jealousy of his rival.

In this way the motif of the building of the Temple is connected with that of sacrificial death and martyrdom. As the development of human culture progresses—and its ultimate goal is the Christianizing of the culture—the initiates who want to further this process, and all others who want to connect themselves with this striving, will have to shoulder martyrdom. The Templars are a conspicuous example of this.

In the centuries that have elapsed between the advent of Christ and the beginning of the current, fifth post-Atlantean epoch, the connection between Grail and Temple can be followed in the so-called esoteric stream of Christianity. This stream consisted of human souls who sought a deeper relationship with the Christ mystery, deeper than was possible through the form the Church had adopted since Constantine. These souls called themselves Johannine Christians.

The Templars may also be considered Johannine Christians. Rudolf Steiner called them the original envoys of the Holy Grail. Elsewhere he says that the Templars wanted to revive the idea of the Temple of Solomon and bring this spiritual impulse to Europe.[63] On the place where the Temple had stood, they were 'initiated by the Holy Grail'. In other words, their Temple idea of a future Christian social order in Europe, which they tried to realize in an impressive manner, was a Grail impulse.

And indeed, centuries earlier a purely imaginative image of a Temple of Humanity had arisen in the souls of the Grail seekers, the Temple of Montsalvat. In the works of Chrétien and Wolfram this Temple is identical with a castle. Some people have tried to identify certain existing castles as the Grail Castle, including Mont Ségur, the castle of the Cathars, but in reality it is not concretely visible, just as the continuation of the Temple of Solomon, the invisible world Temple, is invisible. We may state that the Grail Temple Castle and the invisible Temple are in essence one and the same. In both cases, what is meant is the spiritual enclosure of the New Covenant, the indwelling of Christ in the human being, which will determine the future of the earth and humanity.

Now we will follow the footsteps of the Grail knights and Templars in medieval history.

4. OCCULT HISTORY

1. A World of Images

In Chapter 2 we said that 'there have been essential streams in humanity that converged upon the central event when the Turning Point in Time becomes visible in the Mystery of Golgotha. From there, clearly visible as well as hidden streams of development move on toward the future.' For the great Roman historian Tacitus, Christianity was still a completely hidden developmental stream; it did not come out of hiding until Emperor Constantine not only permitted it in his empire, but also strongly favoured it.

Since then the history of the West was in no small measure determined by the history of the Church, especially in the Middle Ages. In this connection Ernst Uehli, another teacher in the first Waldorf School, who published material about the Grail even before Walter Johannes Stein, postulates in addition to historical Christianity an 'unhistorical Christianity', by which he indicates the esoteric streams I have mentioned already.

Although one may like or dislike his term 'unhistorical', the phenomena he mentions leave no doubt as to what he means. He points to the contrast between the apostles Peter and John, and particularly to the difference in the way Peter's Confession is described in the John Gospel as compared with the three Synoptic Gospels. He emphasizes the fact that in the Synoptic Gospels Peter received the insight that Jesus is really the Christ as a divine inspiration, something that the Father God bestowed on him and to which he merely had to open himself. But in John's Gospel Peter's Confession follows after Christ has revealed His oneness with the Father. The Father revelation therefore occurs here via the Christ being. While this does not change the content of Peter's Confession, it does change the context in which it was uttered.

Uehli's conclusion is that he connects historical Christianity with Peter. It rests on the power of *faith*. For this rock-solid faith Peter was the intermediary and also the example. His mighty personality, which is shown to us in its strengths and weaknesses, is the cornerstone of the Church. Here appears in the Gospel the image of an edifice, a Temple, and certainly all later churches are efforts to make the Church visible as a Temple of Humanity.

Uehli's unhistorical Christianity, Johannine or esoteric Christianity, has a very different character. In a certain respect it is impersonal, because its foundation does not lie in the personal revelation of the Father God received in faith, but in a Christ revelation one has to make one's own through *knowledge and insight*—Gnosis in Greek, which did not mean an intellectual knowing, but an awareness that rested on spiritual *beholding*.

Before Constantine, when Christianity still had a more or less hidden character, the faith and knowledge elements were not yet sharply differentiated. Original Christianity was greatly nourished from the well of Gnosis. Only from the fourth century did an official, orthodox faith develop, regulated and controlled by the Church of Rome. Side by side with this, hidden streams continued to exist that were more connected with the Gnosis element. Because due to the progressing development of the European human being the potential of gaining knowledge through beholding was fading more and more, the human souls who lived in the hidden streams were ever more becoming 'searching souls'.

When at the end of the twelfth and beginning of the thirteenth century the great Grail stories appeared in literary form, an unhistorical Christian element came to the surface which, however, had been continually present; and actually, it had influenced and permeated historical Christianity more than is usually assumed. We may even wonder whether the *essential* steps in the course of historical development did not originate in the unhistorical hidden stream. If we acknowledge the truth of this the subtitle of Stein's book, *World History in the Light of the Holy Grail*, becomes quite real.

In this connection there is another remarkable fact that usually receives insufficient emphasis, also in publications by authors who base their insights on anthroposophical spiritual science. It is not the occult, the hidden aspect that is the most important characteristic of the esoteric stream that as a whole can be called the Grail stream, but it is striking that we find there a *world of images*, rather than concepts. And in this abundantly rich world of images there are three archetypal pictures which, as far as I know, have as yet received little attention *in their mutual connections*.

These are the pictures of the Book, the Altar (the Table in the Grail tradition), and the Temple—the archetypal images that are also of key importance in the Apocalypse of St. John. The first three poets of the Grail, Chrétien de Troyes, Robert de Boron, and Wolfram von Eschenbach all based themselves on a secret book in which they, or their informant, had read the Grail images. It is not impossible that concrete books or manuscripts are meant, but probably the word 'book' has to be taken to mean the lowest level of spiritual consciousness, *imagination*. Whether the three Grail poets themselves possessed imaginative consciousness, or whether they received their knowledge orally from initiates, is something of which we cannot be certain, although their own statements lead us to believe the latter. It is not even very important. They received a knowledge that had been passed on without interruption from the time of the beginnings of Christianity.

That actual, written books also formed a source for the Grail tradition is clear. Well known is the apocryphal Gospel of Nicodemus, the first part of which is called *Acta Pilati* (Acts of Pilate), and which describes the trial of Jesus more extensively than the four canonical Gospels. It also throws more light on the figure of Joseph of Arimathea than the four Gospels of the New Testament. In addition to the *Acta Pilati*, Robert de Boron also used the *Vindicta Salvatoris* (The Rescue of the Saviour), another apocryphal work, as well as the tradition mentioned earlier of the chalice from the Heracles Temple in Tyre that came to Solomon, was used at the Last Supper, and then came via Pilate into the hands of Joseph of Arimathea. Under the cross, Joseph caught the blood and water that flowed out of the spear wound of the Redeemer.

The book as symbol for imaginative vision comes especially to the fore in an old-French prose story that is most often called *The Great Holy Grail*, as distinct from *The Little Holy Grail*, the first part of the trilogy of Robert de Boron. It is about a hermit who, 717 years after Golgotha, had an astonishing experience in the night between Maundy Thursday and Good Friday. The hermit, who was tormented in his religious musings by doubts about the Divine Trinity, had gone to sleep in his hut. In the middle of the night he is awakened by a voice that calls him three times by his name. He wakes up and sees Christ standing before him in a mighty shining light. After admonishing him for his doubts, Christ gives him a little book no larger than the palm of a hand, of which He says that He wrote it Himself. This little book will take all doubt away from him.

The next morning the hermit finds the little book and reads the first words: 'This is the beginning of your genealogical tree...' It is the genealogical Grail tree that goes back to Joseph of Arimathea. The hermit learns in this way that he belongs to the Grail stream. His reading is interrupted by heavenly apparitions, and an angel takes him out of his body up into heaven where he may behold the Divine Trinity. This heals him of all doubt. When he has come back into his normal consciousness he wants to celebrate the Mass, and puts the little book carefully aside. But when he wants to take it up on Easter morning to read it again, it has disappeared.

He is now told to go and look for the book, which can only be found after trials and sufferings. He starts on his way, and after arduous wanderings he finds the little book in a chapel where it is lying on an *altar*. He takes it with him and goes back to his cell. Now Christ appears to him again in a dream and tells him to copy the content of the book. The copy has to be ready on Ascension Day. It is stated that after His resurrection Christ wrote nothing other than this one sublime little book about the Holy Grail.

The story can also be found in the chronicle of Hélinand de Froidmont, a minstrel-author who concluded his chronicle with a year (1204) in which *The Great Holy Grail* had not yet been written, which indicates that the Grail tradition must also have lived among people outside the great Grail stories.

That in this tradition the little Grail book that Christ wrote Himself and gave to the hermit cannot have been meant as a regular book is evident. What is indicated here is a knowing of a supersensible nature. This knowing, this Gnosis, is initiation knowledge that can only be gained through catharsis of the soul.

The second archetypal image that occurs in all Grail stories is the picture of the Grail itself as a stone (Wolfram), or as a chalice (Robert de Boron and Chrétien de Troyes) which either as the chalice of the Last Supper has a direct relationship to the offering in the Mass, or as a miraculous thing brings about nourishment through the Eucharist. Even though the picture of an altar does not appear in the descriptions by Wolfram and Chrétien, everything that involves beholding the Grail as a thing has the sacramental, the altar element in it. It is evident that in their descriptions of the Grail Chrétien, and Wolfram even more so, want to stay away from anything that recalls the ecclesiastical sacrament. This is not the case with Robert de Boron. But that all forms of Grail descriptions involve a kind of cultus is unmistakable.

Robert de Boron is the poet who treats the Grail story most historically by connecting it with Joseph of Arimathea. It will therefore be no surprise that his Grail mystery corresponds most closely with the *mysterion* (the original Greek word for the Latin *sacramentum*) of the historical altar sacrament of the Church. Conversely, it is extremely surprising to hear that in the offering of the Mass a connection is made with Joseph of

Arimathea. The first time this was mentioned was by a certain Amalarius, whose name comes up in the controversies about the Last Supper in
the ninth century. Cardinal Joseph Hergenröther's standard work *History of the Catholic Church* says the following about it:

> ... Amalarius, who wrote a liturgical work in four volumes in which
> he tried to explain all Church rituals, objects and vestments in mysti-
> cal and often fantastic ways. He identified a threefold body of Christ,
> but in such a way that a) the body which the Lord had adopted Him-
> self had to be distinguished from b) the body He has in us as long
> as we live, and c) the body He has in the dead. The Host, he said,
> should therefore be divided into three parts. The part that is put in
> the chalice was to indicate the body Christ bore Himself, the part
> lying on the paten would indicate the body of the Lord in living
> human beings, and the part lying on the altar His body in the dead.
> In addition, he saw in the consecrated bread the body of Christ, in
> the wine His soul, in the chalice the grave, and in the celebrating
> priest Joseph of Arimathea.

At the Council of Quiercy in 838 Amalarius' book was rejected, and the
cardinal pronounced the following judgement:

> ... petty speculations about archetypal images and mysteries in all
> the particulars of the ritual, but especially his doctrine of the three-
> fold body of Christ.

Despite the rejection of Amalarius, the figure of Joseph of Arimathea
does not completely disappear from the official Church. In a theological document from the twelfth century by Honorius of Autun, *Gemma
animae*, it is said that the deacon who, after the words *per omnia saecula
saeculorum*, raises the chalice, sets it on the altar and covers it with a
cloth, represents Joseph of Arimathea—how he took down Jesus' body
from the cross, covered his face with a cloth, laid the body in the grave,
and closed the grave with a stone.

In Robert de Boron's story a Grail table is also mentioned, which
subsequently has its worldly counterpart in the Round Table of King
Arthur. The table on which the Grail cup is placed is at the same time an
altar table, a table of mystical nourishment and moral trial. The pictures
unmistakably express that the companions at the table form a community of human beings who are connected with each other through an
initiation experience. In this regard Robert de Boron is a true representative of unhistorical Christianity, because the Grail community as mystical brotherhood of course does not at all tally with the historical Church
of Rome. About its connection with the Celts I will come back later.

The Grail table had four corners and was made to imitate the table Jesus and His disciples used at the Last Supper. The magician Merlin made for the father of King Arthur, Uther Pendragon, a *round* table that seated 50 knights. Without a doubt, the number 50 is related to the 50 days between Easter and Pentecost; the round table was dedicated on Pentecost. The Arthurian Knights formed a community that had to do with the principle of the Holy Spirit.

When we summarize these Grail pictures with the word *altar*, this expresses at the same time a higher or, if you will, deeper level of consciousness than is expressed in the imaginative idea of the book. We call this the level of *inspiration* where the important point is not so much to know about the origin of the Grail and such, but a direct supersensible experience of the Christ presence *in the heart*. It is in this connection understandable that in the Chalice aspect of the Grail tradition the *blood* of the Saviour is central. To this also belongs the picture of the bloody spear, which is of deep significance and can be esoterically interpreted in several ways. But we cannot go into that here.

The third archetypal image, which has to be viewed in connection with the previous two, is that of the Temple. In the tradition from which Robert de Boron has drawn his *Little Holy Grail* the Grail Temple is missing, but there is an interesting, indirect indication that connects Grail and Temple with each other. We are told that Joseph of Arimathea took the body of Christ down from the cross, caught the blood that again flowed from the wounds in the chalice of the Last Supper, and laid the body bound in linen in his own nearby grave. Immediately thereafter he is arrested by the Jews and locked up in a tower. The Risen One, however, even before He appeared to the women at the grave and later on Easter morning to the disciples, visits Joseph in his dark dungeon. He gives him the chalice with the Holy Blood and teaches him the consecration of the altar sacrament.

Joseph's liberation from the deep dungeon only took place many years later, however, namely by the Roman Emperor Vespasian at the conquest of Jerusalem in the year 70. Vespasian found the old man surrounded by radiating light in his dungeon where he had lived all those years without food or drink, refreshing himself from the holy chalice Christ had returned to him.

The Temple of the Jews was destroyed and immediately thereafter the first Grail community formed itself, for together with his sister, brother-in-law Bron and a small group they had gathered around them, Joseph left Jerusalem to head West, to England. The creation of the invisible Temple that has to shroud the Christ mystery had begun. First the old

Temple had to be destroyed. The Romans who committed this apparent misdeed yet also served an impulse of the future. The Grail tradition incorporated this fact without any prejudice, and clothed the fact that the destroyer of the Temple and the saviour of the first Grail *knight* (for that is what Robert de Boron calls Joseph of Arimathea) were the same person clothed in legendary form.

However, we must not try to find the image of the Grail Temple in all its loftiness and far-reaching symbolic significance in Robert de Boron's work, but in that of the poet of the great Titurel epic, Albrecht von Scharfenberg. This takes us on another Grail path that also leads from Jerusalem to the West, but this time not to England but to Spain.

2. The Grail Temple

We can easily imagine the figure of Joseph of Arimathea, the first Grail knight, as a human being, albeit surrounded by radiant supersensible light because of his spiritual experiences, an initiated mystic who worked in a small circle of followers, but in any case a tangible, even historically verifiable appearance. The mysterious first Grail King, on the other hand, Titurel, the builder of the Grail Temple, seems to come completely out of poetic imagination.

Still, just as many things and persons are treated like fantastic fabrications by materialistic science, for occult historical research they are often real. Sometimes science has to admit defeat, when hard facts prove the so-called fabrications of the poets to be right, as was the case with the archeological findings of Heinrich Schliemann in Troy.[64] The Grail Temple, however, will never be found by excavations, because it is an inner reality that will never leave a visible footprint in the earth.

About the origin of the first Grail King, Titurel, the legend says the following:

> Three of the sons of King Senabor of Cappadocia distinguished themselves in the conquest of Jerusalem by Emperor Vespasian. One of them, Barillus, married a daughter of the Emperor, Argusille, and received as his fiefdom the kingdom of France. The two other brothers also received kingdoms in the West, of which the inhabitants had converted to Christianity. For the three brothers were already Christians before they went West.

This is still a world of images that do not express an outer reality, but an inner one. Fiefdoms and kingdoms must here be understood in an unhistorical sense, and sometimes not geographically.

Rudolf Meyer[65] looks for the origin of this in Cappadocia, a region in eastern Turkey, in connection with the mysteries on the Black Sea, that were mentioned in Chapter 2. Although Cappadocia doesn't border on the Black Sea at all, the legendary royal family of Senabor clearly points to a mystery community or something like it. Barillus and Argusille have a son named Titurison, who marries Elysabel, a daughter of the King of Arragun. The marriage is childless for a long time. Husband and wife embark on a pilgrimage to the Holy Sepulchre in Jerusalem and put all their strength in their ardent prayers. Their prayers are now answered. When the child is born they call it Titurel. An angel tells them at the birth of this son that he will one day be the equal of the angels. As a pure youth he will defend Christianity with fiery strength against the pagans, and as his reward he will be clothed in the radiance of the sun.

The poet Albrecht speaks of the land of Galicia in northern Spain; Arragun also points to Spain. The historical background of this tradition lies probably in the time of the Visigoths who, after a brief stay in Italy, founded an empire that encompassed southern France and the Iberian peninsula (415 AD).

These Arian-Christian Goths fought great battles against invading Germanic tribes, most of which were still pagans. Some centuries later the Iberian Christians had to defend themselves against the invasion of the Arabs. It is extremely interesting that the Grail tradition that puts Titurel in the centre, and not Joseph of Arimathea, still also begins with the destruction of Jerusalem and the Temple of Solomon.

The further history of Titurel relates how he fights for Christianity together with his father, how he extends his youth by chastity and abstinence to his fiftieth year, and how an angel then announces to him that he has been chosen to be the Guardian of the Grail because of his great virtues. He then leaves his parents and is led to an impenetrable forest where a mountain rises up that cannot be found by ordinary mortals. This is Mont Salvat, Mountain of Salvation.

Titurel arrives there together with a company of knights from all directions of the compass. They camp there in tents, and above the camp hovers the Grail, carried by invisible angels. It provides the knights with all the food and drink they need, and later also all the materials and supplies for the construction of the Temple.

First, Titurel builds a castle on the mountaintop, from where he combats the pagans who are trying to invade the area. Then he decides to build a Temple for the Grail that is still hovering above. The rocky ground on which the Temple is to be erected consists of onyx. When it is polished it shines like the moon and is translucent like crystal. One day the ground plan of the edifice that is to appear there is found engraved in mysterious fashion into the sparkling stone surface.

Titurel and his companions then work for 30 years on the construction of the Temple. It becomes a round structure surrounded by chapels that the poet calls choirs, formed from precious stones and gold. In the older literature, and also in Walter Johannes Stein and Rudolf Meyer, we find the figure 72 for the number of chapels. Rudolf Steiner speaks of 72 columns in the Grail Temple.[66] New research into the numerous manuscripts of *Der Junge Titurel* has led to a different understanding. Werner Wolff has recognized a Viennese parchment as the oldest and most reliable manuscript of Von Scharfenberg's epic, and this document speaks not of 72 but 22 chapels or choirs.

On the East side the high altar stands in a chapel that is twice as large as the other 22 spaces of the circle of chapels. If we consider this chapel as equal to two of the smaller ones, the ground plan of the building appears to be defined by the number 24. We also find this number in Wolfram's description of the Grail procession: 24 maidens surround the Grail. In the Book of Revelation 24 elders surround the throne of the Most High.

The large chapel on the East side is dedicated to Mary, the adjoining ones on both sides to John. On the shining, translucent onyx floor in the middle stands a small temple, a likeness of the complete sanctuary. The Grail is placed into this by the hands of angels.

The round structure is crowned with towers raised in a circle like the chapels. A central tower stands out high above the others, and on its pinnacle sparkles a carbuncle, that shows the way to the knights at night. The interior of the Temple distinctly shows a threefold nature.

> The middle zone, which opens out to the surrounding choirs or chapels, is adorned with artificial trees in which birds and angels can be seen, golden green grapevines with moving leaves that generate soft sounds when they are touched by moving air. Close to the ground there is a wealth of roses and lilies, and on the walls green sparkling emeralds are seen. In the main choir there are twines and angels of metal, hollow inside, that can be made to sound with the aid of bellows. In the West, above the portal, stands a great golden tree with branches and leaves, singing birds and trumpeting angels—it is the organ. The central area is therefore like a golden garden filled with vegetative colors, forms and sounds.
>
> The part that lies under it is visible under the translucent floor. It is a crystal sea with fishes and sea animals which are put

in motion through a mechanism of windmills that stand outside the edifice.

The uppermost zone is formed by a vault that portrays heaven, blue of sparkling sapphires and strewn with carbuncles that represent stars. This artificial heaven consisting of precious stones is also moved by a mechanism; the sun and moon rise and set among the twelve signs of the zodiac. Golden cymbals announce the time.[67]

This description depicts the Grail Temple as a cosmos, encompassing heaven, earth, and the waters of the underworld, whereas Titurel himself gives his Grail knights a more moral-allegorical explanation of the Temple building. For a modern human being all of this is a huge riddle. Should we consign Titurel and his Grail Temple to the realm of fantasy? That there would have been such a building somewhere in Spain is not credible, is it? Did the poet perhaps want to create an idealized picture of the Templars, with whom his predecessor, Wolfram von Eschenbach, also tried to connect his *Templeisen* (his name for the Grail knights)?

As regards the latter, the Grail knights do not wear a red *cross* on their mantles like the Templars, but a *dove*, symbol of the Holy Spirit. Identification with the knights of the Order of the Templars was therefore probably not intended.

The mysterious Titurel, of whom the poet says that he may marry a virgin after 400 years, may in my opinion still be viewed as an actually existing human being, not a fabricated figure for a romance. We should picture the individuality of a great initiate whose hidden but wholesome activity works on earth irrespective of the form in which he exists, whether in a material body or a spiritual, non-material condition.

The strange company of knights that help him build the Grail Temple is a group of dead souls, as Rudolf Steiner points out. He says that the young Germanic tribes that in the great migrations of the fourth and fifth centuries invaded the Roman Empire, originally still possessed a strong clairvoyance and, as a result, had a much more conscious connection with the world of the dead than the cultured peoples around the Mediterranean. Their heroes who died in battle stayed with them, as it were.

> ... when they were especially chosen individuals they were called to be brothers of the Holy Grail ... And we will never fully comprehend the Grail saga if we do not realize who the actual guardians of the Grail were.[68]

The saga also points to this connection with the dead by the image of the swan who guides and accompanies the emissary from the Grail. This mighty, winged animal with its pure white colour depicts a being from the sphere of the angels.

In this way, Titurel belongs to this angelic sphere. His edifice is no outwardly visible creation, but really the invisible Temple of the future. Not only is it a threefold sanctuary, as described by the poet, but it can be understood in a threefold way as a spiritual fount of wisdom in which the chalice of love forms the centre.

First, it is the Temple of a new body. For 30 years Titurel builds *on himself*; the Temple of the spirit becomes an etheric reality in him. Just as the material body of Jesus had to be formed during 30 years in order to receive the Christ spirit at the Baptism, for 30 years Titurel has to build the inner life body that may receive the Grail. I consider it not improbable that there is a direct connection between Titurel and Jesus of Nazareth—I do not mean a reincarnation, but in the sense that there may have been a penetration of Titurel's life body by the etheric formative forces of Jesus. Rudolf Steiner spoke about such penetrations, or incorporations, in the case of other great Christians.[69]

The second aspect is the brotherhood of the guardians of the Grail. The Temple is round, like the Pentecost table of King Arthur. It is consecrated to the Holy Spirit, in other words, to the being who wants to bring free human beings together into a community, a brother- and sisterhood. Thirdly, the Grail Temple is a prefiguration of the new earth. It is not the New Jerusalem of the Book of Revelation, but a promise of it, a germ.

People have long thought that Albrecht derived his description of the Temple from the Gothic cathedrals of his time, the thirteenth century. He supposedly had some kind of 'super Gothic' in mind. Modern researchers have come to the opposite conclusion, namely that the builders of the Gothic cathedrals were inspired by what they found in the works of poets and seers. Their highest ideal would have been the idea of the heavenly city consisting of transparent gold and precious stones, the New Jerusalem. Every cathedral was to have been an effort to make this ideal visible.[70]

Be this as it may, the Grail Temple from the Titurel epic most certainly has a future aspect. This third archetypal image, therefore, which we wanted to consider in connection with the two previous ones of the book and the altar, points to an even higher level of consciousness than those of imagination and inspiration, namely to *intuitive* consciousness.

With the word intuition we usually indicate a vague feeling or sensing of something. The spiritual-scientific meaning, however, is a supreme form of exact, knowing insight, in which knowing is at the same time a becoming one with the object of the knowing. One may also say: love as the highest revelation of knowledge, 'mutual touching' of beings.

Imaginative consciousness, the book, enables us to behold the past. For inspiration the experience of the here and now, the direct revelation of a spiritual presence is decisive, as it occurs in a ritual (the altar). Intuitive knowledge, however, reaches into the future; it is an awakening of the will, which is always directed to the future, just as our power of thinking and having mental images is directed to the past.

Spiritual intuition is related to the image of the Temple, for entering the Temple in effect signifies union with the Divine Being, the most profound 'touching', whereas by the ritual at the altar, particularly through the words sounding there, a revelation takes place.

Let us recall once more the representatives of the three archetypal images, book, altar and Temple, as we have sketched them in relation to the Grail. First the hermit in his cell, wrestling with the question with which he racks his *thinking* brain. On him is bestowed the book of the Grail, which also gives him the possibility to experience the highest riddle of the world, the Trinity, by beholding it.

Second, Joseph of Arimathea, a councillor, a merchant according to certain traditions, a man of the world, not a thinker but a man of *feeling*, a direct disciple of Jesus Christ. His loving care for the dead body of the Crucified One and his special attention to the blood cause him to become the first priest of Christianity. Most significant is the fact that the Risen One communicates secret words to him in his dungeon, words that have to be spoken at the consecration of the substances on the altar—an experience of pure inspiration!

Finally the mysterious king, a man of the deed, of action who, however, purifies and sanctifies his power of action by abstinence that is no dark, fanatical asceticism, but an angelic joyful purity, through which his *will* can unite itself with the essence of the world, in which the future lies hidden as a germ.

With their wealth of images the Grail traditions, which only appear at the surface of history for a short time, point the way for seeking souls. The way rises from the imaginative level through inspiration to intuition, the way of every path of initiation.

3. Grail and Apocalypse

Many peculiarities of the Grail tradition indicate that this stream of unhistorical Christianity has an unmistakably Johannine character. In this section I want to point to the connection between the Grail and the Apocalypse of St. John.

The Apocalypse describes the supersensible experiences John went through during his exile on the island of Patmos. In overwhelmingly dramatic pictures he describes the end of the earth—a total upheaval, metamorphosis of that which becomes a new world. As in a gigantic alchemical process we watch how cosmos, earth and humanity are destroyed and born anew in three mighty episodes, each consisting of seven parts.

At the same time, this Revelation may be viewed as an initiation in which the three higher levels of consciousness are clearly marked. These levels of imagination, inspiration and intuition as stages of a spiritual path of schooling or initiation, are also represented in the Grail stories in the images of *book, altar and Temple*.

We might notice in the Apocalypse, however, that initially only the book appears quite distinctly as an image; the altar and Temple images remain more hidden. In Chapter 4, where the throne in heaven is described with the One who is seated on it, the 24 elders, the four living beings full of eyes, and the sea of glass, there is no mention of an altar or a Temple. But we do have to add them in our minds. They are mentioned later, seemingly in passing, as if we had heard about an altar or Temple in heaven long before: 'And when the Lamb opened the fifth seal, I saw under the *altar* the souls …' (Rev.6:9) and 'Therefore they can stand before the throne of God and serve Him day and night in His *temple*.' (Rev.7:15)

Only when the full power of the level of inspiration begins to work— and that is when the angels receive the trumpets and the censer—the altar as image comes to the fore (Rev.8:1-5). Similarly with the Temple. When we approach the highest level of knowledge, that of intuition, the Temple appears in the text (Rev.11), but not as a lofty picture of a heavenly structure with towers or domes, or anything like that. Not at all. John is given a reed with which he has to measure the altar and the Temple. But he must not measure the forecourt, because it lies outside the Temple area proper and is for the pagans. Therefore, the point here is not contemplation, but an inner activity—we are in the sphere of the will!

A little later in the same chapter, when the seventh trumpet sounds and heavenly voices proclaim the Kingdom of Christ, the Temple is opened and the Ark of His Covenant becomes visible. The first consequence of this is that mighty signs, pictures, rise up before the spiritual eye of the seer: the image of the Woman and the Dragon, the double Evil, the two Beasts, the gathering on Mount Zion with the Lamb and, finally, the Son of Man on the white cloud with the sharp sickle.

But only then follows the definitive opening of the Temple. Angels come out of the Temple with bowls in their hands. These 'bowls of God's wrath' (Greek *thumos*) have to be poured out over the earth. In Jon Madsen's rendering of the New Testament,[71] the word *thumos* is translated as 'divine will'. By this deed, which brings the last seven plagues over the earth and humanity, the definitive transformation of the old world into the new is accomplished. That which is not purified in the great metamorphosis is exorcized as evil slag.

When we now place the archetypal images from the medieval Grail poets and those from the Apocalypse side by side, we find a few characteristic differences. In the first place, for the seer John, book, altar and Temple are in heaven, whereas the point of the Grail images is to find heavenly wisdom and love on earth, albeit as supra-earthly experiences. The Grail images relate to a supra-earthly but yet earth-related sphere, namely the world of the life forces, the etheric world. The Apocalypse describes the great alchemical metamorphosis of earth and humanity from a higher spiritual sphere. Heaven here means the astral and devachanic worlds, higher realms of the spirit.

Because of this difference the Grail images and the Apocalypse seem to form each other's complement. The book, for instance, remains rather in the background for the Grail poets. It is as if shrouded in mystery, but is always a revelation of the *past*. It contains the genealogy of the Grail family, the adventures of the first possessor of the Grail, or the heavenly origin of the Grail. But for those to whom it is accessible it is an *open* book, an unhistorical history book.

The book in the Apocalypse, however, is a heavenly book. The One who sits on the throne in heaven has it in His right hand, a scroll *closed* with seven seals. It is the book of the *future* that may only be opened through the sacrificial power of the Lamb.

In the Grail tradition the book is a fount of wisdom, it is Gnosis, knowledge. The apocalyptic book already points to the intuitive sphere of will. Later, in the tenth chapter, it appears in metamorphosed form as the little book in the hand of the mighty angel, who gives it to John *to eat*. It must not be read and understood with the head, but has to be digested, absorbed through the metabolism, in other words, in the sphere of the will.

The last and highest metamorphosis of the book image is the Book of Life, the chronicle of eternity in which human souls *are united in Christ*. Here Temple, altar and book coincide.

Let us now take a look at the aspect of the altar, the image for the consciousness of inspiration. In a ritual it is not only the image that is important, but also an act that is connected with sound. Words and music are sounding. In the Grail stories, everything connected with ritual still has a dominant imaginative character; this is related to the etheric element of the Grail images.

Everything is shown in the sign of the love offering made by Christ. Whether we have to interpret the images as inner experiences that human beings can undergo in their own physiological processes, as is the case for Chrétien; or that we should focus more on the macrocosmic aspect, as Wolfram does; whether we may bring the sacramental element of Robert de Boron to the fore—the point in all these Grail experiences is that the Grail knight should develop a deep relationship with the Mystery of Golgotha.

Just as with the book, however, the Apocalypse shows the complementary side again. The secret of the communion as union with the divine being has its other side in the secret of the trumpets of the Judgement. While in the first instance the trumpet sounds are powerful signs of destruction with which the downfall of the world begins with alarming cataclysms, at the same time they proclaim the revelation of the unconcealed divine presence. It is the birth of the higher being out of the lower. The first four trumpets are but the prelude to the three woes that will follow, the most unprecedented cosmic labour pains, blood and destruction, the opening of the pit of the abyss, hosts of demons. Then comes the appearance of the angel of great strength and all that follows it, an unimaginably dramatic climax.

And in the midst of it all stands John, the great initiate, not aloof but part of this drama of humanity and world, one who knows about the future. All of this is still hidden in the Grail experience. Parsifal stands there as one who knows nothing beside the wounded Amfortas who, because of his egotistic love, brought tragedy over the world of the Grail, stagnation in its development.

But also when the doom of the Grail family is lifted, when Amfortas is healed and Parsifal becomes Grail King, even then the apocalyptic counter-image of the Grail cult remains hidden—as *image*, not as reality. For not long after the last great epic works on the Grail come into being, a woe breaks out over humanity with apocalyptic violence: the destruction of the Order of the Templars.

The Temple of the Titurel epic and the apocalyptic Temple show perhaps the greatest similarity of the three pairs of comparable images in the Grail tradition and the Apocalypse, but even so the complementary counter-image is here also the most notable characteristic. The apocalyptic temple is never described. We might get the impression that the throne in heaven of the fourth chapter forms the centre of the temple; to that extent it is also in the sphere of imagination an invisible temple. If we may view it in this way, there could be a correspondence with Von Scharfenberg's temple in some respects.

We find the sea of glass in the strange translucent onyx floor. The four living beings of the Apocalypse are represented by the four golden statues of the evangelists that adorn the heavenly dome of the building. The connection between the four living beings from the Apocalypse and the four evangelists was already made very early in Christianity in miniatures and icons. In addition, the 22 plus 2 (the double chapel on the east side) chapels could be viewed in relation to the 24 elders. These mysterious figures, imagined as crowned old men with musical instruments in their hands because they sing a new song, are extremely important in the Apocalypse. Rudolf Steiner calls them 'time beings'. They represent the time periods that have already passed in the creation.

The trumpeting angels in the golden branches of the trees on the walls of Titurel's Grail Temple don't exactly make an apocalyptic impression, but perhaps there is still some correspondence.

The complementary characteristics of the Grail temple and the temple in heaven from the Apocalypse are quite evident. In the temple of the Grail the chalice is placed by angels. God's love is expressed in that His Son became flesh. The highest cosmic I-being has connected Himself with the blood of one human being in order to create out of this blood the sun-ferment that will work in all further evolution until the end of the world. This mystery of God's chalice of love must be guarded as a most holy secret to which only the purified ones, those who were tried through suffering, are called.

The temple of the Apocalypse, however, is opened at the end of the world, and out of that one chalice of love come seven bowls of God's wrath, divine will! These are *poured out* by the angels, through which the Apocalypse reaches its highest intuitive level. The interpenetration of being is at the same time the awe-inspiring decision that there will be two realms, that of those who bear the seal and that of the damned. The divine will is love for those who bear the seal; for the damned it is wrath. The chalice of love of the Grail is salutary only for those who seek its blessing. For those who reject it, its love works as burning fire, as destruction.

The history of the Order of the Templars will show us that this apocalyptic truth has been working in the historical course of human development for a very, very long time before the judgement described by the Revelation of John takes place as the Last Judgement. The future works ahead, just as the past has its after-effects.

4. The Ninth Century—Three Streams

When we want to explore the Order of the Templars as a metamorphosis of the Grail stream, we first have to take a look at the ninth century. The ninth century was an extremely important time in the history of Europe. In this period political as well as spiritual decisions were made the influence of which reaches even to our present day. The differences between East and West that had already begun to develop during the Roman Empire are sharpened in the ninth century; the first germs of the later Crusades can already be felt. A theological polarization emerges that will later lead to the great schism in the Church between East and West (1054).

The ninth century is the time period that forms the historical background to the Parsifal story.[72] At that time the Grail impulse also came clearly to the surface of world events through certain figures but still, it largely remained occult history. Individualities of great significance for the development of humanity lived in this age, in part in prominent places in the world of the time, in part also in inconspicuous, or even completely unknown incarnations.

Early in the ninth century the Holy Roman Empire had come into being as the creation of the King of the Franks, Charlemagne. Admittedly, this empire of the West—in Constantinople the East-Roman Emperors still reigned—fell apart immediately after Charlemagne's death, but the idea of the Carolingian Empire continued to play a dominant role in subsequent times, even to our day.

In a lecture given in 1922,[73] Rudolf Steiner describes the ninth century from the point of view that the Pope of the time, Nicolas I (858-867), had to take when he viewed the development of Europe. He could not but observe with a certain uneasiness two streams or spiritual tendencies, against which he felt it necessary to advance from Rome a third, a middle stream.

The first stream, which encompassed much and showed a variety of facets, ran from East to West:

> Nicolas I saw one stream moving, as it were, in spiritual heights across from Asia into Europe. In this stream certain conceptions innate in oriental religion were making their way, in a much modified and changed form, across southern Europe and northern Africa,

to Spain, France, the British Isles and especially to Ireland. In view of what will presently be said I will call this the first stream. Springing from the Arabian regions of Asia, it flowed across Greece and Italy but also across Africa into Spain and then upwards through the West. But its influence also rayed out, in different forms, toward other parts of Europe.

This stream was not a clearly coordinated movement or sect, but consisted more of small, dispersed groups of like-minded human souls who guarded the wisdom of the East, and also handed it on. Not improbably, there were for longer or shorter periods of time persons among these groups who had themselves acquired this wisdom in the East and then brought it to the West.

In these people lived an esoteric conception of the Mystery of Golgotha, in other words, they wanted to approach the events in Palestine reported by the evangelists as a real mystery in the light of the old initiation knowledge they still possessed. For them, Christ was the high divine being who descended into the human being Jesus, and whose incarnation, death, and resurrection could only be comprehended through initiation knowledge, and not by the earthly intellect that is bound to the senses. It was actually Christian Gnosis that lived in this stream, oriental initiation wisdom with which they tried to fathom the Christ mystery.

It has already been pointed out in the foregoing that the contents of this esoteric Christian stream became progressively more difficult to express in ideas and concepts. One had to take refuge in *images*, such as the Holy Grail chalice, the castle, the Temple of Montsalvat.

These images expressed quite precisely what was taking place. When it was related that the angels bore the Grail to western Europe, this meant that the Gnosis of olden times could no longer live in the form of concepts in the heads of human beings, but that it had withdrawn into a higher sphere. The initiate Titurel created a temple for this wisdom, which means that there were individuals who wanted to conserve and guard the deepest initiation secrets, so that the impulse of Golgotha could continue to develop in humanity.

This stream, said Rudolf Steiner in the same lecture, founded schools in Asia where Aristotle was studied and where people tried to comprehend the mystery of Golgotha with the aid of Aristotelian concepts. With this he meant the academies in Antioch, Edessa, Nisibis and Gondishapur, where especially Nestorian Christianity created a connection with Greek thinking.

In the West, in Ireland, schools and academies also arose, where there flourished an erudition that was still completely permeated by mystery wisdom, and where an amazing amalgamation took place of old Druid wisdom, Greek philosophy, and Christian esotericism.

In this East-West stream also worked the best elements that came from the Arabic side. Although this did bring an intellectualistic element with it, which blunted the original stream somewhat, initially this intellectualism was kept in balance by the refined power of fantasy that lived in the Arab culture. The growing barbarism in this, which was worse in Asia than in the western caliphate, has to be ascribed mostly to the influence of the Turks, not the Arabs.

The fundamental nature of the stream discussed here was described by Rudolf Steiner as follows:

> Those who were connected in any real way with this stream of spiritual life, held that the one and only way of salvation—and an echo of this is heard in Wolfram von Eschenbach's *Parsifal*—lay in rising above the sensible and material into the supersensible, in having at any rate some vision of the supersensible worlds, in letting man share in the life of the supersensible worlds, in bringing home to him that his soul belongs in a stream not immediately to be perceived by senses directed to terrestrial events.
>
> The feeling characterizing this gaze upward into supersensible, supra-earthly regions was that, in order to be a full human being, man must belong to worlds transcending material existence, worlds whose happenings are hidden, as were the deeds of the Knights of the Grail, from the outward eye. The mystery implicit in this stream was felt to be somehow imperceptible to the eyes of sense.

Pope Nicolas probably had personal connections with this stream and, in any case, possessed sufficient spirituality to perceive the greatness of this Grail stream, but nevertheless, because of his position as Roman Pope, he had to have his doubts about it, to say the least. For ever since the fourth century Rome had fostered enmity against anything that tended to initiation wisdom. Every form of esotericism in religion and science had to be suppressed and destroyed. They could do no other than treat the seeking souls of the Grail stream as heretics.

The second stream that was observed with no less concern by the Pope arose in eastern Europe. The people living in the regions where later, after the great schism of 1054, the Greek Orthodox Church dominated life, did not feel the need to occupy themselves with esoteric-spiritual conceptions of the Mystery of Golgotha. They were not Grail seekers who wanted to raise their souls to a supra-earthly reality. They too

sensed that the emerging intellect could not comprehend the highest
secrets of Christianity, but they experienced these secrets in the ritual
of the Church, especially when the ritual had at the same time an outer
centre, a kind of concrete geographical focus. Rudolf Steiner:

> And so in the East of Europe, while the esoteric, spiritual reality was
> forgotten, men turned to cult and ritual, clinging with greatest inten-
> sity of feeling to what they held to be the very heart and core of the
> cult: the Grave of the Redeemer. Hard by the Grave of the Redeemer
> in Jerusalem was the place where He had celebrated the Last Supper
> with His apostles, that eucharistic meal which, in metamorphosis,
> became the death on Golgotha, was consummated by His death and
> then lived on—in the central rite, but also in the whole ritual—in
> the Mass.

These people's hearts lived with the greatest fervour into the ritual,
and their greatest experience, the crown on their religious striving and
longing, was a pilgrimage to the tomb of the Redeemer in Jerusalem.
Gnosis, the actual knowing about the mysteries of the redemption, disappeared in eastern Europe; the concepts were insufficient, lacked living power to encompass the secrets. More to the East, in western Asia,
there were still remnants of initiation knowledge in academies, but in
due course, under the pressure of Mongol barbarians, these also had to
disappear. The people of the East, who lived much more directly but
less consciously than western human beings, looked for a Christianity
of the heart.

In Rome, however, the leaders of the Catholic Church considered this
to be a danger. They saw that the peoples of western and central Europe
already possessed the strongly developed intellect to such a degree that
they would never be able to feel completely satisfied just by the ritual,
by devotion to the Holy Sepulchre. Complete absorption of the soul in
the hidden esotericism of the ritual was as unwelcome to the leaders of
Catholicism in Rome as the search for esoteric insight of the heretical
souls in the Grail stream.

For this reason, a middle stream was called into being by Rome,
which was especially intended to meet the needs of the central European peoples. The esoteric content of Christianity was not allowed to
live in human souls as supersensible experience, and therefore it had
to be put in the form of abstract rules, doctrines one could *believe* in. As
answers, the questioning intellect did not receive explanations of the
secrets, but precisely formulated *dogmas*, that made one's own beholding of spiritual realities superfluous.

This choice meant, in fact, that Rome rejected the East, because any strictly handled dogmatism irrevocably had to create conflicts connected with the differences in the way religion was experienced in East and West. Pope Nicolas I was well aware of this and therefore, because he was no fanatic but a noble and wise person, the decision to strengthen the dogmatizing middle stream was an extremely difficult one for him.

In Rome there were other persons, however, who possessed great power and whose intentions the honest Pope was not fully able to see through. Their goal was to push the dogmatizing stream through with the greatest fanaticism. In our context we can only allude to a sinister group in the background that from the fourth century already had actively intervened in the affairs of the Church and the culture. Their negative effect through figures in the immediate entourage of the Pope gave the middle stream an entirely different character than Nicolas had intended. I will come back at length to this 'anti-Grail stream' in Chapter 6.

Shortly after the death of Nicolas I in 867 the conflict between Rome and the East about the faith, which was already growing during his life, came into sharp focus. Now we witness the interesting phenomenon that in the midst of the eastern peoples who lived so strongly in the world of feeling, a person comes to the fore who possesses an almost superhuman intelligence, thorough erudition and, at the same time, great charisma. This was the Patriarch of Constantinople, Photius.

Photius, who received his training in the schools of western Asia, but represented the initiation wisdom that was still living there in a brilliant intellectualistic sense, proclaimed a view of the essence of the human being that sounded like pure heresy in the ears of the western guardians of the Christian faith. He made use of Aristotelian concepts the Roman theologians did not know about. Aristotle distinguished several aspects of the human soul, but in the way the scholarly Patriarch handled these insights, western theologians could only recognize an effort to saddle the human being with *two* souls which they, justifiably, found absurd.

At the Council of Constantinople of 869, Photius' doctrine of the two souls was rejected and the following dogma was adopted: The human being consists of body and soul, the latter of which also possesses spiritual characteristics. This meant that in the Christian Church *the spirit had been abolished.* From that moment it was considered heresy to consider the human being as a threefold being consisting of body, soul and spirit, at any rate, if the spirit was treated as an autonomous entity.

A more weighty decision is hardly conceivable in the course of historical development. This dogma of 869 not only put a dualistic stamp
on theology, but also on science. The denial of the spirit lies at the root
of all later materialism.

Photius' role in this drama was not recognized by his contemporaries, but for us later observers, it is perfectly clear. With all his genius,
with all the power of persuasion of his charisma, which gave him great
respect from the people, he was in fact no more than a pawn on the chess
board of occult history. Because the fireworks of his personality blinded
people's eyes, an attack out of the darkness could be effective. The resolution of the Council of Constantinople was dictated by a power of evil
we have hardly mentioned so far, but of which we have to form a more
and more distinct picture as we proceed.

In the spiritual battle between East and West, which led to the great
schism of 1054, two different conceptions of the Holy Spirit played the
most important role. The West had included in the Creed the famous
word *filioque*, to express the conviction that the Holy Spirit proceeds
from the Father *as well as* the Son (*ex patre filioque*—from the Father and
the Son). The East completely rejected this: the Holy Spirit proceeded
from the Father!

Today we can hardly imagine that in those days there could be
such a fierce opposition between peoples about a religious statement
of faith. But people did not yet have the kind of resignation we have
today as to what is truth. They still wanted to fight for truth, against
untruth. It was in fact a tragedy that the contesting parties often were
no longer able to find the higher spiritual level where the two oppos-
ing views both show their validity as *aspects* of truth and are thus
reconciled.

When people have lost actual knowledge they develop views that
are one-sided and oppose each other. Such loss of knowledge about
the essence of the Trinity, about the relationship of the Father to the
Son, and of the Holy Spirit to both, drove East and West apart in the
filioque battle. When the divine spirit is no longer acknowledged, the
human spirit is abolished. The *filioque* battle and the resolution of the
Council manifested the impotence of human consciousness to penetrate to the essence of the world and the human being. Nevertheless,
it was at exactly that same time that the Grail seekers lived, and that
Parsifal lived. These were actual, living people, but their Grail quest
took place in secret; their connection with the dead was real, but hidden; their Temple of the Holy Spirit was a reality, but hidden.

Did nothing of this come to light? If this Grail stream is a concrete, historical phenomenon, even though the conventional science of history has not really admitted it, shouldn't there be visible evidence?

This does indeed exist, and it is the great merit of Walter Johannes Stein that he found and followed the traces of this stream. In the ninth century, Spain was no longer the centre of the Grail stream, although according to Rudolf Steiner late-Gothic mysteries worked there until the beginning of the Crusades. The hidden Grail castle had moved to central Europe; in the ninth century, therefore, we have to look for the Grail family, to the extent it consisted of living people, more in the central area of the Carolingian kingdoms.

In addition, we see how the three streams described above tended to flow together in subsequent centuries, so that they could no longer be sharply distinguished from each other. For example, the mood that led to the Crusades that began at the end of the eleventh century was clearly coloured by devotion to the Holy Sepulchre, the eastern stream. But the Crusades originated in the West. And the Grail stream did not only reach into the Carolingian realms but also much farther North into Scandinavia, Finland and Russia. The active politics of Rome of course took the middle stream with its dogmatic character also into western and eastern directions.

But all three streams became equally the victims of the gradual erosion of their spiritual content and the materialism that was growing in the period between the ninth and thirteenth centuries. From East to West, the Arabic-intellectualistic approach pushed itself over the original spirituality of the first stream and thoroughly covered it. The esoteric Grail stream could only continue to work in literary form, in the pictures of legends and sagas. The middle and eastern streams also became ever more the victims of materialistic tendencies.

In this situation a new esoteric impulse was urgently needed, a renewed inspiration coming directly from the source of the Christ mystery. This impulse comes to expression in the founding of the Order of the Templars. In a certain sense this Order combined the three streams in itself: the cultus with its centre in Jerusalem, the rules of the Order sanctioned by the authority of Rome, and the Grail stream which remained more hidden, but was the actual core of this impulse.

Before we hear how through the figure of Godfrey of Bouillon this renewed Christian esotericism is directly related to the Grail family, and indirectly to the ninth century, we first have to throw more light on the question of why the first stream (the Grail stream) moved to the West.

5. The Ninth Century—The East-West Movement

For an historical narrative that is based on outer facts and documents the streams described here may perhaps not be so demonstrably evident as other, clearly documented movements, such as the great migrations or conquests, but for such a narrative the *direction from East to West* of the first of the three streams is indeed totally inexplicable.

We may simply observe this East-West movement and leave it unexplained. We just watch how Christianity spreads from East to West. A Christian stream also flowed from Palestine eastward, but it hardly grew to maturity. However, the westward spread of Christianity in general, and of the Grail stream in particular, only become truly interesting when we realize that in the West there seems to have been something that was waiting for it. We can even observe a counter-movement from the Celtic West that went eastward into the heart of Europe to meet the westward movement, as it were. In the Grail saga this is expressed by the connection of the Grail with the Round Table of King Arthur.

King Arthur, the legendary British hero, represents the glory and downfall of the Celts in the West. But in the light of occult history we should view the Arthur figure in connection with the mystery backgrounds that the medieval poets veiled exclusively in pictures, and thus thoroughly concealed them.

Behind the Celts, who came to the British Isles and Ireland only around 500 years before Christ,[74] loom magical cultures that must have had their origin in the far distant prehistoric past. Hints of this can be found in Irish and Welsh mythology of later times and have led several modern Grail researchers to the idea that the miraculous chalice has its origin in these western regions. The view that the Grail sagas have a Celtic-pagan origin and were only Christianized in the Middle Ages, may not be unfounded. In that case, however, the direction of the Grail stream should have been from West to East, and not the reverse. How can we find a plausible explanation of these things?

We have seen that the world of the Grail traditions is one of images, spiritual pictures. Now that we have tried to approach the three archetypal images of the book, the altar and the Temple in a spiritual manner, we have to give our attention to another imaginative element in the Grail world. We are frequently confronted with three other images, namely the *spear*, the *sword*, and the *chalice*; and, although less often, as a fourth image, the *stone*.

The stone in Wolfram's epic, *lapsit exillis*, was considered in Chapter 3. The chalice has also been extensively discussed. The Grail sword is important both to Chrétien and Wolfram. From Walter Johannes Stein we know that this Grail sword is no ordinary weapon, but the 'sword of the word'. The Grail knight was in service of the Christ being, of the Word in the Johannine sense.

The image of the spear also appears in both Chrétien and Wolfram. A squire carries a spear through the hall where Parsifal is received by the suffering Grail King. From the point of the spear blood flows down along the shaft. A connection is made between this imaginative picture and a real historical object, namely the spear with which the centurion Longinus pierced the right side of Jesus, upon which blood and water flowed out of the body of the Crucified One.

In Richard Wagner's opera *Parsifal* the spear is even more important. There it does not appear in the Grail castle, but it has come into the possession of the evil magician Klingsor. He had used it to inflict an incurable wound in Amfortas' lower body. When he hurls the spear to Parsifal it stops and hovers over the latter's head. The weapon and its illegitimate possessor have no power over the 'pure fool'. Parsifal takes hold of the spear and in one stroke Klingsor's whole magical pleasure garden and castle disappear.

When we immerse ourselves in Irish mythology we find there four objects, the spear, sword, chalice and stone as the 'four treasures' of a generation of gods, the Tuatha-de-Danaan. These were an actually existing people that lived in Ireland for centuries before the Celts arrived there. They were not even the first inhabitants, but were invaders from northern Europe. To the later population of Ireland they were as gods who had withdrawn into the invisible.

In his masterful work about Ireland[75] Hans Gsänger has a most interesting explanation of the double aspect of these Tuatha-de-Danaan. How can they be invaders and at the same time gods who play a decisive role in the creation of the world?

According to the tradition about the wanderings the Tuatha-de-Danaan made through Europe, they also dwelled in Greece for some time, in the vicinity of the city of Thebes. Close to this city there was a sanctuary of the Kabiri that had been founded by the Phoenician initiate Cadmus, who also founded Thebes. The original centre of the Kabiri mysteries was in Hebron in old Canaan. From there Cadmus brought the wisdom of the 'great gods' via Samothrace to Thebes. The Tuatha-de-Danaan are said to have learned all kinds of necromancy and magic in Greece, but of course nothing of the sort existed in a mystery place of the Kabiri gods.

Then what did they learn there? They were initiated into the deepest secrets of world evolution. Gsänger writes:

> In the Kabirion of Thebes one penetrated into the secrets of the creative gods who worked in the several stages of world evolution, beginning with world fire, about which the Greek philosopher Heraclitus also spoke. Then came the world light, the world tone, which is hidden in all structures of physical matter, and the last condensation of world matter. The initiates of this group went with their knowledge to Scandinavia where they encountered the offshoots of the Hyperborean (Drotten) mysteries. ...
>
> There it was recognized that their knowledge was more encompassing [than that of the Drotten], which came to expression in the fact that the Tuatha-de-Danaan were given four 'cities', where they founded schools (read: mystery places).
>
> Subsequently, the initiates went to Ireland where they came into contact with the remnants of the so-called Atlantean mysteries. That which arose from this coming together of three mystery streams continued to exist into the first Christian centuries as the great mysteries of Hibernia, which must not be confused with the schools of the Druids.
>
> In the Tuatha-de-Danaan superhuman individualities must have been incorporated who cannot be judged by earthly standards. That is why all events of this period appear like half-earthly and half-supersensible. The old sagas describe the Tuatha-de-Danaan as if they were gods who made use of human bodies to accomplish their intentions. They evidently took on the names of the gods they served.

The mythological pictures of the creation by the Danaan gods are impressive. They possessed the *spear of victory*, the *light sword*, the *chalice of fullness*, and the *stone of destiny*. Without any doubt, these four 'treasures of the gods' were not material objects but imaginations, pictures of cosmic powers.

For someone familiar with spiritual insights into the etheric world, the world of life substances and formative forces in nature and cosmos, it will not take much effort to recognize in the four treasures the symbols of the four ethers: warmth ether, light ether, chemical or sound ether, and life ether. On earth these ethers have their corresponding elements, the states of warmth, air or gas, fluidity and solidity. These four conditions of matter are traditionally called fire, air, water and earth, and can be viewed as condensations of the four kinds of ether. In warmth this condensation is only slight; warmth and warmth ether are more or less one. The light ether corresponds with physical air, while chemical or sound ether corresponds with the fluid element, and life ether with solid matter.[76]

In the story of the earth's becoming, which is described by all old cre-ation myths, etheric substances and forces play an important role. The initiates of ancient peoples knew that the earth did not come into being as a result of a mechanical, dead process, but by the creative activity of higher beings. These beings revealed themselves to the clairvoyant gaze of the initiates as bearers of certain attributes, 'treasures', that were related to the fourfold nature of the etheric world.

The spear of victory was planted by the gods of De-Danaan in the centre of Ireland. It radiated a mighty glow of *warmth*. The light sword expresses in its very name that it is the symbol of the *light* ether. The chalice or cauldron of fullness belonged to the god Dagda who also pos-sessed a magical harp, an instrument that produces sound, and there-fore points to its connection with the chemical or *sound* ether. Finally, the stone of destiny corresponds with the *life* ether which, as the highest ether, is related to the *solid earth*.

Irish myth relates how a dark people, the Fomor led by one-eyed Balor, steal the treasures of the Tuatha-de-Danaan. Impoverished and powerless the Dana people are subjugated and enslaved by the demonic Fomor, until the sun god Lugh comes, defeats Fomor, and returns the treasures to the Tuatha-de-Danaan.

Not only in Wagner's *Parsifal* did one of the Grail treasures, the spear, come into the possession of the evil one; in the beautiful Breton Grail fairytale of Peronnik the Fool both chalice and spear are in the power of the evil magician Rogéar.[77] What in Irish myth is done by the sun god, the redemption of the treasures from the dark power, is in the Grail sto-ries accomplished by the simple, pure fool. Those who are simple and unwise to human beings are wise to God. Peronnik as well as Parsifal vanquish evil by their purity.

What does it mean that the treasures fall into the power of evil? If we may assume that with these treasures actually the four etheric sub-stances are meant, their theft needs to be understood as a loss of the capacity to penetrate into the creative world of the supersensible cos-mos. The sun god, however, or the hero who is the initiate of the sun mysteries, is able to regain this capacity.

In the lecture of 1922 referred to before[78] in which Rudolf Steiner spoke about the three streams of the ninth century he said the following about the searching souls of the Grail stream:

> If that esoteric stream which penetrated to Ireland and died away in later times had been pursued in deed and truth, the souls of those belonging to it would inevitably have experienced union with the

spiritual world. For the great question living in this esoteric stream was in reality this: How is the human being to find his orientation in the etheric world, in the etheric cosmos? The visions which also included the conception of the Mystery of Golgotha were connected with the etheric cosmos.

The Celts as a whole, but primarily in Ireland, Wales and Cornwall, still possessed a knowledge of the etheric cosmos. It stemmed from pre-Celtic times and was nourished from the great Hibernian mysteries, in which the Scandinavian Drotten mysteries and the Kabiri mysteries from Palestine were united. However, this was a hidden source of nourishment that remained in the background.

For the external eye great megalithic structures arose. The sanctuary of Stonehenge, as well as other stone circles or alignments, as they can also be found in Bretagne, point to a cosmically oriented religion, in which the movements of the sun and moon in relation to the earth and the stars were of the greatest significance. These mysterious constructions were not only temples, but equally importantly, they were observatories for the Druid priests. These must have possessed a thorough knowledge of astronomy, geometry and arithmetic, arts that were not yet used to explore mechanical-earthly realities but cosmic-etheric ones. Their observations were therefore not directed to externally revealed light, but to the spiritual side of it, which can be observed where the external light is blocked, namely in *shadow*. In the shadow of the dolmens and gigantic standing stones the Druids 'read' the secrets of the cosmos.

Thus Celtic culture, as well as the megalithic cultures preceding it, were permeated by a mystery wisdom that had the cosmic Sun Spirit in its centre and, because of this, showed a strong kinship with the Egyptian mystery religion, but especially with that of Saba (see Chapter 3). And in Chapter 2 we discussed that the Germanic Baldur myth is also closely related to this.

Now, one of the most important contributions that anthroposophical spiritual science makes to our understanding of the development of the earth and humanity is the insight that the pagan sun god, who was worshipped under various different names by ancient peoples, is none other than the Christ being in His cosmic revelation. Just as the great Church Father Augustine speaks of a pre-Christian Christianity of the philosophers Plato and Aristotle, we may call the source from which pre-Christian wisdom flowed in East and West, namely the sun, the pre-Christian Christ.

When the Grail poets relate that the holy chalice is taken to England (Robert de Boron) or that Parsifal makes a connection with the circle of King Arthur (Chrétien and Wolfram), or that the Arthurian knights themselves go on a quest for the Grail (*Queste del Saint Graal*), this indicates a picture of the encounter of two kinds of Christianity, the meeting of a pre-Christian, cosmic Christianity from the West with a Golgotha-Christianity from the East.

Rudolf Steiner spoke very clearly about this in a lecture given in London in 1924.[79] After describing what the Arthurian knights could observe in the castle at Tintagel in Cornwall as an interplay of light, air and water in the waves crashing against the rocky coast, he said that in this interplay of nature spirits the sun power, the sun impulse manifests itself. The circle around King Arthur was an esoteric community that existed already in pre-Christian times. It saw as its mission to exert an ennobling influence on the as-yet wild population of northern and central Europe in service to the cosmic Sun being. The initiated knights absorbed the sun impulse into their inner being out of nature. This impulse poured into their hearts, most of all their etheric bodies.

> And so, before the Mystery of Golgotha, the knights of King Arthur received into themselves the Sun Spirit, that is to say, the Christ as He was in pre-Christian times. And they sent their messengers out into all Europe to subdue the wild savagery of the astral bodies of the peoples of Europe, to purify and to civilize, for such was their mission.
>
> [...]
>
> Then came the Mystery of Golgotha. What happened in Asia? Over yonder in Asia, the sublime Sun Being, who was later known as the Christ, left the sun. This betokened a kind of death for the Christ being. He went forth from the sun as we human beings go forth from the earth when we die. And as a person who dies leaves his physical body behind on the earth and his etheric body, which is laid aside after three days, is visible to the seer, so Christ left behind Him in the sun that which in my book *Theosophy* is called spirit man, the seventh member of the human being.
>
> Christ died to the sun. He died cosmically, from the sun to the earth. He came down to the earth. From the moment of Golgotha onwards His life spirit was to be seen around the earth. We ourselves leave behind at death the life ether, the etheric body, the life body. After this cosmic death, Christ left His spirit man on the sun, and around the earth His life spirit. So that after the Mystery of Golgotha the earth was swathed, as it were, by the life spirit of the Christ.

Steiner went on to describe how this life spirit of Christ, which permeates the etheric sphere around the earth since the Mystery of Golgotha, was perceptible to the initiates of the Irish mysteries and the circle around King Arthur that was connected with them. In the centuries after Christ these knights saw in the interplay of light, air and water above the rocks of the coast not only the working of the sun, but in it was also spiritually reflected what had taken place on Golgotha in Palestine. This was possible because of the fact that the phenomena of nature in which the cosmic Christ had formerly been perceived, were now permeated by the life spirit of Christ which, when He 'died to the sun', left the sun and now 'swathed' the earth.

Those who had received the required occult schooling were able to decipher in the enveloping sphere of the life spirit the earthly pictures of Christ's life in Palestine as an occult script. These western initiates were thus indirect witnesses of the Mystery of Golgotha. They read the Gospel from nature!

A few Celtic legends retain very interesting traces of this. The most beautiful example is the story of St. Bride of Iona who, on her far western island, was in a mysterious way present at the birth of Jesus in Bethlehem.

However, what was actually happening in Palestine, the incarnation of Christ—the descent of the Sun Spirit, the Christ I, into the body of Jesus of Nazareth—was taken into the hearts of people. From East to West, through Greece, North Africa, Italy, Spain to Europe, the 'real' Christ penetrated livingly into human *hearts*, while the indirect revelation of the Mystery of Golgotha travelled from West to East through *nature*.

The Christianity that moved from East to West—the later Grail stream—worked through the heart and, as it were, took possession of the blood. Not only do we see blood relics of the Redeemer move westward, but a family of Grail Kings formed itself, a group of people who were connected through a common bloodline. When modern researchers, such as the three authors of *The Holy Blood and the Holy Grail*, speak of a royal family (the Merovingian dynasty) that is supposed to carry the blood of Jesus, they indulge in a caricature of reality. What is real was not the physical blood of the *human being* Jesus that had to flow in certain exceptional descendants through sexual procreation, but a spiritual indwelling of the *Risen One* in a group of people who wanted to serve Christ in a particular manner.

In the early Middle Ages this still had to occur through blood relationships; a kind of *Grail people* had to form the connection between the

One and the many, between the Son of Man and humanity. Later this Grail service would detach itself from the blood relationship. The Templars formed a community of individuals in which each member considered his individual blood as belonging to Christ. A vow still bound them to this freely-offered service. A subsequent phase of development would be that free individuals would devote themselves to service of the Grail without an outwardly expressed vow.

The Christianity that came from the West may be called the Arthur stream, for short. But it should make us think not only of the knights of the later Arthur and Grail stories, but certainly also of the Irish and British monks who in the fifth, sixth and seventh centuries embarked on their extremely important and beneficial 'peregrinations' to the continent of Europe. Their form of Christianity still had a distinctly cosmic orientation, just like the pre-Christian and Christian Round Table of King Arthur.

Now, when this Arthur stream and the Grail stream met, what actually happened? I quote from Rudolf Steiner's lecture referred to above:

> The Christ who descended through the Mystery of Golgotha drew into the hearts of men. In the hearts of men He passed from East to West, from Palestine through Greece, across Italy and Spain. The Christianity of the Grail spread through the blood and the hearts of men. The Christ took His way from East to West.
>
> And to meet Him from the West came the spiritual etheric *Image* of the Christ—the Image evoked by the Mystery of Golgotha, but still picturing the Christ of the Sun Mysteries.
>
> Behind the scenes of world history, sublime and wonderful events were taking place. From the West came pagan Christianity, the Arthur-Christianity, also under other names and in another form. From the East came the Christ in the hearts of men. And then the meeting takes place—the meeting between the Christ who had Himself come down to earth and His own Image which is brought to Him from West to East. This meeting took place in the year 869 AD.
>
> Up to that year we have two streams, clearly distinct from one another. The one stream, more in the North, passed across central Europe and bore the Christ as a Sun Hero, whether the name were Baldur or some other. And under the banner of Christ, the Sun Hero, the knights of King Arthur spread their culture abroad.
>
> The other stream, rooted inwardly in the hearts of men, which later became the Grail stream, is to be perceived more in the South, coming from the East. It bears the real Christ, Christ Himself. The other stream brings to meet it from the West a cosmic image of the Christ. This meeting of Christ with Himself, of Christ the Brother of

humanity with Christ the Sun Hero who is there only, as it were, in an image—this meeting of Christ with His own image took place in the ninth century.

Although the view of history sketched here, which is based on spiritual research, may not be acceptable to current professional historians, it does provide us with an extremely concrete explanation of a piece of European history, albeit a spiritual one. It shows us that not only historical facts, but also legendary tradition that has come to us in literary form, as well as the deeper aspects of the Christian religion, are brought into mutual relationship and harmony by these insights.

Other background events that made the ninth century so important in occult history have to remain out of consideration here so as not to overload our theme, but some additional points will be mentioned in the last section of this chapter.

6. The Birth of the Order of the Templars

The birth of the Order of the Templars is a chapter from occult history on which spiritual science has so far thrown little light. But there are notes of a lecture about historical connections of which it is said that Rudolf Steiner gave it to a small circle of people in Hanover in 1905. These contain an extremely interesting statement relating to this subject.

However, it is virtually certain that these notes do not reflect statements by Rudolf Steiner but by Walter Johannes Stein. In that case the date of 1905 cannot be correct, but the content deserves careful attention, because Stein was the one who possessed the most thorough knowledge on the subject. If we take the statements on the Order of the Templars contained in these notes as an historical hypothesis for now, we can form for ourselves a more graphic picture of what took place than the usual story of events, which is so incomplete that we can hardly call it a picture.

The historians who do not view the First Crusade, the conquest of Jerusalem, and the subsequent foundation of the Order of the Templars in the light of the Holy Grail, tell us the following:

> The pilgrimages by Christians to the Holy Sepulchre in Jerusalem were rarely hindered after the conquest of Palestine by the Arabs. Only when the Turks started to dominate the eastern caliphate did the pilgrims meet with serious difficulties when they had to travel through Islamic countries. Toward the end of the eleventh century the violence and robberies of which Christian pilgrims were the victims had increased to such an extent that people in European countries had become extremely worried. The Pope, as the head of Christendom,

preached a fight against the infidels. Under the sign of the cross, with the powerful battle cry 'It is God's will', armies gathered in Lorraine, northern and southern France and southern Italy to march against the enemy in the Holy Land. Peter of Amiens and Walter von Habenichts had already gone ahead with a host of enthusiastic but hardly competent men; by far the largest part of these perished in abominable circumstances.

After a long and difficult march and endless political complications the united army of the Crusaders managed to reach Palestine. Under the command of Godfrey of Bouillon the city of Jerusalem was taken by storm in 1099. The glorious commander was the only one who wanted nothing to do with the gruesome carnage and barbaric pillage the Christians committed in the Holy City. Godfrey refused the crown of the newly founded Kingdom of Jerusalem; he only wanted to call himself 'Protector of the Holy Sepulchre'. His brother Baldwin became king. Godfrey died shortly after in 1100. Baldwin reigned until his death and was succeeded in 1118 by his nephew who was also called Baldwin.

That year saw the foundation of a second Order of knights-monks after the already existing Order of St. John (the Order of Hospitallers). Hugues de Payens and eight knights from northern France made the vow of poverty, chastity and obedience in the hands of the Patriarch of Jerusalem. They took on the task of guarding the roads the pilgrims had to take to the Holy Sepulchre, and to defend the pilgrims from the Muslims. In 1119 the king gave them part of his royal palace for the home of their Order. It was situated where the Temple of Solomon had stood and where the Arabs had in the meantime built two great mosques, the Dome of the Rock with its golden dome, and the Al-Aqsa Mosque. The latter became the residence of the new Order.

In the years that followed only one new member joined the Order, Count Hugo of Champagne. In 1128 the whole group went with Grand Master Hugues de Payens to France, where at the Council of Troyes the Order received its official recognition by the Church of Rome. The rules of the Order were drawn up by the most influential cleric of the time, the Cistercian abbot Bernard de Clairvaux. This marked the beginning of the work of the Order of the Templars.

That is the generally accepted story. However, when we take a more detailed look at the most interesting figure of Godfrey of Bouillon we may be struck by some peculiarities. Conventional historical researchers may be familiar with these, but in connection with the events of the eleventh and twelfth centuries briefly sketched above they have not received much attention.

Godfrey of Bouillon was the son of Eustace Count of Boulogne and Ida, sister of Godfrey, Duke of Lower Lorraine. As a young nobleman he fought on the side of the German Emperor Henry IV against the Pope. At the conquest of Rome Godfrey distinguished himself in a remarkable way. But he incurred a life-threatening wound. He made a vow that if he recovered he would liberate Jerusalem from the yoke of the Saracens. It was said that the aversion he had developed to papist Rome had inspired the idea in him to move the centre of Christianity back to the place where it was born, the city of Jerusalem. History remembers of Godfrey not only his heroic courage and almost superhuman strength, but just as much his great kind-heartedness, piety and humility.

In addition, he was favoured by a circumstance that, seemingly by coincidence, was of decisive significance, for he was extremely wealthy as the result of an inheritance. His uncle, Godfrey of Lower Lorraine, was married to the daughter of the famous Beatrice d'Este, Matilda of Tuscany, who was immeasurably rich. However, their son lost his life at a young age in an accident, while his uncle Godfrey had already died shortly after the birth of the boy. Later, Matilda founded a monastery, named Orval, close to the place where her son was drowned in Belgium, not far from Bouillon where Ida, Matilda's sister-in-law had raised her three famous sons.

It is said that Peter of Amiens, also called Peter the Hermit, was among the first group of monks who established themselves in the Abbey of Orval. He was perhaps Godfrey of Bouillon's guardian, but this is not certain. But what is certain is that Matilda bequeathed a substantial part of her possessions to her nephew Godfrey, and with the money borrowed against these assets Godfrey could equip his army for the First Crusade.

From these particulars one may well conclude that in the idea and preparation of the First Crusade the role of Godfrey might have been a much more crucial one than conventional history describes. In the first place the initiative he took for the whole enterprise is usually obscured or even left out completely. And by emphasizing the part the Roman Pope is supposed to have had in the preparation, no one realizes that the real impulse that led to the First Crusade was clearly a non-Roman one—we might justifiably say an anti-Roman one.

Apart from this, we should not belittle the part of Pope Urban II in bringing about the expedition to the Holy Land. When he preached the Crusade at the Council of Clermont in 1095, he hoped to rid himself of a number of 'heretics' in the Holy Roman Empire who were forming a growing block of opposition to the authority of the Pope. This was successful. In the unruly bands of Peter the Hermit and Walter von Habenichts there were not only villains and adventurers, but also decent people of good families who might also be considered heretics. The same was true for the regular troops of the four European kings who joined the Crusade.

At this point, we should not be surprised to hear that through his mother, Countess Ida, Godfrey was a late descendant of the Grail family. The statements made by Walter Johannes Stein in his lecture referred to earlier add detail to the foregoing in such a way that they give us a better picture, albeit still not a complete one. We have to go back to the ninth century, to a man named Hugo de Tours.

According to the notes of this lecture, Hugo de Tours travelled to Constantinople by order of Charlemagne, and acquired there important Christian relics. One of these, a precious relic of St. Peter, was taken by Hugo's brother to Rome pursuant to a vision. It was brought to a church that was built on the spot where Peter was crucified. Later the great Renaissance master builder Bramante built there a round chapel, *Il Tempietto*.

When the brother of Hugo de Tours died he still had, like all deceased people, a strong relationship with what was happening on the earth, particularly with what was happening in Rome as a result of his deed. He saw how the presence of the relic of St. Peter had the consequence that people undertook pilgrimages to Peter's grave. Then a resolution ripened in him that, when he was born again on earth, he would turn these pilgrimages from the grave of Peter to that of Christ in Jerusalem. And there we have the origin of the Crusades.

This brother of Hugo de Tours was reborn in the eleventh century as Godfrey of Bouillon. He died in the year 1100 and was buried in Jerusalem. On his grave, nine knights from northern France joined hands; they founded the Order of the Templars. Although the lecture notes do not mention it explicitly, one might assume that the impulse to the founding of this Order came from Godfrey's inspiration. For those who view such spiritual research with a degree of skepticism, these statements need be no more than hypotheses; at any rate, they show a clear connection of a series of facts around the development of the First Crusade and the foundation of the Order of the Templars.

The authors of the book *The Holy Blood and the Holy Grail*, which I have mentioned several times before, also call attention to certain connections, for example between the foundation of the monastery in Orval by Matilda of Tuscany, the figure of Godfrey, and the foundation of the

Order of the Templars. It is striking that what in spiritual science is described as a *spiritual* impulse, namely a resolution an individuality makes between death and rebirth, is represented as a *political* impulse proceeding from a mysterious 'Order of Zion'. They profess to be able to justify this based on a number of historical documents. I don't want to be distracted by this and prefer to go back to *The Ninth Century*, Walter Johannes Stein's Grail book.

Here we find Hugo de Tours mentioned side by side with Waldo von Reichenau as the chief representatives of the Grail stream in the circle around Charlemagne. Stein writes extensively about the adventures of Hugo as the legend relates them. After slander put him in a bad light with Charlemagne —who originally held him in great honour—he was imprisoned and condemned to death. The execution, however, did not happen. In a miraculous way Hugo's innocence came to light. Thereupon he received an exceptional gift from Charlemagne, namely a relic with drops of the blood of Jesus. It was not the blood that flowed from the wounds on Golgotha, but the blood that had flowed at the circumcision of the Jesus boy in the Temple, the so-called first bloodshed.

Waldo von Reichenau also received a blood relic, and Stein leaves no doubt that these partly historical, partly legendary blood movements point to the Grail stream. Similarly, the gift of a blood relic to the Flemish city of Bruges in the twelfth century indicates this. The receiver of this relic was Thierry d'Alsace, who took part in the Second Crusade. His spouse, Sybil, was the sister of Baldwin III, King of Jerusalem from 1144 to 1162. Baldwin gave his brother-in-law a part of the blood that Joseph of Arimathea had collected. Thierry bestowed the precious ampoule that contained the drop of blood on the city of Bruges. His son, Philippe d'Alsace, Count of Flanders, was the possessor of the secret book on which Chrétien de Troyes based his Grail epic.

This shows us very clearly that the Templar impulse which, emanating from Jerusalem, wanted to bring a renewed esoteric Christianity, resulted at the same time in the fact that the Grail traditions became exoteric in the twelfth century. For from the fact that Bernard de Clairvaux, who gave the Order of the Templars its rules, was the inaugurator of the Second Crusade we may infer that this Crusade was closely connected with the Templar impulse.

It is to be regretted that we do not find anything more about the brother of Hugo de Tours either in the notes of Stein's lecture or in *The Ninth Century*. We may presume that he was also deeply connected with the Grail stream. At any rate, he finds his next incarnation as one of the descendants of the Grail family along the female line: Lady Ida was a descendant of the Swan Knight.*

Had Hugo's brother during his life in the ninth century been disloyal to the Johannine Grail impulse by becoming too close to the Roman-Petrine element? The presumption is surely justified. If we assume that the inspiration toward the founding of the Order of the Templars came from this individuality—Hugo de Payens was Godfrey's brother-in-arms—we may associate the notorious denial of Christ, of which the Templars were later accused at their trial, with the denial by Peter. Every initiated Templar had to go through the stage of Simon Peter who denied his Lord, just as Godfrey in his previous incarnation had strengthened the Petrine element, which he repented in the spiritual world.

I will come back to this question in Chapter 5.

7. Karmic Relationships

We might imagine that historiography could in the future be based on insight into karmic relationships. History would then not be viewed merely as a process of action and reaction, as a chain of directly demonstrable causes and effects, but as a fabric of karmic connections between individual people and groups of people. In this picture we might discover motives which are inspired by spiritual beings, but yet always have to be brought to realization by people on earth, even though these are usually unconscious of the source of their inspiration. What manifests to the eye as an historical fact will then often be interpreted as a symptom of deeper developmental impulses that may reveal themselves in successive incarnations of one and the same individuality, albeit adapted to the circumstances in which the incarnations take place.

Before concluding this chapter on occult history I want to describe another karmic relationship because it offers, in my opinion, an important perspective of human development. It is the figure of Hugo de Tours, whose brother has been described as Godfrey of Bouillon in his next life.

Walter Johannes Stein says that Hugo was the monk who after long wanderings lived in the hermitage where the lovers of the Grail story, Sigune and Schionatulander, had found refuge. This cannot be anyone other than Trevrezent, the brother of the unhappy 'fisher king' Amfortas. True, Trevrezent was no monk, but he had withdrawn from worldly life to the hermitage in the woods in order to form a counterweight to the

---

* Lohengrin, son of Parsifal.

wounded Grail King, who had harboured a too worldly disposition. He incurred an incurable wound, not in service of the Grail, but because he had gone in search of love.

Of course, if Hugo de Tours was the hermit from the Parsifal story, we may wonder whether Hugo's brother was the Amfortas figure. In other words, was Godfrey of Bouillon in his prior life the historical figure who served as a model for the tragic king in the saga? We don't have a definite answer to this question, but it is not totally inconceivable. The traits shown by figures in a saga do not necessarily have a realistic character, but rather that of imagination, a picture. A family relationship in the saga does not need to point to actual kinship of the historical figures, for the relationship may have been changed in the story. We are on shaky ground here.

The only support we have that may lead us to a positive answer to the question comes from two facts. The first one has already been mentioned in the previous section—in a certain respect Hugo's brother had become disloyal to the Grail impulse when he took the relic of St. Peter to Rome. After all, the Grail stream represented a form of Christianity that was free from Rome.

The other fact is that the graves in Salm and Chiny showed on their heraldic shields three fishes under a royal crown. This gave the saga of Amfortas its origin. The area of Chiny—situated very close to Bouillon in Belgium—belonged to Lower Lorraine. This region, which includes Alsace, is where Hugo de Tours came from, as did his brother. They were descendants of the Duke of Alsace Eticho or Atalric, the father of St. Odile.

Although spiritual science tells us that two successive incarnations are usually very different and rarely or never happen in the same geographical area, it is in this case not inconceivable that this particular individuality, who reincarnated so very soon, came back to the same region, even to the same family, in order to fulfil his historic mission, this time free from Rome.

But still, this impulse also remains problematic in the sense that the fervently pious focus on the Sepulchre in Jerusalem overlooks the fact that this grave is empty. A person who 'seeks the living among the dead' may perhaps not really have understood the message of the Grail. All the enthusiasm with which the European knights went on Crusade, the foundation of the Kingdom of Jerusalem, and all that followed—isn't all of it really a huge historical *and* spiritual error? For now, this is still a riddle.

Not so with Hugo himself. In the lecture notes referred to above a great deal of attention is given to his next incarnation, a Portuguese nobleman, Francisco de Almeida, who conducted responsible missions in service of Spanish and Portuguese kings. These took place in an extremely important time period, namely the transition from the fifteenth to the sixteenth century, the beginning of modern times, the fifth post-Atlantean cultural epoch in which we now live.

At that time we see a revival of the Grail impulse and the Arthur stream, which expressed itself in the movement of the Brotherhood of the Rose Cross, founded in 1459. In addition, two influential Orders were founded, the Order of the Golden Fleece, founded by Philip the Good of Burgundy in 1429, and the Order of Prince Arthur in England. The latter Order was established in honour of Arthur, the first son of King Henry VII of England. The statutes of this Order, which were published in book form a hundred years later, can be found in the British Museum. They were drawn up by Thomas Malory, the famous author of *Le Morte d'Arthur*.

Francisco de Almeida

Sir Thomas Malory is an interesting individuality. As the very young Archbishop of Santiago de Compostela he undersigned in that function the marriage contract of Ferdinand of Aragon and Isabella of Castile. In Santiago he met the Portuguese knight Francisco de Almeida, who initiated him in alchemy. The seventh book of *Le Morte d'Arthur*, for which conventional science cannot find any evident sources, is intelligible only for those who know alchemy as it is to be found in the work of the mysterious Basilius Valentinus (or Basil Valentine).

Valentinus speaks in his writings of a relic he took with him to the North from Santiago de Compostela, where he had gone as a pilgrim. What he called a relic might be better called a treasure, for it was actually the secret knowledge of alchemy that was centred in Santiago and was closely guarded by the Order of St. James.[80] Around 1500 Ferdinand of Aragon was the head of the Order.

The English Crown prince Arthur, born in the old Arthur city of Winchester, married Catherine, a daughter of Ferdinand and Isabella. Not only was thus a political connection made between the two Orders through which one intended to realize spiritual impulses that had to prepare for modern times, alchemy also played an important role in the Arthur Order.

Since the most important rulers of Europe were members of these Orders, it could be expected that they would exert a supra-national influence. One of the most outstanding of these rulers was Maximilian I of Habsburg, the German Emperor, who was married to Maria of Burgundy. Because the Burgundian line had no male descendants, Maximilian inherited this most important realm, to which the Low Countries, Netherlands and Belgium, also belonged. The Burgundian realm encompassed a large part of the centre of Charlemagne's empire that had been divided into three parts after his death. In this middle realm were all the centres that had to do with Grail Christianity. In this way, Maximilian became the head of the Order of the Golden Fleece. He was also a member of the Order of Prince Arthur.

The English Crown prince Arthur died at a young age, but King Henry arranged things in such a way that Arthur's widow Catherine remained in the family. She became the wife of Henry's second son, Henry VIII, who later cast her off in order to marry Anne Boleyn.

When we now wonder what the significance of the above facts is, why suddenly alchemy appears on the scene, and what role the Portuguese nobleman De Almeida played in all of this, we come to surprising results. First of all we have to realize that the statements made by Walter Johannes Stein about this subject are esoteric contemplations of historical relationships. It should therefore not surprise us that conventional history, which knows nothing of occult history or just rejects it, is silent about this.

We can find more about it in three articles by Stein dated respectively in 1934, 1935 and 1936. In the third one Stein describes the events in which Francisco de Almeida was involved in the same way as in the lecture mentioned earlier. But the second article has a version of this that differs on one most essential point. The third article might perhaps have been a correction on the former one.[81]

In his lecture Stein speaks of the relic of St. Peter that the brother of Hugo de Tours brought to Rome. On the place where Peter was crucified a wooden church had at one time been erected. Eventually it was replaced by the round stone chapel of Bramante, says Stein, which happened by order of Ferdinand and Isabella as a thank offering for the miraculous recovery of their grandchild, the later Emperor Charles V, from a mortal illness. This miracle came about by an appearance of St. Peter, and in memory of this Ferdinand wanted to build a chapel in Rome.

Francisco de Almeida, who served King Ferdinand at the time, went to Rome, obtained permission from Pope Alexander Borgia to build a chapel, and gave the money for it to Bramante, the greatest master builder in those days. On the spot where according to tradition Peter's cross had stood, Bramante built a round chapel, the first round structure that functioned as a Christian church. It was called *Il Tempietto*, and can in a certain regard be considered as the archetype of the later Church of St. Peter, the dome of which was executed by Michelangelo following Bramante's original plan. It was De Almeida's destiny to make a contribution to the fact that, on the same place where the brother of Hugo de Tours (De Almeida's previous incarnation) had brought a relic of St. Peter, an important Petrine impulse could take effect in modern times.

So far, the statements agree. But then Stein writes in the article of 1935:

> A Portuguese knight [the name De Almeida is not mentioned] brought the holy object from the court of Pope Alexander VI to Santiago de Compostela. [...] He took with him the object that the Pope had granted him. The Order of St. James believed it had a claim to it, since the knight was a member of the order. But the knight ensured that the holy object was passed to Basilius Valentinus who carried it to the North. The conflict which arose between the knight and the order as a consequence led to the death of the knight in March 1510. But the holy object traveled to the North.[82]

When we read the article of 1936, however, the origin of the holy object is a completely different one, and the story is more in agreement with the notes of Stein's lecture. According to this version, the Portuguese knight does not at all receive the object out of the hands of Pope Alexander Borgia. It came from a Moorish ruler who, when the knight had been mortally wounded in the Battle of Granada and was captured by the Moors, had lovingly cared for him, cured him and initiated him in his profound alchemical wisdom. For the Moors in Spain possessed an extremely rare book and a holy object, an alchemical relic in the form of a pearl. The book contained the *alchemy of Aristotle*, the esoteric document of the Greek philosopher that had not reached the West at the time.

After De Almeida had fully recovered from his wounds he managed to escape from the Moorish camp and took both holy objects, the relic and Aristotle's book, with him. He should have given them to his Order, but he didn't do that. He arranged that they were given to the 'rightful possessor', Stefan Rautter from the Rhineland, who used the pseudonym of Basilius Valentinus. The person who gave the relic and the book to this greatest initiated alchemist was De Almeida's wife, who was murdered out of revenge by the Order of St. James. De Almeida himself was also executed. Stein speaks here of two expeditions to India that De Almeida had undertaken.

The article of 1936 not only agrees with this but supplies a few important additions. De Almeida is the one who conquered the Portuguese possessions in India for the Portuguese crown after Vasco da Gama had opened the sea route around the Cape of Good Hope. His work was finished by Alfonso de Albuquerque. De Almeida was made Viceroy of India by King Manuel of Portugal. He wrote letters to the king about his measures and justified them. First of all he wanted to make the sea route to India safe with strategic points along the coasts. The interior did not need to be conquered because 'we now have to wrest the trade to the Orient out of the hands of the Arabs and take their place.'

On the way home from his second stay in India he was killed by unknown hands in Saldanha Bay on the south coast of Africa. A lance of a peculiar form pierced his face. The assumption is that natives killed him, but the form of the lance contradicts that. He was not murdered but executed because according to the Order he had committed treason by putting secret knowledge into foreign hands. However, he did this fully on his own responsibility because, in his opinion, bringing the alchemical mystery wisdom to middle Europe would create the possibility to make this wisdom fruitful for the future. The Order of St. James would never have been able to do this to the same degree. De Almeida knew that by this 'treason' he would break the power of the Order, and that he would have to pay for it with his death. He bore the consequence of his deed with knightly dignity.

If we now pay attention to the manner in which Stein wrote these articles we receive the impression that he approached his subject in a very restrained manner, yet with evident emotion. And this should not be a surprise to us, because *he described his own karma there.*[83]

There really cannot be the slightest doubt that Walter Johannes Stein knew, through his own occult experiences and confirmed by his teacher Rudolf Steiner, that his individuality was incarnated as Francisco de Almeida in the fifteenth century, and as Hugo de Tours in the ninth century (Trevrezent). In the Introduction to the second edition of Stein's Grail book Johannes Tautz carefully, but unmistakably, indicates this karmic relationship.

It often happens that a similar karmic motif appears in different incarnations of exceptional individualities. Here we see the motif of slander out of jealousy. Hugo de Tours is condemned based on false accusations by envious vassals of Charlemagne. De Almeida's gravestone disappears after his death. Stein:

> The gravestone of the knight who gave Basilius what belonged to him because he was initiated, has disappeared. It had written on it: 'Here rests the knight *sans peur et sans reproche.*'* The inscription, the whole grave has gone. Jealousy pursued him even after death. But history is eternal. It progresses and reveals in later periods the knowledge of earlier times which has been extinguished.[84]

In Stein's own life slander and jealousy also played an important role. This is not the place to write about that, but he is the one from the immediate circle around Rudolf Steiner, who advocated in the most radical manner for a renewed Grail- and Arthur impulse in the twentieth century. He is the one who in the masterful articles cited above, written in a simple, crystal clear style, sketched the importance of the 'last knights in Europe'. And by his intensive study of the work of Basilius Valentinus, he could describe alchemy as a spiritual path of schooling that can contribute to the *healing* of the human being in body, soul and spirit in modern times. One could also say: to the healing of the wounded King Amfortas in us. I quote:

> I once asked Rudolf Steiner whether Basilius Valentinus was out of date. 'No,' he said, 'you approach him with new sentiments and the path he describes is the same as that represented in my book *Knowledge of Higher Worlds.* His path contains the esoteric substance of Anthroposophy and his conception of the world is ours too.' He recommended the book to me as a book for meditation. He referred to it as a compendium of higher knowledge. He said that its view of nature was Aristotelian.[85]

---

* Without fear and without blame.

Stein's work as a teacher at the first Waldorf School in Stuttgart, his role in the movement for the threefold social order, his later work in England, where he developed a wide-ranging activity—including, and by preference, as a *healer*!—all of this stood in service of the Grail.

I want to conclude this section with another quotation from the articles referred to above, from which we can have some idea of the great relationships in occult history:

> Knighthood had its own specific impulses. A kind of school, a school of the fifteenth century is revealed at work here. The impulses which introduced the new age were disseminated through the symbols of alchemy and the romances of chivalry. What was clothed in the story of John, the priest-king in the South, was at work in the North in the symbol of King Arthur. But they were linked by a common concern: the preparation of mankind for the modern age. The honorable attitudes of the chivalry of old were affirmed once more in order then to take leave of that chivalry forever in exchange for journeys over the oceans, the discovery of new lands, the encirclement of the world with the instruments of technology. That is why Maximilian is the last knight. That is why the knights of St. James, of Calatrava, of the Wing of Michael, of the Order of Christ are the great explorers. A new conception of the world was emerging.[86]

5. The Order of the Templars

1. Knights and Monks

The purpose of the following observations about the birth, growth and downfall of the Order of the Templars is not to repeat once again all kinds of generally known facts, but to place the known facts in a new light, to stand up to old, persistent prejudices, and to take the ground from under new prejudices. With the help of Rudolf Steiner's spiritual science we will try to build up as complete a picture of this subject as we can so that, hopefully, a fruitful historical vision becomes possible.

When the Order was created two important impulses of medieval society were combined, the impulse of knighthood and that of monasticism. When we try to penetrate to the sources of these two social phenomena, it does not suffice to point to the polarity between renouncing and embracing the world. Behind these two inclinations in life stands what we today call a concept of the human being.

In the typical Germanic-Celtic picture of the ideal human being lived the sun hero with his twelve paladins. Whether this hero is called King Arthur or Charlemagne, he is the representative of the cosmic Sun Spirit, surrounded by his helpers who represent the forces of the stars. He reigns over them, but on the other hand he is the first among equals, the leader in whom the strengths of the paladins are concentrated, but who also can only exist because this circle around him exists. The meaning of this existence is battle, but not battle for their own benefit; selfless battle through which light triumphs over darkness.

The medieval knightly romances, although they date from times when the cosmically oriented knighthood was already in decline, still clearly show in their norms and honour codes that this knighthood originally was an esoteric community. The knight is not merely a valiant warrior, but he is an initiate in the northern and north-western mysteries (see Chapter 2). His Christian archetype is the heavenly warrior Michael, the archangel of the sun who finds his earthly representative in St. George fighting the dragon.

The imagery is clear; the knight protects the weak and defenceless; he fights for the pure virgin who is threatened by the power of the dragon. The esoteric brotherhood of the Round Table fought for order and justice, and in old times that was still a salutary battle. The knight fought monsters and demonic beings, which means that he freed the 'virgin' in himself through inner trials and schooling; he purified the star-being from the cosmos in his soul.

In the knightly ideal the European human being of the Middle Ages experienced the awakening I-force that in the Germanic peoples was very strongly connected with the fact of being embodied, with physical, natural life. This was a completely different experience from that of the Greek or oriental human being, who felt his I to be much more a heavenly being. But when in the course of time knighthood lost its original initiation impulse this same physical, natural I-experience easily led to an extremely malicious egoism. When the knight did not out of his own initiative give his I a spiritual orientation he would tend to degenerate and become a robber-baron or commit violence. Raising the I to the spiritual was the way of the Grail knight.

Thus a distinction has to be made between the knights of the *sword*, the defenders of justice, the protectors of order—and what counted there were concrete human rights, no abstract legal disputes—and the knights of the *word*. The latter were most often 'invisible' knights, because they sought and served the Unseen. They did not openly exhibit their Grail knighthood; they were called and sent out from a spiritual centre, a secret Lodge, which of course had a physical home somewhere, but was hidden from unknowers.

If we want to comprehend the essence of knighthood we have to try and gain insight into courtly love and music. This is another subject about which Walter Johannes Stein made some interesting observations. Both the Germanic Gudrun saga and the Celtic Tristan saga speak of the mysterious power of music in connection with courtly love. Both music and courtly love have to do with the higher human being—the 'Valkyrie', as Stein writes in his article about Tristan.[87] The fact that creating music as an expression of courtly love is connected with the deeper essence of the human being, and not with his heredity, was recognized in the culture of knighthood in the courts of southern France. Those who were born with the talents of poet-composers were considered equals to princes, even if they were born as serfs. The troubadour, the Minnesinger did not belong to a social class; he was the 'finder' of the truly human.

The power of courtly love found its expression in poetic words and in the music of the harp or lyre, the Apollonian instrument *par excellence*. Whoever was able to play the harp like Orpheus, David or Tristan, found the way to his higher being, the soul bride. With music he could subdue and overcome the lower nature that manifested itself in beastly wildness.

All these elements demonstrate that the knightly impulse is related to the northern, Apollonian mystery stream (see Chapter 2). We should therefore not be surprised when we come across alchemy in the milieu of the knights; for alchemy was a typical path of schooling that sought the higher human being in the deepening of *natural processes*, a metamorphosis of the northern, macrocosmic path. In the *Chymical* (meaning *Alchemical*) *Wedding of Christian Rosenkreutz* we find the expression *Knight* of the Golden Stone, with which a degree of initiation is meant.

In its different forms of manifestation the nature and inner essence of this mystery stream did not at all correspond with the kind of Christianity that had been developed in Rome since the fourth century. In Roman Catholicism a facet of ancient Rome worked on that has to do with the legal element, with power and organization. Bureaucracy, officialdom—nightmares of modern society—date back to Rome. Via the Roman Church this influence has permeated Europe. In knighthood we see this happening already in Charlemagne's time—a beginning of decline, because the office clerk is of course the complete opposite of the true knight.

The various cultural impulses now interpenetrate. In the realm of the Franks it looks as if knighthood is in league with Rome, but always when true knighthood shows itself a careful observer will find traces of an anti-Roman tendency. This is true for the Celtic Arthur stream— which we can recognize in a certain respect in the legendary stories that were woven around the Germanic Emperors Charlemagne and Frederic Barbarossa—and equally for the knightly cultures in southern France and northern Spain in the eleventh, twelfth and thirteenth centuries, the culture of the troubadours.

The several knightly Orders also showed this anti-Roman disposition in a variety of ways but quite unmistakably, and from the viewpoint of history it is extremely interesting to see how they handled the Roman element or, rather, how Rome dealt with these Orders.

Ultimately, this knighthood was to become a literary phenomenon that almost necessarily had to end in the formidable anti-knight epic *Don Quixote* by Cervantes. But even though knighthood is ridiculed in this book, the hero of the story is so great in his madness, so human and so noble, that at the end of the book we have the impression that it is he who represents the true human being, and that all others, the so-called normal persons, are but sad figures.

The other cultural stream that worked in the Order of the Templars, monasticism, was of a totally different nature. When we look for its origin, we do not find the cosmic sun hero but the world-renouncing ascetic. Was this view of the human being in agreement with original Christianity? The figure of Jesus Christ as described by the evangelists is by no means that of an ascetic who withdraws into the loneliness of the desert. Jesus lived for the people among the people. Monasticism has its roots rather in an oriental attitude to life although, as is well-known, Buddha also rejected strict asceticism.

It is not insignificant in the polarity between knighthood and monasticism that the first Christian anchorites (hermits) in the third century AD, Paul and Anthony, lived in the Egyptian desert. As compared with the northern impulse of knighthood, monasticism has a distinct southern signature. The hermit or monk sought by the *inner way* the mystical connection with the divine world. The temptations of St. Anthony, often depicted by painters, are clearly mystical experiences of the catharsis of the soul through trials and schooling, but in a different way from that of the knights. The knight went in search of adventure; in the confrontation with the world he had to overcome evil, also in himself. The hermit withdrew from the outside world and sank down into his own inner world.

Besides mystical renunciation of the world, however, monasticism also developed a number of other aspects because of which it was able to become for a thousand years a most important cultural factor in European human society. It dedicated itself to science and saved the literary legacy of Greece and Rome and also of the Christian Church Fathers, not only by collecting, preserving and studying the ancient manuscripts, but also by carefully copying them. What had been taught in the Catechumen schools[88] in beginning Christian times could thus be handed on by the monks.

For centuries the visual and musical arts were practised and developed by monks in their monasteries. Architecture and sculpture, although not executed by the monks themselves, were fostered by the abbots. Music, poetry, miniature paintings, astounding precision work—even today a joy to eye and ear—everything cultural that was not of Arabic origin was generated in monasteries.

But just as important was their role in economic life. They went into agriculture and viticulture, as well as all kinds of crafts and trades. The later Cistercians applied themselves to the development of desolate areas, and mining was sometimes also in the hands of monks. However, we do have to realize that most of the necessary physical labour was not performed by the actual monks, but by lay brothers. Finally, a particularly important aspect of the monasteries was the care of pilgrims who travelled along the famous routes to Santiago de Compostela, Rome or Jerusalem. Especially the congregation of Cluny encouraged Christians to undertake the journey to Santiago.

Benedict of Nursia (480-547) founded the first regular monastic Order in Europe in 529. He introduced the vow of poverty, chastity and obedience, and gave the first monastery on Monte Cassino a number of monastic rules that were adopted by subsequent monasteries as they were founded. Although monastic life was very strongly based on authority, it also had a germ of community life in which the participants were not bound by a shared bloodline. But it was only at the end of the Middle Ages that brotherhoods could come into being in which people dedicated themselves to communal life as free individuals without a vow; an example of this was the Brotherhood of the Rose Cross.

Monasticism has been of great importance for the development of the Church, but just as with knighthood, the origin was in fact anti-Church of Rome. In the organization of the Church in Rome, Christianity had taken on a form that was often repugnant to the truly faithful Christian. The whole political, legal-dogmatic element, the regulation of everything relating to spiritual life, had to give birth to a need to withdraw from it, in order to dedicate oneself to religion in pure piety.

Renunciation of the world was therefore actually a flight from the growing political character of Christendom fostered by the Roman clergy. But a mutual influence between the clergy and monasticism did take place. Rome did everything it could to keep the work of the Orders under its control and use them as much as possible to serve and increase its power. Strong independence and autonomy existed especially in the monks who came to the European continent from Ireland in the early Middle Ages.

Celtic or Irish Christianity, still nourished out of the Hibernian mysteries (see Chapters 2 and 4) also developed monastic communities early in the sixth century, but of a very different nature than the Benedictines. First of all, the monks did not take a vow. Also, around their very simple huts, which were arranged around a little church that was the centre of their sacramental life, members of their families were living whose lives were more worldly. At any rate, this was the case in the larger settlements. The way the Irish monks lived was extremely strict and ascetic. Frequently there was one of them who excelled in erudition, piety and leadership capacities, who stepped out of the original community to establish a new settlement somewhere else. Monastic schools also came into being comparable with the ancient Greek academies, where wisdom of the ancient Greeks and early Church Fathers made a glorious mixture with the lively traditions of the Druid schools and the bards.

In the course of the sixth century interesting spiritual leaders with twelve followers began to travel to the continent of Europe. Among the best known are Columbanus and Gallus who founded monasteries in France, Switzerland and Italy. These Celtic peregrinations had great influence. They settled in areas where most of the population were still pagans. They worked in a totally different way from the missionaries from Rome, who tried to eradicate all pagan traditions, religious images and customs root and branch. The Celtic Christians did not take any pagan piety away from the people, but succeeded in leading it over into a true, deeply felt Christianity. In this sense they strove, just like the Arthurian knights, to ennoble the still wild population.

It goes without saying that the leadership of the Roman Catholic Church left no stone unturned to assimilate the Irish centres in Europe in the course of time. But still, many of these places, for example Reichenau on the Bodensee between Germany and Switzerland, were able to preserve their special, free and spiritual sphere.

The further development of monasticism in European Christianity took place in waves, more than that of knighthood. An incredible flourishing of the impulse of Benedict came with the foundation of the monastery of Cluny in Burgundy in 909. The rules of the Order, which were hardly, or not at all, followed in preceding years, were now very strictly applied by abbot Berno. This resulted in a general improvement of monasticism; the honour and prestige of the monks increased again after it had been minimal for a long time. The Church could do no other than applaud this revival and accept the sovereignty of this 'monarchy of monks'.

For two and a half centuries Cluny was the spiritual centre of Europe, but this glory also had an end. The resplendent and art-loving spirit of Cluny had to cede its place to the rigorous austerity of Citeaux. The Order of the Cistercians, founded by Robert de Molesme in 1098, took the torch from Cluny under the leadership of St. Bernard de Clairvaux. And thus the stream that Benedict had put into movement centuries earlier then merged with the Grail stream that revealed itself in the

Order of the Templars. Bernard gave the new Order its rules and wrote the following immortal words in *In Praise of the New Knighthood*:

> A new knighthood has appeared in the land where Christ lived. It is new, I say, and not yet tried in the world, where it conducts a double battle, now against opponents of flesh and blood, then again against the spirit of evil in the heavens. And that the knights resist physical enemies through the strength of their bodies does not surprise me, because I do not consider it exceptional. But that, armed with the forces of the spirit, they make war on vices and demons I call not only marvelous, but worthy of praise with all the respect due to monks.[89]

2. Initiation

We now have to pose the question which has been asked through the centuries regarding the Templars, namely whether they had a secret and, if so, of what did it consist? In the immense number of books about the Order this question is answered as often with yes as with no. It appears to be a matter of personal preference whether people join one party or the other. And yet, this aspect of the problem is not so very hard to solve. One has to say yes on the basis of the objective fact that those who wanted to destroy the Order, and did indeed destroy it, played into the existence of esoteric secrets of the Templars in extremely cunning ways.

But that does not say anything about the nature of these initiation secrets. One can learn nothing conclusive about the essentials of initiation, unless an initiate is willing to divulge something about it. The Templars possessed initiation secrets they did not betray, not even under the most terrible torture. But during the torture certain 'confessions' were made that were related to the secrets of their initiation. How that was possible, and why so many contradictory statements were made at the trials, also without torture during the interrogations, will be discussed later.

It is doubtful that there would have been *written* secret rules, because in occult communities all initiation knowledge and secret rituals were communicated by word of mouth. This was true in antiquity as well as in Christian times. That which was written down about mysteries in the latter days of Greece and Rome is usually still of an esoteric nature, meaning that the written words could only be really understood by initiates. Even if something might actually have been put into writing, it would be in the form of signs and symbols, and as such we have to regard the graffiti that were found on the walls of dungeons in castles and prisons where Templars had been kept. If these were really occult signs, which is doubted by some, their interpretation is hardly possible for non-initiates. There have been very clever explanations, but in most cases these evoke more questions than they answer.

In this case we cannot do better than to consult initiation science. And although anthroposophical spiritual science does not give us a lot of information about the esotericism of the Templars, it does enable us to form a somewhat satisfactory picture of what this initiation must have been like. It places the known historical facts in a broad perspective, and some inexplicable facts that have led to all kinds of theories become understandable in ways that are, on the one hand, less sensational than some had thought or perhaps hoped while, on the other hand, they reach much further than conventional science *wishes* to reach.

The picture of the Templars I have sketched at the beginning of this book, and that was derived from the knightly Order in Rudolf Steiner's second Mystery Drama, is an idealized picture, an imaginative but not historical reality. I did draw a preliminary conclusion from it, namely that in the Templars an initiation impulse was working that was oriented toward a future Christian culture, which showed unmistakable traits of Manichaeism.

I also pointed to a passage from a lecture by Rudolf Steiner (Chapter 3) that makes the connection between the Grail stream and the Order of the Templars abundantly clear. He calls the Templars the original envoys of the Grail. On the place where the Temple of Solomon had stood they established a 'place of wisdom' and 'after they had been prepared they became servants of the Holy Grail and were initiated by the Grail'. We saw that this rather mysterious statement throws light on the enigmatic first ten years (1118-1128) when a very small group of French noblemen prepared themselves for a world-historic task. Their mission was not to explore the Temple Mount for archeological treasures, but to prepare the Christian culture of the future.

The following final passage from the notes of the lecture mentioned above are of particular significance regarding the question as to what the 'initiation by the Grail' consisted of. First we are told that a preparation for a new cultural epoch was intended, the fifth post-Atlantean epoch, our time. How does Christianity have to be taken up in modern times?

> We understand what the Templars professed, what their secret cult meant. They recognized: The Christ, as the Church of Rome represents Him, has no meaning for us. We, however, proclaim the Christ who went around in Jerusalem and who received His

initiation from John the Baptist. Our teachers who proclaim Christ
are therefore not the teachers and padres of the Church, but John the
Baptist himself, Christ's initiator.

Then there is mention of a second principle, which relates to the place
of the human being in the world-all that is reigned over by the laws of
the stars and nature. These two fundamental principles of the Templars,
the new Christianity and the view of nature, are connected with Protes-
tantism and natural science, in which the culture of modern times has
found its breeding ground. The notes end with a brief remark about the
Rosicrucians who guarded the common premise of the two principles
of the Templars, because our culture lets them grow apart into a purely
worldly science and a materialistic religion.

The Rosicrucians care for the true development of the fifth cultural
epoch and thus prepare for the sixth cultural epoch. I have mentioned
the second principle and what follows it only for the sake of completion,
but do not want to go into it further at this time. I will come back to it
in Chapter 6.

According to these remarks, the initiation of the Templars consisted
of two components that shared a common premise: a teaching from
the direct source of esoteric Christianity, separate from all traditions of
the Church, and a teaching that was related to old mystery knowledge,
spiritual star- and nature wisdom. To understand this we have to let go
of the common usage of the word teaching. We would form an incorrect
picture of such an initiation if we would think of anything like teaching
in a school, although the element of instruction will certainly have been
present.

In the first instance, however, the initiation demanded a way of life
consisting of *total surrender to the Christ Being*. It is in this sense that
we should understand the expression 'initiated by the Grail'. That in
this regard John the Baptist is mentioned as the initiator is understandable. The word of the Baptist, 'He must increase, but I must decrease'
(John.3:30) is the premise for this complete surrender.

The Templar had to fill his heart and soul 'to the brim' with the Mystery of Golgotha. He had to be ready to sacrifice every drop of his blood
to bring the holy places where Christ had dwelt on earth into the power
of the European-Christian world. His blood did not belong to him; it
was dedicated exclusively to this holy task. He must never take flight in
battle, even if the enemy was three times as strong. He was not allowed
to have any personal property; what he acquired belonged to the Order
as a whole.

This brought about a profound experience of Christ, a deep spiritual experience, not only in the souls of the knight-monks, but it also penetrated into the social provisions that came into being in Europe through the Templars. For some individuals—and their number should not be underestimated—such total surrender to the Christian ideal truly signified a rebirth of the soul being. It resulted in frequent out-of-body experiences of such people so that they penetrated into the spiritual world where they learned profound initiation secrets.

The most extensive passages Rudolf Steiner dedicated to the Templars can be found in his lectures about *Inner Impulses of Evolution.* [90] There he describes what in the previous paragraphs was summarized and then adds that by the circumstance referred to something 'remarkable and powerful' took place in the Order of the Templars, namely that a substantial number of these knights truly underwent the Christian-Johannine initiation, without knowing and applying its rules.

This Christian initiation was based on a similar complete surrender to the Christ Being, but then in the form of meditation on the seven steps as described by John in his Gospel, beginning with the washing of the feet and following the stages of the Passion through to Ascension. Rudolf Steiner spoke repeatedly about this path of initiation.[91] In the course of his esoteric schooling the candidate penetrated into the higher regions of spiritual knowledge. Besides this deepening of the soul life that led to initiation experiences, however, there must also have been secret teachings and rituals about which nothing is said in the lectures in *Inner Impulses of Evolution*. Rudolf Steiner did speak about these in earlier lectures given in the First Esoteric School before 1914.[92]

Another important source of information is the lecture by Walter Johannes Stein that I have referred to in connection with Godfrey of Bouillon and Hugo de Tours. It mentions three grades of initiation. The first was the grade of St. Peter. It was related to Godfrey of Bouillon, the inspirer of the Order, who in his previous life was the brother of Hugo de Tours who did not go to the tomb of the Redeemer in Jerusalem, but to Peter's tomb in Rome. The Petrine grade is directly related to the denial of the crucifix, the most sensational accusation against the Order during the trial. This will be discussed more extensively in section 4 of this chapter.

The second grade was the grade of St. James. It was connected with St. James, the apostle who went to Spain, the patron saint of Santiago de Compostela. He played an important role in the battle of the Christians against the Moors in Spain. There are descriptions of visions in which the saint appears as a knight seated on a white horse, with a fire-spewing lance, who goes before the Christians in the battles. Even Arab sources mention these apparitions.

According to Stein's lecture, the Order of Santiago built a round *tempietto* on the tomb of St. James for the knights who were going on voyages of discovery at the beginning of modern times.[93] The gold with which these explorations were paid was the gold of the Templars. But before this happened, 54 knights and their Grand Master Jacques de Molay had to die at the stake. Then follows a mysterious statement: this second degree will be fulfilled when the gold will find its way back under similar catastrophes.

The third degree is the degree of St. John. But this can only be put into practice in our time. It has to do with the world economy. The economy has to be governed by truly Christian love, but so far it has been moving in the opposite direction.

In the three degrees of initiation we find an expression of the three stages of human consciousness. The pilgrimage to the tomb of St. Peter was a matter of *faith*, the foundation of Christianity as an historical stream. For this one had to go through the stage of denial. St. James, however, kindles the flame of *hope*. In his sign the voyages of discovery were undertaken, and it is no coincidence that the 'storm cape' was renamed Cape of Good Hope once it had been rounded and the way to India was open.

The degree of St. John expresses that true Christian love has to come into existence. This is the third 'cape', the cape of catastrophes that threaten us if we do not succeed in bringing this Christian love to realization—the only thing that will enable us to round this cape of catastrophes.

These indications are supplemented by statements from lectures of *The Temple Legend* by Rudolf Steiner that I referred to before. He speaks there about the so-called Great Mass that was celebrated after the regular Mass in which everyone participated. This second part was meant only for those among the Templars who wanted to go through an occult schooling. In this Great Mass a direct connection was made between the sacrifice of Christ and the cosmic development that is expressed in the relation of the movements of the sun with the fixed stars on the one hand, and the development of human consciousness in the different cultural epochs on earth on the other.

When the sixth cultural epoch (3573-5733) begins the sun will be in the sign of Aquarius. This is the sign of John the Baptist who baptized with water in order to prepare human beings for the baptism with fire by Christ. In the age of Aquarius, the seed of Christianity will sprout to full maturity like the little grain of mustard seed.

> The coming of a 'John/Aquarius' who would first confirm the old John and announce a Christ who would renew the Temple, once the great point of time should have arrived when Christ will again speak to humanity—this was taught in the depths of the Temple mysteries, so that the event should be understood.

This shows us that the preparation for the future stretched not only to our cultural epoch, but even to the next epoch. It also throws light on the place John the Baptist occupied as 'initiator' in the esotericism of the Templars. The lecture continues:

> Moreover, the Templars said: Today we live at a point of time when men are not yet ripe for understanding the great teachings; we still have to prepare them for the Baptist, John, who baptizes with water. The Cross was held up before the would-be Templar and he was told: You must deny the Cross now, so as to understand it later; first become a Peter, first deny the scriptures, like Peter the Rock who denied the Lord. That was imparted to the aspirant Templar as a preliminary training.[94]

Later we will go into what follows from this, the significance of the cross and the symbolic figure of the divine Father who was shown afterwards to the Templar.

Finally, we find in this same lecture a most important indication that provides a distinctly esoteric background to historical facts. It is known that the Order of the Templars gave to Mary, the mother of Jesus, a central place in its devotion. This is clearly connected with Bernard de Clairvaux who, as the 'protector' of the Order must have instilled his deep devotion to Mary into the Templars. But behind this devotion to Mary, certainly for a man like Bernard, stands much more than a pious love for the Mother of God. Half of the impressive number of prayers the Templar had to say every day were devoted to Mary. They had to say the prayers while standing. The rule of the Order says: '...because our Lady was the beginning of our Order, and in her and in her honour, if so please God, the end of our order will be...' Rudolf Steiner says in the lecture quoted above:

> When one follows the teachings of the Templars one finds in their centre the worship of a feminine being. This feminine being was called the Divine Sophia, Divine Wisdom...

Even behind the popularized Mary worship sanctioned by the Church still stands in the Middle Ages the memory of the cosmic archetypal image of the human soul, the heavenly Virgin of the stars. It is the Wisdom Being who was venerated in antiquity under various names, such as Isis and Demeter, and who took on human form in Mary, the mother of Jesus. There existed a living, real striving for the Sophia in the Johannine esoteric stream of Christianity.

All esotericism actually has to proceed from this being, because the initiate must first of all transform his own soul into the Virgin Sophia. This purified astral element of the human being can then be fructified by the spirit self, which in Christian esotericism is called the principle of the Holy Spirit. The child the Virgin gives birth to is the Logos, *Christ in us*. At the same time the Mary-Sophia being is the guide—Stella Maris, the Star of the Sea—on the path toward knowledge of higher secrets. Dante depicts this being as his Beatrice, and in so doing he stands in the same stream as the Templars, the stream of Grail Christianity or esoteric Christianity.

The heavenly knowledge the Virgin bestowed on the candidate for initiation, Gnosis, was in the Middle Ages still a heritage from long lost times. Also when a candidate had his own actual experiences of the spiritual world, for normal consciousness these could at that time only be clothed in old images. Truly new esotericism suited to modern times still had to be born.

This fact, however, namely that the contents of mystery teachings mostly still dated back to Egyptian-Babylonian times, such as all knowledge of the stars, enabled certain spiritual beings, who together are referred to as Lucifer, and who prefer to nestle themselves in everything of the past, to infiltrate the esoteric streams. There is every reason to believe that some of this influence also worked into Temple esotericism, even if unnoticed by anyone. In any case, the arrogant attitude displayed by some Templars, and for which the entire Order was unjustifiably blamed, was undoubtedly due to this luciferic element.

The idea that Islam had a particular influence on the 'secrets' of the Templars, is not true. Not Mohammed's Islam, in which esotericism actually hardly plays any role, but occult streams from areas where Islam was dominant have obviously had an influence on the Order. But we should guard here for erroneous ideas. True initiation secrets are given by masters to individuals who are mature enough for them. These masters may, living on earth—often as unknown, unassuming figures—find their followers and teach them, but they may also reveal themselves out of a spiritual sphere. We have already heard that the true Grail knights were inspired by heroes who had died (Chapter 4). I imagine that this was also the case with the Templars.

It should also not surprise us that there lived a Manichaean element in the Order, because around 1100 this teaching was already widespread in the West. Moreover, it is part of the esoteric Grail stream, since this stream directly emanated from the Manes council in the fourth century (Chapter 2).

3. The Mystery of the Templars' Gold

Although the statements from the lectures by Rudolf Steiner and Walter Johannes Stein regarding the initiation of the Templars give us a more coherent picture than most other authors, we are still left with substantial problems. In the first place there is the question of how we should imagine the four degrees of initiation.

It is clear that these degrees should not be regarded in an outer sense as three ranks within the knighthood, but that they represented inner stages of spiritual maturity. The fact that the degrees of St. James and St. John related to future developments in humanity—the stage of St. James was also still a future stage with respect to the era in which the Order existed (c. 1100-1300)—of course does not mean that these degrees of development could not be reached earlier by certain individuals.

In the history of the Order we see a sequence that corresponds with these three degrees in a certain sense. The first degree, the stage of St. Peter, could be represented for the Order as a whole by the relationship the knights had to find with Rome and the Roman Catholic faith. This meant for each individual knight the trial of the denial of the cross. By the way, it was a *Pope* who gave them the white robe of the Order with the *red cross* on the back.

The degree of St. James corresponds with a strong urge to action, with the fighting character of the knights; the relationships they had to forge with worldly power, with European rulers and the kings of Jerusalem, are part of this picture. When the Holy Land was lost to them they had to live more than ever in the *hope* of winning it back.

The third stage is reflected in the way they unfolded social activity in Europe that anticipated developments in modern times, the age in which the economy acts as a world power. Part of this was the manner in which the Templars worked with money.

However, before we immerse ourselves in this aspect of the Order I want to point again to the *Divine Comedy* by Dante in which a kind of initiation in three degrees is described—those of faith, hope and love. In cantos 24, 25 and 26 of *Paradiso*, before the poet can reach the highest experiences in the heavenly worlds he has to pass an 'exam'. The apostle Peter interrogates him as to his faith; James examines him as to hope, and before John Dante, who is briefly blinded by the spiritual sun radiance of the 'Eagle of Christ', shows his profound insight into the essence of love.

That with his three confessions the great Florentine not only shows that he is familiar with the essence of the Pauline virtues of faith, hope and love, but that this heavenly exam also proves that he may be regarded as a bearer of these virtues, was undoubtedly intended by him. Whether he alluded with this to the initiation of the Templars is hard to say. In any case, Dante had a close personal connection with the essence of Temple knighthood. More about this in section 6 of this chapter.

When we contemplate the overall influence that emanated from the Order of the Templars we are struck by the contrast that existed between their political-military operations and their social activities. Even though they were exemplary warriors, who with legendary courage and contempt for death stood up to an often much stronger enemy; even though their thorough knowledge of the East enabled them most often to strike the right diplomatic attitude in addition to their military capacities, they did not succeed in stopping the superior power of Islam in the Holy Land nor in protecting the little Christian kingdoms that had developed in the area.

When we study the volatile history of the twelfth and thirteenth centuries in Palestine, and of the Templars between 1118 and 1187, the re-conquest of Jerusalem by Saladin, and further to the year 1291 when because of the fall of Acre the Holy Land was definitively lost, we see a long string of triumphs and defeats, heroic courage and narrow-mindedness, mutual wrangling and intrigues. All of this makes it abundantly clear that the Templars were in fact powerless amid the divisions among the Christian rulers and their intolerance and selfishness. Even the great figures among these kings and princes—Richard the Lionheart, Saint Louis, Emperors Frederick I (Barbarossa) and II, some favourably, some unfavourably disposed to the Order—despite their personal prestige, were not able to offer effective support to protect and keep the Holy Land in Christian hands. And again the question that was posed earlier thrusts itself upon us: was the whole effort to which Godfrey of Bouillon had provided the impetus, the re-conquest of the Holy Sepulchre, perhaps a mistake?

By contrast, the social-economic work of the Order in Europe was an extremely successful undertaking. Immediately after the Council of Troyes in 1128, when the Order was officially confirmed and had received its rules from Bernard de Clairvaux, knights came flocking in, and also ordinary citizens who took more subordinate positions as *servientes*. All kinds of people joined them who were not taken into the Order, but who enjoyed its protection or served it as manual labourers, peasants or serfs.

The properties the Order received as gifts or acquired for itself—primarily rural estates—grew substantially in a short time. In Europe a powerful network of social-economic enterprises was formed. There were nine provinces: France, Portugal, Castile, Aragon, Majorca, Germany, Italy, Apulia/Sicily, England/Ireland. The activities were centred in *commanderies*, local and regional centres of which there were ten thousand at the beginning of the fourteenth century. In addition there were many farms, often fortified or in the immediate vicinity of a castle.

The work on the land with the concomitant trades, the storage, distribution and trade of produce, management and administration—everything was organized in practical and rightful ways. Unimpeded by the greed of princes and prelates, the enterprises of the Templars were able to prosper in safety and welfare because the Order was independent of both worldly and clerical powers. They were exempt from taxes and from tithes to the Church, and were not subject to the judiciary of either Church or ruler. With its own priests, who answered only to the Grand Master, the Order formed a church within the Church, just as it also formed an international state transcending all national states.

It is of course universally known that the Templars developed an international banking network with their system of drafts. They loaned money to kings and princes against good collateral, and they competed with the Italian banking firms, which did not always enjoy the trust and confidence people experienced from the Templars. The Order was immeasurably rich, but each member was poor. When any money was found on him after his death he was posthumously punished which meant exclusion from funeral ceremonies and burial in unconsecrated ground like a slave. This even applied to the Grand Master.

Ever since Louis Charpentier proclaimed that the Order of the Templars supposedly financed the construction of the Gothic cathedrals in France, many others have repeated this. Apart from the fact that Charpentier dreamed up more of such theses of highly questionable calibre, so that one has to take his financing story with many grains of salt, his representation is typically French-centred. Why only the French Gothic cathedrals, whereas the Order was clearly international? Moreover, it is quite well-known from descriptions or administrative documents that were preserved how these buildings were in fact financed.[95] These sources never mention any income that could be connected with the Order. If this had been the case it would not have remained a secret, for what would have been the reason?

The building of the Gothic cathedrals was an affair of the cities and more especially of the powerful chapters of the canons. That the Templars would have maintained any special relationships with these partly secular but yet unmistakably clerical groups, is not likely. What is much more probable is that the Templars had relations with the builders' Lodges which, just as the Templars, were bearers of esoteric knowledge and traditions. The truth is that in the twelfth and thirteenth centuries the Templars contributed to a rise in the general level of prosperity, particularly by creating safe channels for trade and for pilgrimages, as well as through sensible measures for grain storage because of which famines due to failed harvests could be avoided.

Another thesis of Charpentier has it that the Templars got the silver they put in circulation in Europe from America, but I don't want go into that. This idea does solve some riddles, such as the disappearance of the archives of the Order which, after their transport in carts to Rochelle just before the Templars were arrested in Paris, were supposed to have been shipped to America. There is also the so-called 'Atlantic fleet' and more of such mysterious things, but in the overall picture one has to form of the Order based on normal historical as well as occult-historical facts, the America thesis is just a bit too romantic to satisfy our sense of truth. Based on material found to our day, the confidence with which some authors propound this thesis as a fact is certainly not justified. But of course, we do have to keep the possibility open that the improbable will prove to be true after all, even if it comes from a doubtful source.

However, it is more important to direct our attention to the manner in which the Templars worked with money, and especially with gold. From there we will come to the mystery of gold as such, and eventually also to America, where in pre-Columbian times gold was still sacred. The Spanish conquests of course put an end to that. These conquests, by the way, were a direct consequence of the impulse of the Templars (see Chapter 4).

It is my deep conviction that the role gold played for the Templars is related to the way they regarded their own blood. The initiated Templar regarded his blood not as his own, but it belonged to Christ. Blood is the physical expression, or the physical instrument, of the human I. The *red* blood is in a certain respect bound to the lower ego nature. The victory over the self-centredness of the ego found its highest expression in the words of St. Paul: 'Not I, but Christ in me.' The motto of the Order says this in a slightly different manner but means the same: *'Non nobis, Domine, non nobis, sed tuo nomini da gloriam'*—'Not to us, Lord, not to us, but to Thy name give glory.' In other words: Not our own I, burdened with lower impulses, work in us, but Your Name, meaning the I-AM, the Christ I.

Because of his initiation, the Templar knew that Christ was the Sun Spirit, the Logos according to St. John. The relationship of gold with the sun was an alchemical secret which, however, was an open secret in the Middle Ages. In the human being the blood that flows through the blood vessels is the same as the gold that was 'frozen' in subterranean veins or is still flowing in rivers on earth. For that reason the egoism of the human being can become so strongly attached to the possession of gold.

When gold is brought to the surface it has to be dedicated to the gods as was done by the Indians in Central and South America; it must be worked into beautiful objects by artists, or else it is desecrated by the greed of human beings. When that happens a curse rests on the gold. The only way a person can be released from the curse of gold is by Christianizing his own being. When not the egoistic I, but the I-AM can work in this I, then gold can circulate in human society free from the curse. That is the degree of St. John in the Templars' initiation.

Gold did not become a means of payment until quite late in human development. It happened in Greek/Roman times. Previously it had a sacred significance; it was connected with religion and priesthood, and when kings decorated themselves with it or created gold coins stamped with their image, they could do so because those kings were also the high priests of their people. In the distant past of Atlantean times there must have been mysteries in which the initiate was brought into contact with the secret of the subterranean forces that work in the formation of metals and precious stones.[96] These mysteries continued to exist into post-Atlantean times, and many aspects of them must still have lived in post-Atlantean populations in the Americas.

With the growing consciousness of self, the I-awareness and the concomitant awakening of a rationalistic-materialistic disposition, such as gradually developed in people during the Greek/Roman period, the role of gold also changed. The coins became money, and the possession of such coins meant power.

When the young Germanic tribes invaded the Roman Empire around the year 400 AD, their objective was clearly to capture gold. Earlier many of them had already served as soldiers in the Roman legions because of the pay, the possession of money and plunder. These tribes hardly made any use of money as a means of payment; they still lived at the stage of barter. But their mythology and sagas show that they did have a notion of the mystery of gold. They were therefore attracted to gold by a powerful desire. This is without a doubt connected with the elementary, but strong I-awareness in the Germanic souls, whereas they also knew the dangers of gold, the curse of gold.

The myth relates how Loki, the Germanic equivalent of Lucifer or the devil, forces the dwarf Andvari (or Alberich) to give him his gold, including one ring Andvari implored him to be allowed to keep. Thereupon the dwarf pronounces his curse on the gold, which henceforth will bring calamity on everyone who possesses it. In the saga of the Nibelungen we see how the gold curse not only causes the end of the hero Siegfried, but then also the awful destruction of all the Nibelungen. Virtually the only one who at the end of the story is spared in the general slaughter is Dietrich von Bern,* the legendary figure who is identical with the historical king of the Goths, Theodoric the Great. Why does Dietrich not go under, but stands as the human representative of the Germanic god Vidar in the wild downfall of the Twilight of the Gods? Because he has no desire for gold.

The figure of Dietrich also appears in other traditional stories, for instance in the saga of the dwarf king Laurin. Laurin is said to possess all the gold and precious stones of the world and to have the power to imprison the human soul that is possessed by desire for gold in a subterranean cave in the depths of a mountain. Dietrich, who is entirely free of any thirst for outer riches, is able to liberate the imprisoned soul from the depths.

The Templars tried to counter the doom of gold by Christianizing their souls at a time when the battle between East and West had become acute again. The Turks were steadily advancing in the direction of Europe and the Mongol hordes of Genghis Khan were invading from the East deep into the Western world. In those times the Order of the Templars was building a supra-national Christian empire that rested

---

ᛉ Bern is German for Verona.

on the selfless power of gold. This empire could not be the *Imperium Romanum*, which was founded on egoistic gold power. The gold belonged to Christ, just as the blood belonged to Christ. A non-egoistic money policy had to form the foundation of a Johannine realm of Christian brotherliness—a grand ideal of the future.

It goes without saying that such a spiritual and profoundly Christian ideal was an unprecedented challenge to the powers of darkness. Since this ideal was cherished and pursued at a time that was not yet ripe for it, the adversary powers were inevitably able to find opportunities not only to destroy the bearers of the ideal, but also to initiate an effective counter-stream in European culture. In this counter-stream, which since then has increased egoism, greed and the desire for money power a hundredfold, today's humanity is pulled along, without any insight, like a boat without a rudder, to catastrophe. It is of the greatest importance that we develop insight into what is really going on in humanity, so that we can begin to discover the greater connections and more deeply lying impulses and streams in the course of history than is commonly done in materialistic historical research.

The Christian impulse of the Order of the Templars was destroyed in an outer sense by the French King Philip, called the Fair, whom one might call an initiate of the anti-Christian powers. His pathological greed and thirst for gold are well-known. Through all that occurred in the Templars' trial in the beginning of the fourteenth century, the counter-stream mentioned above formed itself, and little by little it gained in strength. This did not show so much in clearly demonstrable phenomena, but rather in a gradually proliferating change in mentality—one might call it the cancer of greed.

After the Order had been disbanded by Pope Clement V, the European rulers and prelates pounced upon its possessions like hyenas. The Order of St. John, the official 'heir', never received the riches of the Order of the Templars. Only a small part of the gold could be kept from human greed. In Portugal the Order of Christ came into being in 1319 as the successor of the Templars, and the gold that was present there was used for the exploratory voyages to India. Henry the Navigator, Grand Master of the Order of Christ, gave the most direct impulse for these voyages which, in a certain sense, can be considered as important contributions to the fight against Islam, because the discovery of the sea route to India eventually pushed the Arabs out of their monopoly on the trade with that country. A remnant of the original Temple and Grail impulse was still living in the Portuguese discovery voyages until the sixteenth century.

The discovery of America by Columbus in 1492 is only indirectly linked with this. In the conquerors who went from Spain to America after Columbus—who, by the way, died convinced that he had reached India via the western route—there was not a trace left of the Christian ideal of the Templars. Greed seized these souls in the most unrelenting way, and the treasures of gold of the Indians, who had no greed for gold at all and at first never expected any harm, were barbarically plundered. Ever since, the gold curse has worked its destructive effects through the history of humanity more than ever before.

After the destruction of the Order of the Templars, the Grail stream as an esoteric Christian stream, of which the Templars were part, continued in a different, more hidden form. However, our discussion of this continuation has to wait until we have first made for ourselves a clear picture of the demise of the Order and of the signature of the counter-force.

4. The Trial

On October 13, 1307, before daybreak, all the Templars in France were arrested by order of King Philip. Guillaume de Nogaret, Philip's loyal chancellor and sinister accessory, accompanied by a strong escort of soldiers, demanded access to the 'Temple' in Paris where Jacques de Molay, the Grand Master of the Order lived, and took him into custody together with another 130 Templars. Without any resistance the knights and *servientes* let themselves be taken. Accused of heresy and sodomy they were interrogated and tortured by functionaries of the king, and only ten days later handed over to the Inquisition.

This attack on the Order, counter to all law, was carefully prepared and kept strictly secret to the day it was executed. We, contemporaries of dictators and extremists, witnesses of leftist and rightist coups, seizures of people, disappearances of political prisoners, torture and murder, intimidation and false propaganda—we are familiar with the methods and recognize their signature in the machinations of the French king that were used to destroy the Templars. People went to sleep in the Middle Ages and in the morning seemed to wake up in the twentieth century. At one stroke a 'modern' principle of absolutely inhuman behaviour had become operative in European history.

One wonders with astonishment and consternation how it was possible that one man was able to bring down an all-powerful organization, an Order that enjoyed universal honour and respect and was protected by exceptional privileges from all interference in its affairs by worldly and clerical sources—an Order that owed allegiance only to the highest office in the Church in the person of the Pope. Not only did this man, King Philip the Fair, bring the Order down, he was also able to defame it to such an extent that there continue to be people even today who believe in the culpability of the Templars. There are still those who simply assume that the accusations are grounded in truth. Don't we have those confession, supposedly also from Templars who did not make them under torture?

But one thing is abundantly clear. Not only King Philip and his accomplices, but also later enemies of the Order have purposely made the affair of the Templars inextricably confusing. The fact that the most important documents of the trial disappeared in the course of time is certainly no coincidence. Precisely because the Order was a movement that was in fact grounded in secrets of initiation it was possible for intended and unintended mystifications to come into being. One has the impression that at the time, and perhaps even today, the enemies of the Order seemed to be driven by an occult power that was able to represent the Christian esotericism of the knights in such a way that the appearance was in many respects against them.

Needless to say, as in every organization there will also have been weaker individuals and misfits, but whoever base their judgement of a spiritual movement on such exceptions not only commit an injustice, but also become guilty of falsification of history when they assert their one-sided judgement as if it were objective history.

At first, King Philip was favourably disposed toward the Templars. He gave preference to the Order and praised it for its exemplary qualities. However, he needed the Templars, in the first place because he was always short of money for his turbulent politics, and also because he thought he was entitled to their support against Pope Boniface VIII, whose aspirations were certainly not in line with the Templars.

Undoubtedly the Templars will have viewed the 'friendship' of Philip with the necessary skepticism. When the king asked to be admitted to the Order as an honorary member, his request was refused. That this refusal must have particularly irritated the haughty and ambitious king is quite certain, but he did not immediately undertake any measures against the knights. On the contrary, he entered into a kind of financial alliance with them, to which he was actually more or less forced by the miserable situation into which he had brought his country. Starting in 1303, income from the whole kingdom was deposited with the 'Temple' in Paris, and for four years the order managed the finances of France together with functionaries of the king.

However, when he had succeeded in getting a Frenchman of his choice elected as Pope, who then continued to reside in France and took no steps whatsoever to move to the Holy See of St. Peter in Rome, he was able to fulfil his long-cherished wish to destroy the Order of the Templars. Pope Clement V was to his death in 1314 a willing, although sometimes vainly resisting, instrument in Philip's hands that allowed Philip to legitimize his plan of destruction. Indeed, he controlled Clement to the point that at the Council of Vienne in 1312 the Order was abolished.

In a personal conversation very soon after the Pope's election, Philip accused the Order of heresy because of reports that had reached him as well as the King of Portugal, of supposedly shameful practices committed by its members. The King of Portugal ignored the matter, knowing full well that the informers were unreliable figures, but Philip ordered an investigation of those Templars who had been expelled from the Order because of bad behaviour.

The Pope, who initially did not believe a word of the accusations, still promised to take the affair in hand. In 1306, Grand Master Jacques de Molay was ordered to France from the headquarters of the Order on Cyprus, not so much to hear the allegations, but rather to consider the merger of the Templars with the Order of St. John. The latter subject did not come from Philip, but did fit in with his original ambitions.

From a document by a certain Pierre Dubois, one of the king's dedicated servants who found smooth legal formulations for the king's intentions, we know what Philip was actually after. He wanted to merge the Orders of St. John and the Templars, put himself at the head of this new spiritual and worldly power and abdicate as King of France on behalf of his 16-year-old son, in order then to reign as King of Jerusalem. The incredible riches of both Orders would be in his hands, and he would also receive a large part of the income from all prelacies, bishoprics and spiritual Orders. It would be a supra-national monarchy in which all the financial resources of the Christian West would be under his control. That Jerusalem had to be the capital of this realm is telling. We can clearly see that King Philip's ideal was the ideal of the Templars turned upside down, for it is of course self-evident that the manner in which this king wanted to use gold was diametrically opposed to the selfless mission of the Order.

The Grand Master of the Templars came to France, but the head of the Order of St. John sent his regrets. Jacques de Molay visited the Pope in Poitiers where he was then staying. He brought two memorandums, one regarding a new Crusade, and the other about the merger of the two Orders, which he strongly rejected. In a personal conversation he had with the Pope the allegations the latter had heard from King Philip must undoubtedly have been discussed. The king himself, however, although expected for a conference with the Grand Master, did not show up.

Jacques de Molay departed for Paris, where a meeting of the leaders of the Order had been called. During his absence King Philip arrived in Poitiers in a magnificent display and openly articulated his accusations against the Order in the presence of the Pope and his dignitaries. In addition, he demanded a trial of heresy against Clement's predecessor, Boniface VIII, blackmail of the first order with which he threatened whenever he wanted to force his way with Clement. Great consternation—all the prelates that were appointed by Boniface felt threatened in their positions. Clement's shaky health failed; the king left in a bad mood. Jacques de Molay visited the Pope a second time in Poitiers and demanded that the allegations against the Order be carefully investigated. Clement promised to appoint a commission of six cardinals to take up the affair.

In the meantime the king was preparing his attack. All over France, government officials were informed under the strictest secrecy of the command that all Templars had to be arrested. In Paris, the king's sister-in-law, Catherine of Valais died. The king asked Jacques de Molay, together with the highest nobility of the realm, to hold a slip of the shroud at the solemn burial that took place on October 12, 1307. The next day the same Jacques de Molay was arrested like a criminal.

A royal manifest, dripping with 'righteous indignation, profound alarm, and Christian emotion', was read to the people in which heresy and the most awful offensive practices of the Order were made public—the beginning of a stream of false propaganda that would remain unequalled until the twentieth century.

The trial that took place ten days later in Paris under Guillaume de Paris, Grand Inquisitor of France, was clearly a mock trial. In the previous days the royal functionaries and plenipotentiaries of the Inquisition had done their work of interrogating the prisoners with the aid of a list of questions in order to get confessions from them. First they promised forgiveness if the accused would admit all the allegations; if this was refused, he was subjected to the most horrendous torture.

The accusations were the following:

1. When making the vow, everyone who was admitted to the Order—and the admissions always took place at night—had to deny Christ, spit on the crucifix and tread it underfoot. With the leader of the admissions ceremony kisses had to be exchanged on improper places of the body.

2. At their meetings the Templars venerated a devil's head from which they implored wealth and happiness.
3. The priests were not allowed to pronounce the words of the consecration when celebrating the Mass.
4. Newly admitted members of the Order were forbidden to have contact with women, but homosexual intercourse with brothers in the Order was emphatically permitted and encouraged.
5. The heads of the Order asserted that they, as lay brothers, were permitted to give absolution to their members.
6. Because of these things the Templars in general had a bad reputation.

Grand Master Jacques de Molay and Geoffroy de Charney, precept of Normandy, admitted the principal point of the charge, the denial of Christ. Even though there continue to be historians who persist in denying that De Molay was tortured, written documents by contemporaries are perfectly clear on this point. Other dignitaries of the Order also gave in under the unbearable pains the expert torturers submitted them to. Jacques de Molay was even forced to sign a letter addressed to all imprisoned Templars in which they were encouraged to confess the misdeeds of which they were accused, like their Grand Master had done.

The king and his chancellor Nogaret won the first battle, and this would prove to be decisive; the poison of their smear campaign has been working ever since in history, even to our own time.

The affair of the Templars dragged out for another seven years; we will not describe all the details of this degrading and humiliating history. Pope Clement tried to take the investigation into the supposed guilt of the knights out of the hands of the French king, but because of his weak position and equally weak character he failed. Philip's supremacy over the Pope, whom he all but held as a prisoner, and especially his total unscrupulousness, superior intelligence and satanic obsession, time and again gave him the advantage in the macabre chess game.

In 1308 hope briefly revived for the Templars when the Pope announced that he wanted to make an investigation of his own, by which he declared the judgement of the Inquisition invalid. But then the king immediately unleashed a storm of pamphlets against Clement that, by portraying him as a protector of the heretical knights, placed him in an unfavourable light. The king called an assembly of the three estates of the realm in Tours, and received a motion of confidence from them—a slap in the face of Clement. The king allowed Jacques de Molay and the heads of the Order to be taken to Poitiers in order to be interrogated by the Pope himself. However, their transport was blocked in Chinon, where they remained in prison under the pretext that they were too sick to complete the trip. Seventy Templars selected by Philip did reach Poitiers and were subjected to interrogation. None of them dared openly declare themselves not guilty.

Clement issued a papal bull in which the rulers of Europe were encouraged to submit the Order of the Templars in their countries to an investigation. The findings in the countries outside France virtually without exception showed the Order's innocence, but the poison of the accusations was working. Even more than this worked the poison of greed; the possessions of the Order were too attractive to let an opportunity pass to seize them with an appearance of justification.

In France confusion and uncertainty reigned. The most noble knighthood of the country had disappeared into the royal dungeons. Confessions made in the torture chambers were recanted, but many knights maintained their initial statements out of fear of repeated torture. And all the time new interrogations were taking place under the unmoved eyes of the king's functionaries.

The Pope started a new investigation, and 546 Templars were willing to defend the Order. The commission made slow progress and the king did not hesitate to stymie their work with one stroke. He forced the Pope to appoint the brother of one of his completely dedicated henchmen as bishop of Sens. Independently of the committee of the Pope this man sentenced 54 'apostate' Templars to death. These had indeed persisted in their innocence. They were burned at the stake in Paris in 1310.

The will of the imprisoned Templars to defend their Order openly before the commission then evaporated. On June 5, 1310, the second trial was concluded. The findings accumulated; the Pope accepted them but postponed his decision. Urged by the king, Clement then assembled a council of the Church in Vienne that began in the fall of 1311. The question of the Templars was on the agenda, and the Church Fathers were leaning toward deciding in favour of the Order. But the dark power of Philip was hanging over the assembled priests. The council was adjourned.

In the spring of 1312 the discussions were resumed. On March 20 Philip entered the town with an impressive display of his retinue. The decision had to fall. What was going on behind the scenes is easy to picture. Two weeks later, in the presence of the Pope, the king and all clerical and worldly authorities, the papal bull *Vox clamantis* was read, by which the Order of the Templars was dissolved. Clement was clever enough to avoid declaring the Order guilty; he dissolved it 'with a bleeding heart' because due to the trial it had become too severely compromised. Clement's decision was not a judgement but an 'apostolic ordinance'.

Thereafter followed the decisions regarding the possessions of the Order. The papal bull assigned these to the Order of St. John. Only a relatively small part of the immeasurable riches Philip had hoped to get his hands on ended up in his possession.

At this point, the Grand Master and three other dignitaries were still alive, imprisoned in the castle of Gisors. The king insisted that they be sentenced. In spite of his earlier promise to personally interrogate the Grand Master, Clement gave this last weighty job to three cardinals. The four prisoners were brought to Paris and the original accusations against them were read to them, as well as the confessions they had made: denial of God, insults to the cross, idol worship, and sodomy. The sentence: life imprisonment.

But then the Grand Master spoke up. Facing death he could but say the truth. He accused himself of the worst crime, namely to have been a witness against his own Order. It was to stop the unbearable pains of the torture that he confirmed the accusations. Now however, he declared all the allegations to have been lies and completely recanted his confessions. The preceptor of Normandy agreed with him; the other two remained silent.

Immediately Philip ordered the Grand Master and the preceptor to be burned at the stake on the western tip of the Ile de la Cité in Paris, which was done right away. It took place in the evening of March 18, 1314. It is said that, standing in the flames, the Grand Master called God's judgement on the Pope and the king, both of which died that same year.

5. The 'Guilt' of the Templars.

More important than the questions of whether the Templars indeed imported their silver from America and financed the construction of the Gothic cathedrals with their gold, is the question of whether the Order was guilty of anything. For what we today think of heresy and sodomy is irrelevant; the point is to know what is the truth in this case. If we can give a satisfactory answer to the question of guilt, not only is then the riddle of this piece of history resolved; it also breaks part of the power that at the time in the person of Philip IV of France destroyed the Order and, through this destruction, was able to exert a disastrous influence on further historical development. In Chapter 6 this power of evil will have to be discussed at length. The influence of evil can only be kept within bounds by the truth.

The Order of the Templars had its rules that were drafted by the Cistercian abbot Bernard de Clairvaux and confirmed by the Church at the

Council of Troyes in 1128. These rules, which included the old Benedictine vow of poverty, chastity and obedience, were later expanded with articles relating to the organization and discipline of the community of Templars. The bylaws were written down, but were kept strictly secret, just as was customary in all communities such as guilds, building Lodges and the like. The Pope, however, who officially recognized the Order, was fully familiar with the contents of the bylaws.

Only three copies of the rules have been preserved, probably by accident. When one assumes on good grounds that every house of the Order had a copy, we might wonder what happened to all those thousands of other copies. Most probably King Philip had those in France destroyed because the rules were in clear contradiction with his accusations. In other countries they may have been destroyed by the knights themselves when the Order was dissolved. In any case, we may assume that the rules of the Order were known to all those who acted as judges at the trial.

Barring rare exceptions, which were severely punished by the Order itself, there has been no evidence that the Templars did not completely faithfully follow the extremely demanding rules of the Order in the two hundred years of its existence. The profoundly Christian tenor of the brotherhood was fully acknowledged by the Church, which came to expression in the robe of the Order that was given them by the Pope: the white robe with the red cross. Their black-and-white standard with the words *Non nobis, Domine, non nobis, sed tuo nomini da gloriam* (Not to us, Lord, not to us, but to Your Name give the glory) may similarly be regarded as an expression of the unconditional surrender to Christ that characterized the Templars.

Due to these official but secret rules the Order was untouchable. But were there no truly secret rules, besides the official ones, that could provide proof that all the Templars were committing heresy and indecent behaviour under the cover of their supposed Christian character? King Philip left no stone unturned to find such a document. He never found one, and therefore we officially still do not know whether there existed *written* rules of an occult nature besides the bylaws of the Order. But we may confidently presume that they did not exist, because in esoteric communities the secrets were always communicated orally.

But the Templars did have an *unwritten esotericism*; I tried to make that clear in the previous sections. Hardly any of *this* esotericism came out at the trial. What did come out were the shadow images that are part of every occult development. The inspirations of the French king that enabled him to bring to the surface what was hidden in the unconscious grounds of the souls of the knights as 'guilt'—these inspirations came from the shadow realm of evil. And Philip knew how to communicate these inspirations to his henchmen as interrogation methods. The torture he ordered was of such a nature that the unbearable pain clouded the victims' consciousness so greatly that demonic pictures rose up out of the shadow realm of the soul.

In every occult schooling, certainly also in the path of initiation of the Templars, the potential arises to experience not only the spiritual in its good aspect, but also the dark side of it. The process inevitably opens the door to counterforces of a diabolic and satanic nature that want to estrange the human being and cut him off from his divine origin, tempters that try to get hold of the soul through terror and allurements, and want to prevent it from connecting with the true divine world.

Every virtue the candidate succeeds in making his own through arduous trials, exercises and detachment has its counterpart in a *vanquished vice*, which is banished as a 'guilt shadow' to layers of the soul that remain completely unconscious as long as the soul is functioning normally. Every deep insight into the Christ mystery and every deep experience of total surrender to Him are victories over the inclination to deny Christ and desecrate what is holy; it is the work of the shadow, an inclination that is an inseparable part of the light of a path of initiation.

Many a Templar may on his path of schooling have suffered from visions and dream pictures that showed him that a diabolical urge can work in the human being that wants to desecrate Christ, and deny the holy symbol of consecration. He had to overcome these temptations, as well as that of falling back into worshipping pagan godheads and, in so doing, misjudging the progress Christendom had brought to humanity. Because of his strict renunciation of every sexual contact he may have had visions of perversities that he had to control and overcome by constant exercise and prayer.

King Philip himself was not an initiate in the good sense of the word, but he possessed an instinctive knowledge of these things that was given to him as a kind of satanic initiation. That he was the right person for this was partly because of his pathological thirst for gold, which makes a person accessible to such inspirations. He knew so much that he was able to put together a kind of script that contained just the right suggestive questions, which under hellish torture called forth from the clouded consciousness of the victim the shadow images of guilt as necessary answers, and in effect forced him in this diminished state to confirm the question.

The priest of the Order, Pierre de Boulogne, who defended the Order before the papal commission in 1310, and who had himself made confessions under torture that he later recanted, declared: 'Under such torture the freedom of the human being is lost.' Many knights retracted their confessions when normal consciousness returned; they were extremely upset when their confessions were read to them, and said that they must have said those things unconsciously. One of them even precisely indicated what had happened to him: 'Whoever confessed this was no Templar but a devil who had invaded a human body.'

All of this has to place conventional historians before insoluble problems, for only occult science is able to have insight into the soul conditions of both the martyred Templars and their sinister enemy. Think of all the things that have been concocted to explain the denial of God, the spitting on the crucifix, the pagan symbol of Baphomet, and the supposed omission of the words *hoc est meum corpum* ('this is my body') during the altar sacrament. And think of all the luciferic-gnostic heresies the Templars were alleged to have committed and how they were supposed to have been influenced by Islamic vices and mysticism. Then there are all the old wives' tales many people still believe, including apparently Jacques de Mahieu when he quotes the saying: 'Watch out for the kiss of the Templars.' Everyone who really studies the Order of the Templars knows that these knights-monks did not even kiss their own mother and sister, in order not have any 'contact of the flesh', no matter how innocent.

All incriminating statements about the Templars were put into the world by King Philip. In other countries it was only when the Order was dissolved by the Pope that the poison of all the allegations began to work. Before that no investigation had ever turned up any culpability.

If we really want to talk about a guilt of the Templars, it was at the same time their highest honour and undying glory. They wanted to bring about a Christianization of society, admittedly before the low point of anti-Christianity had been reached, and therefore perhaps too early. They aimed for a future Johannine Christianity, but their striving was so ascetic and so strictly spiritual, that the powers of evil could pounce on those very characteristics. Their 'guilt' was perhaps their excessive challenge of the powers of darkness, which were therefore able to respond with the diabolical practices described above.

We may state without having any doubts about it that the Templars served God and did not deny Him, that they gave themselves body and soul to Christ and felt the greatest reverence for the symbol of the cross and for the Crucified One. They were no disguised Muslims, nor worshippers of a pagan idol. They celebrated the holy Mass without any omissions and received the consecrated host just like any pious Catholic, and they observed the Benedictine vow of poverty, chastity and obedience in the strictest possible way.

What was said in section 2 of this chapter about initiation does not contradict this. The fact that the lowest grade of this initiation was the stage of St. Peter, in which the denial of Christ figured as a trial, of course absolutely does not mean that the Templars denied Christ. Asserting this is just as absurd as saying that Peter was a denier of Christ. Neither is the anti-Church, or rather anti-Roman element—which, as we have seen, was connected with Grail Christianity in general and with the figure of Godfrey of Bouillon in particular—any proof of diabolical heresy and vice. For that matter, the anti-Roman element did not consist of opposition to the Church of Rome in some form or other, but of the development and protection of a future Johannine Christianity. It was a preparation and was done in solidarity with Rome and loyalty to papal authority.

With the destruction of the Order darkness fell over Europe; ever since, evil has been able to nestle itself deeper and deeper in the culture of the West. But at the same time a resurrection force was born from the martyrdom of the Christian knights. The first one who must have sensed this, and who could give the highest poetical expression to it was the Florentine poet Dante Alighieri. The first apotheosis of the drama of the Templars can be found in Dante's *Divine Comedy*.

6. Human Tragedy and Divine Comedy

In my book *Dante's Openbaring* (*Dante's Revelation*) I propounded the thesis that the *Divina Commedia* was the first form in which the esoteric Christian impulse of the Templars was resurrected after their destruction. Several authors who wrote about the *Divine Comedy* in the twentieth century also noticed that Dante has to be viewed in relation to the Order of the Templars. Rudolf Steiner spoke about Dante in terms showing that he also recognized this relationship. In the 1905 lecture referred to earlier he said in relation to the Sophia Being that played a central role in the esotericism of the Templars:

> This wisdom is exactly what Dante sought to personify in his Beatrice. Only from this viewpoint can Dante's *Divine Comedy* be

understood. Hence you find Dante too using the same symbols as those which find expression in the Templars, the Christian knights, the Knights of the Grail, and so on.[97]

The unprepared reader will probably wonder how the poet Dante (1265-1321), with his fantastic descriptions of Hell, Purgatory and Heaven, can have any relationship with the Christian knights of the Temple of Solomon, who focused their activities so distinctly on the earth. To understand this we first of all have to realize that Dante was a statesman, who in the year 1300 was a member of the governing body of the city of Florence and as such held an extremely important position in Italy at the time. His exceptional gifts and his high ideals for human society predestined him in a certain regard for a highly influential role in the spiritual and social-political development of the fourteenth century, which began when he had reached the age of 35, by tradition the midpoint of life.

In addition, his most important teacher, Brunetto Latini, had shown him the developmental path of initiation, which we may conclude from the expression Dante uses in the *Comedy* to characterize Brunetto: 'You taught me how man makes himself eternal.' (Inf.15:85) 'Makes himself eternal' is surely meant here as connecting with the eternal already during life; crossing the boundary in a 'withdrawal' of the spirit, therefore, from the earthly sense world to supersensible realities. Dante connected this striving for initiation with a deeply Christian disposition which, through his theological-philosophical studies and universal knowledge regarding humanity and the world, had matured into an all-encompassing view of the world, true wisdom.

According to René Guénon,[98] Dante was an initiated leader of an occult organization that had a direct connection with the Templars. This organization, indicated with the letters F.S., *Fede Santa*, was said to contain the higher degrees of the *Fedeli d'Amore*, a kind of secret brotherhood to which Dante's older friend, the poet Cavalcanti, also belonged. Guénon does not explain what the connection with the Templars consisted of, but it is entirely possible that various esoteric groups that all had a more or less Johannine (anti-Petrine) character—and that was certainly the case for *Fedeli d'Amore*—had connections with each other. Be this as it may, Dante's striving as an initiate and statesman was directed toward the same ideal as that which the Templars wanted to prepare, so that it might be realized in the future, namely the Christianizing of human society.

What Dante saw as the principal cause of the un-Christian nature of human society in his time was clearly the 'wolf of greed' that devours the true humanness of people. The curse of gold, the selfish passion of wanting to possess—Dante viewed them as the greatest social evil. In the *Divine Comedy* the advent of a Saviour is foretold, one who will over-come the 'old she-wolf,' in the figure of a hunting-dog, the *Veltro*. This Saviour is also indicated with the number 515, which in Roman figures looks like this: DXV.

A modern Italian professor, Rodolfo Benini, explains this enigmatic symbolic number as follows: D = Dante, X = Christ (from the Greek letter X for Latin CH), and V = Veltro. Thus DXV or DVX means *Dante Veltro di Christo*—Dante is supposed to be the Saviour himself, the fighter against evil. Of course, other scholars contest this, but without decisive arguments. The only thing that makes this brilliant solution of the riddle of the *veltro* and the 515 questionable—assuming that these are two different symbols of the same thing—is the characterization Dante himself gives of the *veltro*. This being does not nourish itself with earthly food but with 'wisdom, love and virtue'. Therefore it clearly does not refer to a mortal human being.

Another Italian, Roberto Passaglia who, inspired by Rudolf Steiner also tried to fathom the *veltro* secret, views the *veltro* as the higher I of the human being, the self that nourishes itself with virtues and that comes into being through ennoblement and catharsis of the soul. This view, which Passaglia advances in a convincing manner, also based on expressions in Dante's text that are difficult to understand, is in my opinion correct, but I don't think it contradicts Benini's finding that DXV is *Dante veltro di Christo*. For Dante was himself on the path of 'eternalizing' his being, developing the eternal self that is related to Christ.

And this initiation principle, which he wanted to make into the guiding principle in human society, was also the basis of the initiated Templars on which to realize their work on the erection of the Temple of the future.

But then human tragedy struck in Dante's life. Charles of Valois, a brother of Philip IV of France, intervened in the affairs of Florence, and Dante was expelled from the city in 1301. Until his death, 21 long years, he was forced to wander as an exile, watching powerlessly how a disastrous party-war continued to tear Italy apart, while the she-wolf of greed kept doing her destructive work.

In these years, remarkably parallel with Dante's fate, the tragedy of the Templars was taking place in France. But while the Templars through torture and death by fire made the sacrifice of their lives dedicated to

Christ—which enabled them to work out of the divine world as inspiring spirits into the future—Dante, the 'Templar who does not die', sublimated his burning suffering, his dead ideal, his unheard-of genius that had to remain idle in social-political regard, into his *Divine Comedy*.

This poem, in one hundred cantos, which describes a journey through the realms of the hereafter, has been analysed, explained and admired by commentators throughout the centuries. The stirring pictures of the Comedy have made a deep impression on countless human souls of many peoples and races, but we also have to understand that even after seven centuries this work is a mighty call on the human being of the present and the future. For too long it has been considered only as a summary of antique pagan and medieval Christian wisdom—of course it is that too. But when we discover that the *Divine Comedy* also harbours a Templar impulse, only then can we recognize the future, the prophetic nature of this work.

During the years in which the trial of the Templars was dragging out, events of far-reaching significance took place outside France, in the Holy Roman Empire, which included Italy. When in 1308 Emperor Albrecht von Habsburg died—whose only object was to increase his family possessions—King Philip IV of France tried to make his brother, Charles of Valois, acceptable to the Electors of the empire as a candidate for the position of German emperor. The gold of the Templars, with which souls could be bought, was of course not scorned in Germany, but the Electors preferred Henry of Luxemburg, who was crowned Roman Emperor in Aachen in 1309.

Just as in 1308 the hopes of the Templars were revived that their case would develop in a favourable direction, Dante also put all his hopes in the newly elected emperor, the noble figure of Henry IV. He viewed him as a sovereign who, standing above the parties, would be able to bring justice and peace in his realm. Dante made the round of the Italian cities, exhorted people, wrote admonitions, letters, pamphlets, and summarized his ideas and ideals in his treatise on the monarchy. This document brings the Templars' ideals to expression. Probst-Biraben writes about this: [99]

> Dante, who proves to be well-informed about the ideas and methods of the Templars, expounds views in his *De Monarchia* that accurately summarize these ideas:
>
> – An overall unifying governance under a sovereign who is recognized by the other princes and is elected, whose power therefore is not hereditary, just as the German emperors and the Grand Master of the Order were elected by a council of equals, like the chapters of the Order;

– elimination of personal interests that are the causes of wars
  between rulers and countries, on behalf of the peace that is necessary for the happiness of all;
– striving for social freedom by liberating all individuals (abolition of
  serfdom).

> The Tuscan poet also expounds the thesis of the Templars of the
> mutual independence of the imperial and papal powers, and he cer-
> tainly means with this that the holder of worldly power may never
> be the tyrant of his subjects. In such a case the ones who chose him
> would be obligated to depose him and choose another.
>   Above the Emperor and the Pope he places a mysterious author-
> ity—perhaps the representative of the priest-king John according to
> the tradition of the Knights of St. John—because a political-worldly
> government is also not qualified to interfere with worldly authority.

Initially, Henry was indeed received as a liberator in Italy, at least by
the Ghibellines who had anyway always supported the international
empire. But when the victorious new emperor-to-be wanted to march
on Rome to receive the imperial crown, revolts broke out in the northern
Italian cities which were financially supported by the Florentine Guelphs
(the 'Blacks' who opposed the 'Whites' to which Dante belonged). Only
after time- and manpower-consuming sieges was Henry able to continue
to Rome, where he was crowned in 1312. Pope Clement was in Avignon,
and the coronation was performed by the cardinal of Ostia.

Immediately after, Henry had to prepare for a battle against Robert of
Naples, who was leading a force of anti-imperial troops of the Guelphs.
However, Henry died unexpectedly in 1313. It was rumoured that he died
of a poisoned host served to him at the instigation of Pope Clement by
a Dominican during Mass. This was a devastating blow for Dante; even
worse than his own painful exile from his home city did he feel the grief
of his lost hope and expectations. But the powerful verses of the divine
poem were forming themselves already and filled his contemporaries
with respect and admiration.

Thus we see how between 1307 and 1314, the period in which the
Order of the Templars was destroyed, a destruction also takes place
of that which could have formed a basis for a European society with
a balance in power relationships. First of all this would have needed
an emperor who could end the conflict between worldly and spiritual
power that had existed for centuries already. In this power struggle the
French kings, as 'protectors of the faith', usually supported the interests of the Pope, or acted as if they did while, fishing in the troubled

waters of the Italian party fights, they looked solely after their own interests.

Henry IV indeed harboured the right disposition needed to be such an impartial emperor. It remains a question whether the poisoned host was indeed served by order of Pope Clement, or whether we should once more have to look in the direction of King Philip of France.

As an initiate, Dante was thoroughly acquainted with the workings of evil. He even had the unprecedented courage to depict the relationship of the French king with the Pope as a direct expression of evil in his *Divine Comedy*. We find this in the last cantos of *Purgatorio* when the poet, reunited with his Beatrice, is shown the grand allegorical images of good and evil in earthly paradise. Also for his contemporaries it must have been evident that with the giant and the whore, whom the giant in turn caresses and molests as she sits on the dragon, the French king and the depraved Pope are meant.

Maybe less evident to non-initiates of his time is the direct allusion to the Templars at the end of *Paradiso*, where Beatrice points to the heavenly hosts with the words:

> Now see how many are in the convent
> Of the white robes.
>> (Par.30:129)

And a little later:

> Then, in the form of a white rose, the host
> Of the sacred soldiery appeared to me,
> All those whom Christ in his own blood espoused.
>> (Par.31:1-3)[100]

The connection with the Order of the Templars is expressed overtly when St. Bernard de Clairvaux appears on the heavenly stage. When Beatrice has taken her place in the heavenly rose, Dante lets him who bestowed on the Templars the rules of their Order, and from whom the first group of knights surely also received esoteric indications, be the mediator between the highest divine secret of the Holy Trinity and the human soul that thirsts for beholding it. Bernard's prayer to Mary (Sophia), one of the most beautiful poetic creations of humanity, enables the poet to have a brief impression of the Trinity.

Dante, who composed these last verses of the *Divine Comedy* shortly before his death in 1321, expresses with these words his most profound esoteric experience, a true Grail experience. Serving the Trinity is

Grail service, service in the temple of creation. The whole *Divine Comedy* is permeated by the secret of the Trinity, also in its content. Dante describes the realms of Hell, Purgatory and Heaven in such a way that he does not speak directly of the earth while yet placing it fully in the centre. The principle of the Trinity reigns in the realms of the hereafter; although Hell is the anti-Trinitarian world, still it is formed according to this immanent law—the realm of the shadows of guilt. But on earth human beings, as sovereign I-beings, have to learn to build the divine laws of the Trinity into their society. To achieve this they have to overcome lasciviousness, greed and power-hunger; they have to be *poor, chaste and obedient.*

Dante was no monk and no knight; he was a free citizen of a free city, at least, a city that wrestled to realize its republican freedom. Not as a vow, but as a free spiritual decision, human beings of the future have to observe a threefold purification in order to make it possible for the principle of the Trinity to work on the earth. Obedience no longer means to obey an outer superior, but our own being, the *Veltro*, the higher self that can in freedom make true St. Paul's words: 'Not I, but Christ in me.'

7. The Mystery of the Cross

Among the most precious treasures of the Templars was a cross with inlaid pearls, rubies and sapphires, and at the crossing of the two arms a little case closed with a crystal door containing a splinter of the cross of Christ. King Philip had taken possession of this rare relic and at his death left it to the Abbey of Poissy, where also his embalmed heart was kept (of which it was said that it had the size of a child's heart). Apart from the strange way in which both the cross and the heart were lost—lightning caused a fire in the abbey's church which destroyed both objects in 1695—this splinter may lead us to discuss a most important aspect of Temple esotericism about which we have so far not spoken.

At this point it may have become evident that the Temple knights wore the red cross on their white robe with the greatest respect. They venerated it even more deeply than the average pious Christian because they knew the profound significance of this symbol. The sign of the cross can be found in virtually all peoples and in all cultural epochs, which tells us that this is a universal human symbol. Just like all important signs and symbols in art, religion and science, this symbol too is rooted in the knowledge of initiates, and has spread from the old mystery centres all over humanity.

When we want to fathom the cross as a specifically Christian symbol and want to understand the teachings the initiated Templars connected with it, we first of all have to know what the four letters I.N.R.I. signify, that were nailed to the cross of Golgotha. The explanation Iesus Nazarenus Rex Iudaeorum—Jesus of Nazareth King of the Jews—does not touch the essence of the matter. In the lecture of 1905 mentioned before, Rudolf Steiner spoke about this, but the notes are incomplete and unclear. When I compare these notes with those, also mentioned before, of a lecture by Walter Johannes Stein, I arrive at the following. The four letters on the cross indicate the following Hebrew words: Iam (water), Nour (fire), Ruach (air) and Iabeshah (earth). The cross thus symbolizes the four elements. Fire relates to Jesus, air to John, water to James, and earth to Peter (Greek *petra* means rock).

The cross expresses what we described in section 2 of this chapter about the initiation of the Templars. They had to go through three stages, the Peter stage, the James stage, and the John stage. The totality of the four letters I.N.R.I. gives the name of Christ Himself—the Celts called the Risen One the Lord of the Elements.

Christendom first had to root in the Peter element, the solid earth. The Temple of Solomon too, the House for God's Name, first had to be built of stone and wood. The development of humanity has progressed so far that the higher I-principle can descend into it, but the outer temple has to be demolished so that the inner Temple of Man can be erected. Similarly, the outer body of Christ had to be destroyed in order to release the resurrection body. Christianity is going through a phase of becoming more and more materialistic, and this is an expression of the developmental process of the human I on earth. In this path of development the I has connected itself with its sheaths—a threefold connection has come into being: with the astral body (the soul), the etheric body (the life forces), and the physical body (the material sheath). In this way the I has, as it were, three times 'denied' the higher, cosmic I-being. But the cosmic I-being, Christ Himself, went this way into the depths of earthly incarnation. He made this sacrifice in order that the human I can move again in an upward direction.

Christian initiates have to prepare the upward path to complete unification with Christ for humanity. They must know the future goal, but first they themselves have to go through the Peter stage of the denial of the cross. The Templars were unable to explain this profound teaching to their judges; actually they were never given the chance to do so.

But after they had 'denied the Cross' in order to find it again in a deeper sense, they were shown a symbolic figure, the venerable form of a man with a great beard as the symbol of the Father God. They learned that future masters of humanity will speak the Word of the Father to human beings in order to raise them to full understanding of Christ. And they were told:

> When you have understood all this, you will be ripe for joining in building the great Temple of the Earth; you must so cooperate, so arrange everything, that this great building becomes a dwelling place for our deeper selves, for our inner Ark of the Covenant.[101]

In the Middle Ages there was also a legend about the wood of the Cross of Golgotha, which can be found in *Golden Legends*.[102] Rudolf Steiner discusses this legend at length in *The Temple Legend*.[103] He does not explicitly say that the esoteric aspects of this legend were known especially to the Templars, but we may assume that the core of this story was part of the wisdom of the Templars. The Christian legend is as follows.

> When Adam and Eve were expelled from Paradise, the Tree of Life remained behind, but later Seth was allowed to receive a shoot of this Tree. This son, conceived with Eve by Adam after Abel had been killed by Cain, planted the shoot of the Tree of Life in the earth. Out of this shoot grew three trunks that were partially fused together. From the wood of this Tree the famous staff of Moses was made. Centuries later, when the Temple of Solomon was being built in Jerusalem, one tried to create a pillar from this same wood, but for some miraculous reason the pillar did not fit into the building, no matter what one tried. Eventually the efforts were stopped and the wooden pillar was laid across a pond as a bridge. It served its purpose there without anyone noticing it.
>
> When however the Queen of Saba visited the Temple and walked across the wooden bridge from one side of the pond to the other, she noticed that the bridge was made of an exceptional kind of wood, and she predicted that on this wood the World Saviour would be crucified. Ultimately this did indeed happen, and afterward many other things happened to the cross.

The three trunks that grew out of the shoot of the Tree of Life indicate the three higher spiritual aspects of the human being: manas, buddhi, and atman, called by Rudolf Steiner spirit self, life spirit, and spirit man. These higher spirit principles, which in Christian esotericism are called Holy Spirit, Son, and Father underlie the three lower principles of the astral, etheric, and physical sheaths that envelop the I on earth. The development of the three higher principles out of the three lower ones is the goal of all striving of the human race. Initially the threefold higher nature of the human being is still veiled, hidden behind the outer sheaths of the lower threefoldness.

Rudolf Steiner uses an analogy with a work of art: we should imagine that the triad of the physical, etheric and astral bodies is something like the outer picture of the higher forces of atman, buddhi, and manas. Just as an artist creates outer forms, expresses a particular idea in colours, these three lower sheaths express like a work of art what the three higher principles have in them as idea.

The I first had to learn to feel at home on the earth in its three lower sheaths. That was the purpose of all outer living arrangements, the way life was organized, and the norms and regulations of a moral nature. The sons of Cain were the ones who looked after this aspect of human society. The Abel-Seth stream in humanity guarded the connection with the divine world, for Seth had planted the shoot of the Tree of Life. In the edifice of Solomon these two aspects had to be connected. The outer building enveloped the Ark of the Covenant with God; the higher (manas) principle could now make a connection with the lower sheaths.

And yet, this was all still preparation. First there was the staff of Moses; it meant no more than the law. Everything in the world is built according to laws. Humanity first has to learn to obey the law, but subsequently this outer law has to be no more than an expression for the inner law. Even though the holy law of Moses, with its origin in the Tree of Life, was kept in the inner, most holy part of the Temple of Solomon, it did remain an outer command, until Christ truly transformed the law into grace and love.

The next phase of the preparation is again described in the form of a searching image in the legend. The pillar made of the Wood of Life does not fit in the Temple, because although the Ark of the Covenant is placed in the innermost part of the building, the Living Word of God had not yet incarnated. The Wood of Life becomes the bridge that leads from the lower realm to the higher, just as in Goethe's fairytale the Green Snake sacrifices itself to become the bridge between the material and the spiritual realms.

Finally, the third metamorphosis of the Wood of Life signifies the complete connection of the higher principle with the lower, of the inner with the outer. Christ creates the veritable union of the two streams which in Hiram, the son of Cain, and Solomon, the son of Abel/Seth, were still separate, although the construction of the Temple already indicated a preparatory connection of the worldly with the religious stream.

Christ is united with the forces of the Tree of Life. He is Himself the Living Law and the Living Bridge, which He unifies into the vertical (staff) and horizontal (bridge) of the Living Cross. Henceforth human beings can find life in their higher nature as Christ bestows it on them; their lower nature becomes the wooden cross that they shoulder in imitation of Christ. For that is the mystery of the cross in a Christian sense: that an inversion takes place. In the legend the higher principle is symbolized by the three trunks that grow on earth out of the shoot of the Tree of Life. The lower principle is a reflection, an expression of the higher, but because of the advent of Christ on earth the higher principle of the human being has come to life in Him, and the Trunk of Life that Seth had planted becomes the outer cross that Christ carries on His back and erects on Golgotha as reconciliation for the expulsion from Paradise.

The black wooden cross becomes the symbol of the lower principle, which must now be carried by a living force from within. The cross must be carried; then human beings can take it into their being; then the pillar fits into the Temple.

In the oft-mentioned lecture of 1905 even more far-reaching aspects of the symbol of the cross are mentioned, but we cannot go into these here. A discussion of these would require a description of evolution in a spiritual sense, which would far exceed the framework of this section and would also go beyond the intention of this book.

The secrets of the cross referred to above were without any doubt an important part of the teachings of the Templars. When we are able to immerse ourselves meditatively in what was merely briefly summarized here, we will come to realize the immeasurable depths and heights of the Christian mysteries. The Templars were Cross-Bearers in the fullest sense of the word. We can understand that their last Grand Master, Jacques de Molay, before he let himself be tied to the stake, took off his white robe with the red cross and folded it lovingly, so that the most holy symbol would not be burnt by the fire.

6. World Future

1. Evil: Grail and Anti-Grail

When we now, as part of our theme, want to cast our eyes onto the present and the future we need to direct our attention in particular to the workings of evil. This is uncomfortable, but inevitable—uncomfortable, because people tend to be interested in the manifestations of evil out of sensationalism, but rarely does anyone want to hear concretely what evil is and how it works; and inevitable, because a deeper penetration into the mysteries of evil belongs to the world historic tasks of our time. So far, the aspect of evil has been mentioned only in passing. Now that in our review of history we have arrived at the threshold of modern times, it becomes necessary to develop a more comprehensive view regarding this question.

The current cultural epoch, which Anthroposophy calls the fifth post-Atlantean epoch, began in the fifteenth century when the Middle Ages, which still belong to the fourth, the Greek-Roman epoch, drew to an end. The well-known cultural movements we indicate with the words Renaissance, Humanism and Reformation are manifestations of a much stronger awakening of human consciousness than existed before. The pillars on which this consciousness of self rests, which we may also call a feeling of individual maturity, or freedom of the human spirit, are exact sense observation and abstract-rational thinking that is more or less bound to the physical matter of the brain. These two capacities of the soul, of which exact sensory observation is a truly new property in human development, unfolded with incredible speed, first in Europe, and primarily in the western part of this continent, but gradually also across the earth, although there always remained gradations, as is the case with every kind of development. Natural science arose, and in its wake came technology, both of which challenged the human intellect to its highest achievements.

This development brought about the complete descent of the human I into the lower three members of the human being. The part of the soul in which the I can now, conscious of itself, feel at home on the material earth is in Anthroposophy called the consciousness soul. Sensory observation and abstract thinking are making the I of the consciousness soul free—free to ..., but first of all free from ... The I frees itself from spiritual traditions, from religion and faith, free from God and commands. The I becomes 'Faustian'. But we know what happened to Faust; he had to make a pact with the power of evil. More than ever before, in the era of the consciousness soul a power of temptation, of counter-guidance insinuates itself into human affairs. We have to recognize this and learn to deal with it *consciously*.

Toward the end of the previous chapter we made the following statement: 'The development of the three higher principles out of the three lower ones is the goal of all striving of the human race.' Such striving is inconceivable without freedom. But then there necessarily also has to be a principle that works against this striving, and tries to make it fail. For if it could not fail, if the achievement of the goal would be absolutely certain, there could hardly be a question of striving. Striving always means overcoming resistance.

Now, the development of the higher principles of manas, buddhi and atman out of the three lower ones, the astral, etheric and physical bodies, can only come about through the activity of the self-conscious I. The I is, as it were, the mathematical top of a cone through which all the lines run that form a double cone, one pointed up and one pointed down. It is therefore understandable that evil aims its activity at the human I, as a power of resistance to test human striving.

To begin with, evil appears as a *double* power. Thus we find it described in all mythologies, sagas, fairytales, and spiritual messages: Midgard serpent and Fenris wolf, Leviathan and Behemoth, the Devil and Satan, a *luciferic* and an *ahrimanic* power. The luciferic spirits want to draw the human I away from the earth and capture it in their own luciferic spiritual realm, whereas, by contrast, the ahrimanic power wants to chain the human I to the earth, imprisoned in matter. Ahriman is the one who in the Gospels is called 'the prince of this world'.

One might say that Lucifer strives for a weakening, a volatilization of the I, and Ahriman for a hardening. In both cases it is a pulling away of the I from the top of the cone, in Lucifer's case upward, in Ahriman's case downward. In either case the goal of the development of the earth is thwarted. The workings of these two powers are, of course, much more complicated that can be indicated in this brief description, but the fundamental idea given here will help us in our contemplations.

The two powers work against each other and thus keep each other in balance in a certain respect; but they also play into each other's hands. Because of the work of the one, the other gets a chance to intervene.

In the Templars, for instance, we saw such a strictly ascetic and high spiritual ideal that the knights as individuals, but also the Order as a whole, continually came close to Lucifer's 'flight from the world'. This made an ahrimanic intervention by King Philip IV possible. In revolutions we often see a fiery luciferic element, which may well be noble and idealistic, and which then is followed by an extremely cold ahrimanic counter-movement. Witness the French Revolution followed by Napoleon, the Russian Revolution followed by Stalin as clear examples.

The malicious characters of Lucifer and Ahriman are relative to the extent that both powers also have positive aspects. Lucifer is indispensable in everything for which enthusiasm, fantasy and inspiration are needed, for example in the arts. Ahriman's influence is justified in everything of the nature of densification, materialization. These two spiritual powers have not only received their place in the great plan of the world because of these positive aspects, but just as much because of their necessary role as counter-strivers, which make human freedom possible.

However, when the double power of evil appears as a unity, such as the dragon in the twelfth chapter of the Book of Revelation (12:13-18), which is called both the Devil and Satan, we may have the impression that behind the two there stands a third, higher power, the power of absolute evil. This is certainly the case with the Beast in Revelation, symbolized by the number 666 (Rev.13:18).

It sounds as if I accept as a matter of course that the powers of evil are concrete spiritual beings. However, this is not due to a rash, uncritical assumption, but a well-considered contemplation of the problem. In Anthroposophy the spiritual world is described as an extremely complicated and differentiated world of higher and lower beings. For conventional, materialistically oriented science and for the superficial view of public opinion, this may be an unprovable phantasm. But for those who carefully and without prejudice go further into it, and who use it to test life and history, these spiritual contents become useful, highly plausible ideas, to say the least, ideas that have as much, or more, justification as any other ideas with which we try to explain the riddles of the world.

When we now contemplate the trial of the Templars in relation to the question of evil we may come to the following. At the beginning of the fourteenth century an ahrimanic power took possession of the King of France with his henchmen in such a way that, because of this, the Order of the Templars was destroyed and its fame stained to our time. The fact that Philip IV could be such an opportune instrument in the hands of Ahriman was, apart from the king's particular nature, caused in part by the general human vice that governed him to a pathological degree: greed. The events that took place between 1307 and 1314 imprinted the curse that rests on the sacred sun metal when it is not consecrated to the spiritual, but put in the service of an egotistic striving for power, into the soul configuration of Europe, as it were. The destruction of the Templars and all that which followed from it, was aimed directly at esoteric Christianity. If we regard the Templars as 'the original envoys of the Grail', the attack on the Order is to be understood as an anti-Grail impulse.

Just as the history of the Grail has been shown to go far back into the past, even to pre-Christian mysteries, we also have to look in the past for the origin of the anti-Grail impulse to understand that its later working was the result of its earlier preparation. In this connection it is important to realize that evil arises when good is moved in time, so that it either comes too early or too late. Spiritual powers that serve progress at a particular stage of development will hold progress back and oppose it if in a later stage they want to hold on to things as they were. Such retarding influences may have either a luciferic or ahrimanic colour.

Thus even in our time there are still influences working from the old Atlantean era of human development. In Asia these have adopted a more luciferic character, in America a more ahrimanic one. Both had their effects in Europe already in pre-Christian times, but their influence becomes more distinct in the Middle Ages and later—the one from Asia in the Mongol hordes, the one from America after its discovery in 1492 in completely different forms. With all this, we should not lose sight of the fact that together with the evil aspects, there are also good influences that serve the progress of humanity. It is particularly necessary to emphasize this to people who think that when someone points to ahrimanic influences from the West, the person is therefore necessarily also anti-America.

As regards the advent of Christ on earth and His relationship to evil, it is evident that the revelation of the Christ being evokes the full power of the adversary. Christ does not annul the effects of Lucifer and Ahriman, but overcomes them by showing their being in His light. Making evil visible to the insight of human beings is necessary to give us the freedom to reject evil or follow it. The history of Christendom teaches us, however, that acquiring insight into evil is no simple matter.

It is a generally known fact that from its very first beginning Christianity has had to cope with a double opponent. On the one hand there is the luciferic power that shows in the decadent mysteries and the murkiness of old occultisms such as the sibyls, speaking in tongues, magic, etc. On the other hand, but also in combination with this, we see the power of the 'prince of this world' that was concentrated in the Roman Caesar. We can read in the *Acts of the Apostles* how these two powers of evil harassed the beginning Christian communities in Palestine, Syria and Asia Minor. However, these were attacks from outside which the first Christians were still able to ward off—even if at the cost of their lives—in the name of their Lord, since He had vanquished both of these powers. But it did not take long before the adversaries penetrated into the ranks of the Christians themselves and their influence became much more effective once they could work from the inside.

Church history shows only one side of these invading enemies, the luciferic aspect. The many sects and streams of a Gnostic nature, the 'false doctrines' that were still impregnated with old mystery wisdom—the Church that was acknowledged in the fourth century by Constantine had to push all of this out the door. That which, because of this, remained more or less hidden, was the effect of the ahrimanic enemy that was able to bring the Roman anti-spirit into the Church, the legal-organizational element, the Caesarian power impulse that was now transferred from the Emperor as High Priest to the Bishop of Rome, the Pope.

Dante pointed to this ahrimanic impulse in the Roman Church when he fulminated against the worldly possessions of the popes, that began already in Constantine's time. This meant the entry of the 'wolf of greed' into the Church organization.

One thing that remained completely hidden from conventional history, which very early on already adopted a standard pattern like a *fable convenue*, was the existence of a group that dated back to the fourth century, whose object was to destroy everything that connected Christianity with the wisdom of the old mysteries. Rudolf Steiner calls attention to this anti-Grail collegium in the fourth century and places the centre of its activities in central Italy.[104] This group, which of course never came into the limelight of history, had great power. Due to such people not only were pagan documents, temples and artworks destroyed, but especially also documents of an esoteric Christian nature. In this connection, Steiner mentions a large poetic work about the event in Palestine, in which the Christ being is depicted as the Sun Spirit who unites Himself with the human being Jesus at the Baptism in the Jordan.

That this special knowledge of the relation of Christ with the cosmic Sun world had to be eradicated according to the intentions of the anti-Grail powers within the Church, is also shown by the fact that the 'apostate' Emperor Julian was eliminated by this sinister collegium. This emperor, who was initiated in the mysteries of Eleusis, was no enemy of Christianity at all. Only, in the 'imperial' form Christianity had adopted since Constantine he did not find what he was looking for. As we saw already in Chapter 2, he wanted to acquire a deeper insight into the secrets of the Sun being. He expected to be able to learn more about this in the Near East, where there were still remnants of Zarathustra's sun wisdom.

The area where he went with his Roman legions was the region where the great initiate Mani had been working. If Julian had come into contact with Manichaeism, which would have been entirely possible, he would have discovered that in this stream there existed complete insight into the relationship between the Sun being and Jesus Christ. For this reason the encounter of Julian with Manichaeism had to be prevented. An unknown hand hurled the spear that killed him; the murderer fulfilled the deed by order of the anti-Grail collegium.

That we are witnessing a strong anti-Christian power in this case becomes evident when Rudolf Steiner describes an exceptionally moving aspect in this regard, namely that due to the activity of these individuals, who were of course mere instruments in the hands of Ahriman, the Christ being experienced a kind of second crucifixion in supersensible spheres.

Still, this was only preparation for the awful attack of the evil powers around the middle of the seventh century. Here we witness the chilling sphere of the absolutely anti-divine power that the Book of Revelation indicates with the number 666.

In the section about Aristotle in Chapter 2 a city in the neo-Persian Empire was mentioned where there was an important academy. The name of the city was Gondishapur, the same place where Mani died in prison and his body was shamefully exhibited at the city gate. The Greek philosophers who had been expelled from Christian areas because of their pagan philosophy and science, had fled to Gondishapur. In the course of time the city had become a splendid centre of Hellenistic culture that excelled especially in knowledge of astronomy and medicine.

Rudolf Steiner says, based on his spiritual research, that from there an extremely malignant attack on humanity was undertaken around the year 666. It was the intention of the power that in the Apocalypse is indicated with the number 666 to spread such a brilliant intellectuality from the Academy of Gondishapur into the culture that certain parts of humanity would go through an accelerated development that would anticipate the stage in which we are today. Such an advanced development of the consciousness soul in part of humanity would in the course of time strongly radiate out so that its effects would reach all over the world. As a result, through this accelerated development the human soul would be made so strongly aware of the physical earth that it would become chained to the mechanistic-material. The proper development of the I of human beings would then be cut off, and human beings would come under the power of the Beast as hardened robots.

This design of evil failed, or rather, succeeded only to a very limited extent, in the first place because the Christ being accelerated His advent on earth due to this satanic attack. He came 333 years before the originally intended time, which was the year 333 AD, right in the middle of the fourth post-Atlantean epoch, 'in the middle of time'. The advancement of the Mystery of Golgotha had a spiritual influence on all of humanity, as a result of which the soul was bound less strongly to the body and became more open to the spirit. Although this did not take away the greatest danger of the impulse of 666, a certain equilibrium was created.

Another cause of the partial failure was the appearance of the Islamic Arabs. In a certain respect these people served the intentions of Gondishapur, but they also weakened their effect. The Arabs, who conquered the neo-Persian Empire toward the end of the seventh century, eagerly took in the brilliant scholarship of Gondishapur and did indeed spread it into the world. They intellectualized the Aristotelian wisdom of the Academy of Gondishapur and, in doing so, laid the foundation of our later European, materialistic science. The great extent to which Arabic erudition, particularly in Moorish Spain, anticipated our current science, and even our technology, is much too little known, but it confirms what Rudolf Steiner says about Gondishapur: The intention was to accelerate the development of our current soul condition, the consciousness soul.

But in what respect did the Arabs weaken this impulse? We have to imagine that the intended intellectuality would have been implacably sharp and icy cold, truly a deathly force. The sultry, imaginative soul life of the Arabs, coupled with the character of the religion of Mohammed, contributed to the moderation of the extreme character of the impulse.

In the meantime the actual influence of this impulse of evil was great indeed. Rudolf Steiner points out that since then the sting of atheism is present in every human being; the denial of God was planted into humanity like a disease. The decision of the Council of Constantinople in 869 to abolish the spirit also has to be regarded as a fatal consequence of the Gondishapur impulse. The anti-Grail collegium in Rome, which must have had a hand in this, was before the year 666 already an instrument in the hands of the power of evil.

Now, we need to wonder whether over against the mostly ahrimanic attacks described here we can also discover the workings of Lucifer. That is most certainly the case. In the ninth century there was an anti-Grail activity that was reflected in the later poetic traditions. Everything Chrétien and Wolfram described as the grotesque realm of Chastel Merveille with its temptations and terrors has an unmistakably luciferic character. We see here not so much the icy cold of deathly intellectuality, but the heat of lust and desire. Due to this power, King Amfortas is suffering from his incurable wound inflicted in the groin by a poisoned lance.

The mysterious master of this magic realm, the magician Klingsor, is put on stage in Richard Wagner's opera *Parsifal*, but in Chrétien and Wolfram he remains invisible in the background. They describe how the hero Gawain manages to live through the trials and terrors and, because of this, becomes the lord of Chastel Merveille; and through these poetic pictures of Klingsor's realm, they tell the reader or listener that we have the ability to control and overcome the element of desire and lust in our own soul. However, that does not mean that there have not been any objective, even historically discernible anti-Grail activities in connection with the figure of Klingsor.

This character can probably be indentified with Landulf II, Duke of Capua (825-879) who was held in great respect by Emperor Ludwig I. His brother, Pando, had called the Arabs, who had already conquered Sicily in 827, to Apulia in southern Italy, and Landulf also allied himself in a certain way with the Arabs. The saga of the Grail speaks of Klingsor's relationship with a 'pagan' queen, named Iblis, by whose husband he had been emasculated when the latter surprised the lovers in each other's arms. This castration had caused Klingsor's profound hatred of man and woman. It happened in Kalot Bolot, or Kalta Bellota, a place in southwestern Sicily.

Interestingly, Iblis is the name the Muslims use for Lucifer. We should regard Kalot Bolot as an occult centre from where the Grail stream in Europe was opposed. The fact that Klingsor was called a magician indicates that he used black-magical forces, and therefore also showed ahrimanic traits, because the lord of black magic is Ahriman.

In the sphere of evil there is no arbitrariness or caprice; everything takes place according to plan and design. The future is prepared long, very long ahead. All moves on the chessboard of world history are conceived and considered with absolutely waterproof logic. And yet, time and again Lucifer and Ahriman are disappointed in their expectations. It often looks as if evil triumphs, but on closer examination their victory is never complete; in fact, many times the result of their anti-human interference ends up being a strengthening of the true essence of humanity because it has led to a forward step in human evolution. But still, it is understandable that the powers of evil never give up in spite of their disappointments. For as humanity progresses in the direction of freedom the chances of success increase for these powers. As human beings more and more fall away from God—for that is what freedom means in the first instance—they become more receptive to evil. And evil has no need to improvise; it took its measures already centuries ago.

The blow that destroyed the Templars was a rhythmical repetition of the impulse of 666. When we take this figure as a number of years it returns in 1332 and 1998.[105] I have already pointed out that the diabolical cunning of Philip IV strikes us as something very modern. The absolute inhumanity that was intended in the impulse of Gondishapur was directed first of all to human thinking. An ice-cold intellectuality had to create the potential of an effective separation from the divine world. This intellectual 'fall into sin' did not fully happen until modern times, but it was thoroughly prepared.

The second attack was aimed not so much at thinking but more at feeling. The Knights Templar were no scholars; they lived more out of the forces of the heart. The mysteries of gold and blood, which they guarded, now had to be desecrated and turned into their opposites. It is evident that corruption was brought into the sphere of feeling. The slander, insults, and disgrace of the noble knights worked like corrosion on the feelings of posterity.

In the meantime a seed for a truly Christian social order was thwarted for many centuries. Over against this, however, we should also consider the positive working of the Grail romances; the esoteric Christian stream came to a halt, but withdrew into the imaginations of the epics. And concurrently, the renewal of the Christian mysteries of modern times was being prepared, namely the stream that is connected with the name of Christian Rosenkreutz.

The third attack is the one we stand in since the late twentieth century; it is aimed at the will. Because of this the powers of energy in matter have been unleashed. In this third surge of evil the two previous ones are clearly recognizable, only they are even more radical and have global dimensions. That which in previous times had been prepared in East and West, and had already clearly announced itself in the transition of the Middle Ages to modern times in the Mongol hordes and the discovery of America, comes to sharp manifestation in a gigantic struggle between East and West.

2. The Rosicrucians

When we now wonder whether the spiritual impulse of the Templars was in any way continued, the answer is on the one hand rather simple, but on the other hand extremely complicated. We can point to one clearly demonstrable continuation, namely the Order of Christ in Portugal. This Order, of which Henry the Navigator was the most important Grand Master, was not only a direct continuation of the Order of the Templars, but in a certain sense also a renewal of it. For it made a strong contribution to the characteristics of modern times with their *global economic* nature after the opening of the sea route to India. However when toward the end of the fifteenth century the way to the West was also opened, the original impulse of the Order of Christ was no longer working. On the contrary, the conquest of America by the Spaniards gives us an eloquent picture of the curse that rests on gold when the 'wolf of greed' reigns supreme.

The other knightly Orders that existed already when the Templars were all-powerful, the Hospitallers, the Spanish Orders of Santiago and Calatrava, and several similar brotherhoods, remained active in the fight against the Moors or the Turks, but a continuation of the esoteric stream of the Templars did not really develop in these Orders. We have already seen that the first Portuguese Viceroy of India considered it necessary to keep the most important treasure that destiny had given him, out of the hands of the Order of Santiago.

But while the last revival of the knightly ideals in the Order of the Golden Fleece prepared the rulers of Europe for modern times, a hidden metamorphosis of Christian wisdom was already growing, which would become the stream of the Rosicrucians.

There are some authors among the Freemasons who spread the view that there is a direct connection between the Templars and the Freemasons. To test the verity of this view we have to trace the origin of the Order of the Freemasons. But this does not really lead to an evident *direct* connection. The researcher of occult history does, however, find an indirect connection when he considers the 'guardians of the Holy Grail', and particularly the mysterious figure of Christian Rosenkreutz.

Regarding this person, however, and also all that is connected in some way with Rosicrucianism, there are if possible even more misunderstandings and false pictures than regarding the Templars. Even apart from the extensive scientific and quasi-scientific literature about this subject—most of which does not penetrate to the essence of the matter, because this essence cannot be found anywhere in available documents—modern societies and associations that call themselves Rosicrucians create so much confusion that it is almost impossible to get a true picture of the original stream of the Rose Cross. To find our way out of the labyrinth we have to consult exact initiation science as Rudolf Steiner represents it.

In the Middle Ages already was being prepared what would be the new phase of human development in the fifth post-Atlantean epoch, namely on the one hand, penetrating the outer cosmos and nature by *natural-scientific* means and, on the other hand, searching for a connection with the divine world by means of a personal *religion*. But this natural science and personal religion, both of which would in our time develop a strongly materialistic character, would also have to be able to connect in the future with a spiritual stream that could then be taken up by human beings in complete *freedom*.

This spiritual stream is the ongoing working of the Christ mystery. And this has incredible implications. For instance, in the future, human beings will have to develop capacities to master the living forces of nature, just as they now possess power over dead matter in nature. The latter capacity was developed over thousands of years through the indefatigable striving and labouring of the Sons of Cain. Science, art, and social organization came into being because in the course of time people have worked on the world and transformed it. All large buildings and technical inventions, but also sculptures and paintings; all the treasures the different arts have generated through the ages, and all social measures, laws and rules—all of this rests on control of the physical world, in the sense of the *inorganic* world. The pillars of culture, wisdom, beauty, and strength carry the temple of humanity. The ones who built this since time immemorial are the mason brothers, the Freemasons, whether or not they called themselves by that name.

Control of the forces of life, however, still needs to be developed. The first germs will have to come into being in our time in connection with social life, the area where human beings will first come to the insight that control of *inorganic* forces generates nothing positive for social life.

Here the Grail principle of self-sacrifice, which also lived in the impulse of the Templars, will have to come to social realization. From our present time, the one-sided masculine element, which has until now been the dominant factor in the control of the dead forces in nature, will have to be overcome. In the feminine, the forces of the future of all that lives are much more present than in the masculine; men will therefore have to make great efforts to get these living forces within their reach.

The original Freemasons and Templars, and also the true Rosicrucians, are very closely connected with each other, in the sense that all three were at the same time spiritual and social movements that wanted to represent the mainstream of human development, and thus serve the progress of humanity. These movements were inspired by great initiated masters, who belonged to the White Lodge of humanity, which may also be called the Grail Lodge.

We came to know one of these masters in our contemplations on the Phoenix and the building of the Temple of Solomon (Chapters 3 and 5); this was Hiram Abiff. He was born again as 'the disciple whom Jesus loved', Lazarus, whom Christ initiated by raising him after an initiation-death lasting three and a half days. As John, he lived through the Christian initiation again in overwhelming spiritual experiences, which he described in the Book of Revelation. Later he described the sevenfold path to this initiation in his Gospel.

In preparation for his future mission this individuality incarnated in the eighth century as Charibert de Laon, whose daughter Berthe ('with the big feet') was the mother of Charlemagne. About Charibert as a historical personage not much is known, but the saga that was woven around him belongs to the best-loved stories of the Middle Ages. It is the romance of Flor and Blanchefleur.

Behind the 'youth of the rose' who loses his 'bride of the lily', and then wins her back, we have to look for one of the greatest initiates of humanity, just as in the case of Parsifal. The saga came from Provence, where also Kyot, Wolfram's informant, came from, and not from the East, as is often alleged. Flor was no Christian prince but is described as born from Islamic parents or, as was said at the time, 'pagan' parents. His father had the name *Fenus* or *Phoenix* and reigned in Spain. This indicates without any doubt that we have to do here with Grail-related motifs. Blanchefleur is the daughter of a Christian woman who had become a hostage. The mother is of noble birth but in spite of the kind treatment she receives from the queen, she is regarded as a female slave at the court of Fenus.

King Fenus is upset by the love between Flor and the daughter of a slave. He wants to kill her, but at the insistence of his spouse this does not happen. The beautiful girl is then sold to merchants who take her to the East, where the Emir of Babylon buys her. She is locked up with many other women in a curious tower in the middle of the city. The Emir loves her fervently for her exceptional beauty and sweetness, and wants to make her his queen.

The men who had sold Blanchefleur to the oriental merchants received great treasures for the girl. One of these was a golden chalice on which the history of Paris and Helen was depicted in relief. When Flor goes in search of his beloved he takes this cup with him, and largely because he is willing to part with this object, he manages to get the guard of the tower to let him into the seraglio, hidden in a big basket with fresh red roses.

When he is discovered, the Emir wants to put the two lovers to death by his own hand, but because of the advice of his wise vassals, who are moved by the beauty of the two and are also deeply impressed by the unwavering faithfulness of their love, the drama is happily resolved. The Emir forgives them and allows them to marry each other. Not much later Flor and Blanchefleur leave the Emir and return to their country, where King Fenus has died. Flor becomes a Christian and, with him, all his subjects.

Behind this touching love story much is hiding. In the various pictures that make the story so rich and mysterious, people who are familiar with these things will easily recognize an alchemical element, for example in the empty grave of Blanchefleur that is described at length; similarly also in the miraculous horse on which Flor rides, and in the women's tower of the Emir. It is also no coincidence that the cup with the history of Helen appears in the story. Helen is Selene, the moon goddess who is abducted from West (Greece) to East (Troy) because of her beauty, and is then reconquered after a cruel battle. In the case of Blanchefleur, however, love brings this about. No powerful fleet and grim heroes accomplish the deed, but a seemingly weak youth, really still a child, innocent as a lamb.

Just as in the Grail symbol, the story is about the union of the moon being (the white lily) with the sun being (the red rose). The pure, still selfless wisdom element as the virginal silver-mirror and the modest beauty of the lily date back to the mysteries of the distant past; they still came from heaven. The noble soul of the oriental person admires this being, but the red rose from the West symbolizes warm personal love that can bloom on earth, and transforms the impersonal wisdom element into a new stream of spiritual power.

Why do these children love each other so much? Because they were born on the same day, Palm Sunday, the day when Jesus entered the city where he was to bring the great love offering.

The story of Flor and Blanchefleur contains not only the germs of the Parsifal saga, but of everything in the history of Europe that is related to the profound symbolism of the lily and the rose. And in this regard the movements from West to East, and from East to West, are again of decisive significance.

Walter Johannes Stein believes that behind the first embassy that was sent to the Arabic court of Al-Mansur in Baghdad in the time of Pepin, Charlemagne's father, lived an inspiration from the great initiate *Flor*. His purpose would not so much have been to forge a political alliance with the eastern caliphate, as to explore a spiritual connection with the Arabic eastern world in order to 'rescue' the spiritual wisdom that was still living there for Europe.[106]

One of the forms in which we can experience the union of 'rose-love' with 'lily-wisdom' is the fairytale. Berthe, the daughter of Flor and Blanchefleur, also called 'Berthe with the goose feet,' grew in popular tradition into 'Mother Goose', who told fairytales. This notable circumstance throws light on the way certain esoteric streams worked in the Middle Ages. The Cathars, Templars, and Rosicrucians spread fairytales among the people. Originally, these brief stories were not only told to children, but also to adults—maybe even only to adults. In forms of imaginative pictures, teachings of great depth and beauty, seasoned with light humour, were handed on to the people. This was like educational material that was given to the people by initiates and wise men, side by side with the teachings of the Church.

We often don't realize—not surprisingly given the nature of our culture—to what extent esoteric elements still influenced medieval culture, despite the fact that there were no more mysteries where initiations took place as in antiquity. Extremely small brotherhoods, completely hidden from historical researchers; lonely initiates such as the Friend of God from the Oberland, inspirer of Christian mysticism, formed a spiritual bridge from ancient to modern times. But the same was true for the widely known teachers of Cluny, Chartres and early scholasticism who, in a certain regard, also drew from hidden mystery sources, and also for the Templars, alchemists, poets, cathedral builders, and all who had a deep longing for supersensible knowledge.

But in addition to this, a truly new spiritual impact had to come. This could only happen if the old ways of gaining access to the spiritual worlds were closed for a time. Rudolf Steiner mentioned the year 1250 in this connection.[107] For a short time, he said, even the highest initiates on earth were unable to make direct spiritual observations, although they could remember their earlier initiation experiences, also from former lives. The reopening of the spiritual worlds coincided with a new initiation of the individuality Hiram-John-Flor, who in subsequent times was called Christian Rosenkreutz.[108]

Around 1250 there were twelve wise men living in central Europe who were called to become the bearers of a new Christian esoteric impulse. Seven of the twelve had been Atlantean initiates who had worked under the leadership of the great Manu spirit in several oracles that were dedicated to the gods of the planets. As the Holy Rishis, the great teachers of the ancient Indian cultural epoch, they again became disciples of Manu. In them the entire cosmic wisdom of Atlantis was concentrated and they were able to call this up out of their memory. In addition, four of the twelve were representatives of the four post-Atlantean epochs, the old Indian, old Persian, Egypto-Babylonian, and Greco-Roman times. The twelfth was the one who was most intellectually formed. He mastered the knowledge of his time, but because of his strong intellectuality he represented the fifth epoch that was still to come (our time).

These twelve wise men came together in order jointly to lead a thirteenth. This was the individuality who was to receive the new initiation. As a child he came under the guardianship of the twelve who instilled their wisdom into him. Each of these twelve was a profound Christian, but they were conscious of the fact that the outer Christendom of the Church was but a distortion of true Christianity. Each of them could illuminate one aspect of Christianity out of his specific mystery experience. It was their joint striving to harmonize the wisdom streams they each separately represented. Their purpose was to create a synthesis of all religious streams and world views of humanity, and for this to happen the thirteenth was necessary.

The child, who had in the meantime grown into a youth, and who had no other contacts with the world than the care and teaching of his twelve masters, absorbed everything with the greatest heart forces and earnestness. The initiation procedures worked deeply into his physical constitution; at a certain moment he no longer took in food, and fell into a kind of death-like condition that continued for a few days during which his body became completely transparent. Rudolf Steiner said about this:

> Then an event occurred that could only happen once in history. It was the kind of event that can take place when the forces of the macrocosm cooperate for the sake of what they can bring to fruition.[109]

While he was in this condition the twelve stood around him and let their wisdom flow into him, summarized in brief, mantric formulations. After some time the youth awoke from his death-like sleep. A profound change had occurred in him. His soul was as if born anew out of the harmony of the twelve wisdom streams. His body, which came to life again, was incredibly transparent and radiated light. Out of the mouth of the youth the twelve now received their wisdom back again in metamorphosed form, the form that was given by Christ Himself. During his initiation sleep the youth had gone through St. Paul's Damascus experience. What he was now able to reveal to his teachers was called by them true Christianity, *the synthesis of all religions or world views.*

The youth died relatively soon after this most holy mystery that had been enacted in him. The twelve men dedicated the rest of their lives to taking down the wisdom that had been bestowed on them from the mouth of the youth. This could only be done in the form of symbolic figures and pictures that indicated the supersensible, imaginative content. Only toward the end of the eighteenth century did these symbolic figures of the Rosicrucians appear in print.

As the fruit of the initiation, the etheric body of the thirteenth remained intact and did not dissolve into the world ether as usually happens. This etheric body could then continue to work on earth in an inspiring capacity, not only for the twelve first teachers, but also for their followers and students. From this arose the stream of the Rosicrucians.

Not much more than a century after these totally hidden events, the individuality of the thirteenth was born again. He then lived more than a hundred years (1378-1484), and ever since he has had the name of Christian Rosenkreutz. This is a mystery name, and for that reason cannot be found in any baptismal register. Initially he was brought up in a similar way to the child of the thirteenth century. His teachers were students and followers of the original twelve, but this time he was not kept away from the outside world, as he had been before.

When he turned 28 he travelled to the East. Before Damascus St. Paul's initiation experience repeated itself for him. The imperishable etheric body that had formed itself in the thirteenth century penetrated him again in this incarnation, as it has in all subsequent embodiments that have taken place every century since then. Because of this, the etheric body, which can also inspire and even penetrate other people, grows in lustre and power.

After he had for seven years absorbed all the wisdom of that time on his travels in the East and West, he returned to middle Europe and took the most developed students and followers of the twelve as his brothers and disciples. Thus began the work of the Rosicrucians.

It is of course difficult for the materialistic feeling and thinking of modern human beings to find what was described here credible, and it is understandable that virtually nothing of this ever became known outside a small circle of initiated followers. In the *Fama Fraternitatis* by Johann Valentin Andreae (1616) something was written about the biography of Brother Christian Rosenkreutz in the fifteenth century. But to non-initiates the deep esoteric backgrounds of the Rosicrucian movement only became accessible by the work of Rudolf Steiner.

A most important addition to what was described above—which was derived from Rudolf Steiner's lectures in Neuchâtel in 1911[110]—are the notes Steiner gave to the French author Edouard Schuré in Barr, Alsace in 1907.[111] These say, among other things:

> ... the initiation of Mani, who also initiated Christian Rosenkreutz in 1459, is considered to be of a 'higher degree;' it consists of the true understanding of the nature of evil. This initiation and all that it entails will have to remain completely hidden from the majority for a long time to come.

This shows that the esoteric stream of Mani, which was mentioned earlier in this book, also had a connection with the Rosicrucians.

3. Esotericism and World History

The notes mentioned above also contain the following:

> In the early part of the fifteenth century Christian Rosenkreutz went to the East to find a balance between the initiations of the East and West. One consequence of this, following on his return, was the *definitive* establishment of the Rosicrucian stream in the West. In this form Rosicrucianism was intended to be a strictly secret school for the preparation of those things which would become the public task of esotericism at the turn of the 19th century, when material science would have found a provisional solution to certain problems.

These problems were described by Christian Rosenkreutz as:

1. The discovery of spectral analysis, which revealed the material constitution of the cosmos.

2. The introduction of material evolution in organic science.
3. The recognition of a differing state of consciousness from our normal one through the acceptance of hypnotism and suggestion.

Only when *this* material knowledge had reached fruition in science were certain Rosicrucian principles from esoteric science to be made public property.[112]

In connection with this we have to give our attention to a number of extremely important matters.

We may regard Christian Rosenkreutz as the high and mysterious 'Christ Knight' who works as the hidden spiritual leader of our time. His stream has the cross with the roses as its holy symbol, which means that the Christian human being has to direct his gaze from the crucifix onto the black cross with the seven roses, in other words, that from death he has to go to life. But this 'going to life' means going through sacrificial death in order to come to the life of resurrection.

Rosicrucianism is based on the connection of the spirit of the East with the spirit of the West. This brings to expression that this stream is the metamorphosed Grail stream (and Temple stream). Everything that drives East and West apart, everything that works in a polarizing manner between East and West, works in opposition to the Rosicrucian principle. With this I also mean that people who assert that 'spirit' can only be found in the East, and that it is needed to 'save' the West, go against the principle of Rosicrucianism just as much as those who say that spirit, especially oriental spirit, is superstition, and that what matters is the superiority of the materialistically and practically thinking West.

The stream of Rosicrucianism had to remain secret until the transition of the nineteenth to the twentieth century. Why was this needed? In the course of the five hundred years between the fifteenth and the twentieth century our epoch had to be thoroughly confronted with the materiality of the world. This must not be prevented by any occult influence, because the *freedom* of the human being depends on it. The leadership of Christian Rosenkreutz consisted in the fact that he fully accepted the evil that is irrevocably called into being together with materialism and human freedom—and with this, his own martyrdom in *Imitatio Christi*.

During his five hundred year hidden activity he has emanated a continuous esoteric stream of inspiration in world history leading, on the one hand, to progressive ideas in external culture, which has become more and more alienated from the spirit and, on the other hand, to the development of truly healing counterforces.

Because of Rudolf Steiner's spiritual research we are able to gain an impression of this hidden work. It is only with the greatest respect, but also in astonishment that we can see in what forms and manners, and through which individuals and movements, the inspiration of Christian Rosenkreutz manifests itself. It is also evident that Rosicrucianism, as it is brought by the great initiated leader of our age, cannot be judged according to one definable standard. In each century the inspiration differs because it has to be adapted to the moment in history, to the ever-changing reigning conditions.

The stream of esoteric Christianity can never move in one fixed channel, it can never be represented by one religious confession; it is much too all-encompassing. This is the reason why it is so difficult for a church-oriented person to develop a relationship to it. Such people are usually, without knowing it, so dogmatically influenced that they see no Christianity where it is most present without the need to be openly acknowledged or confessed.

Another problem in evaluating Rosicrucianism is the fact that there is a virtually inextricable confusion of true and false Rosicrucianism. Especially in the eighteenth century there were Rosicrucian associations, Freemasonry Lodges of different kinds, alchemists and adepts, secret societies and circles, which not only fought each other tooth and nail, but also in many cases had little or nothing to do with the true intentions of Christian Rosenkreutz. And yet, in his eighteenth century incarnation as the Count of Saint Germain—also a highly controversial figure—he exercised an influence on such groups.

How can we understand this influence, since it took different forms from century to century?

In the first place we have to think of *alchemy*. Medieval alchemy was a Christianized continuation of the mystery wisdom of antiquity. It was a path of initiation that formed a contrast with the path of *mysticism*. Admittedly, the old alchemists could no longer directly penetrate to the higher spiritual beings who work in the stars ('intelligences' they were called), as ancient initiates were able to do. But their connections with the nature spirits (the beings of the elements of fire, air, water and earth), which they came to know in natural processes and which still spoke to them of cosmic secrets, not only gave them profound knowledge of the human being and nature, which enabled them to help humanity as *healers*; but through this they also prepared a *science of nature* that had to be developed in modern times. In alchemy was present a knowledge of nature, or rather, a wisdom of nature that created a direct relationship between the sensory, material processes the alchemist brought about in his laboratory and the moral, inward processes in the human being. Nature and spirit had not yet parted ways.

We have the impression that the initiation that Christian Rosenkreutz experienced at an advanced age in 1459, which is described in *The Chymical Wedding of Christian Rosenkreutz* (the German original of which was published in 1616), and which Rudolf Steiner connects with Mani and the mystery of evil, had to do with the riddle of matter as the bearer of evil. However, the 'alchemical wedding' also has a connection with the social question. I will return to this later.

The original brotherhood of the Rose Cross, founded after the return of the initiated master in the fifteenth century, consisted of a small group of alchemists. Through these individuals and their successors Christian Rosenkreutz had a direct, inspiring influence on the development of true alchemy as a Christian path of schooling. This lasted from the fifteenth to the eighteenth century; after that, alchemy lost its significance. Something else had to take its place.

Another aspect of the Rosicrucian inspiration, often connected with the first-mentioned one, was its influence on more or less *secret* brotherhoods. The Freemasons' Lodges are of course the best known. In Chapter 3 it was already pointed out that the Temple legend, which plays such an essential role in these Lodges, came from Christian Rosenkreutz. But there were also completely secret brotherhoods that sent their initiated 'missionaries' among the people. These often appeared as unknown, mostly unassuming persons who did not in dress, language or manners distinguish themselves from the people around them. A single word, a brief conversation with the person they had chosen for their inspiration sufficed. The person who was thus approached was often hardly aware of the significance such an encounter had for him and for the world, but in such a way ideas, insights and impulses had their influence in history. The best known and most honoured thinkers and authors took up the core of their spiritual work from such inconspicuous meetings. This was the case with Voltaire, Rousseau, Lessing, and others.[113]

Great artists also received important impulses for their work from such unknown people. It was the master himself, or one of his brother-adepts, who inspired Hieronymus Bosch to his remarkable works that are so rich in esotericism.[114] Rembrandt van Rijn was visited by a man who taught him the secret of light and darkness. Rembrandt painted him as the *Polish Rider* (Frick Gallery, New York) and as the *Knight with shield and lance* (Kelvingrove Museum, Glasgow). It was Christian Rosenkreutz in his Dutch incarnation in the seventeenth century.

Whether William Shakespeare had a personal encounter with Christian Rosenkreutz is not known. However, his work is steeped in Rosicrucian wisdom, and Rudolf Steiner mentioned the great English poet as someone who received the inspiration of the master.[115] He also mentioned Jacob Böhme, the shoemaker-philosopher, whose mystical works had an incredibly deep influence in central Europe. Remarkably, Francis Bacon of Verulam also took in Rosicrucian inspiration, but he turned it into its opposite.[116] 'Baconianism' became the principal pillar of modern materialistic science, one could say, the arch-enemy of esoteric Christianity.

But that qualification would not correspond with the Rosicrucian impulse, according to which the adversarial forces also need to be part of the progress of evolution. The higher principle that works in this impulse, the Manichaean principle, teaches the redemption of evil by entering into a certain relationship with it. Additional known and lesser known historical figures could be mentioned who came to their most important thoughts or deeds, directly or indirectly, under the influence of Rosicrucianism, but in all of them the occult influence they received, consciously or unconsciously, in no way diminishes their own greatness. The forms in which they cast the inspirations that came to them were always realized through their own talents and capacities. They did not sleep through the gifts the spiritual world bestowed on them, but put themselves in service to that world.

In order to fully comprehend the scope of the hidden work of Christian Rosenkreutz, however, we should not only consider what happens on earth, but also in cosmic worlds. In one of his lectures given in Neuchâtel, referred to above,[117] Rudolf Steiner says that the development of natural science, specifically Copernicus' view of our solar system, made it necessary for Christian Rosenkreutz to take a contrary position to this in an occult sense. The Copernican system, no matter how useful for a materialistic view of the world, is insufficient for a true comprehension of reality, because the very concepts on which the theory stands are illusory.

In order to determine the position of Christian occultism regarding this new world view, Christian Rosenkreutz called a meeting at the end of the sixteenth century, in which the great spiritual leaders of humanity could deliberate together, whether or not they were incarnated on earth at the time. One of these spiritual leaders was Gautama Buddha who, although no longer embodied in an earthly incarnation, continued his lofty mission in service of humanity in non-physical form. He had worked in this way in the Christian mystery place on the Black Sea, where his most important disciple had been the later Francis of Assisi.

In his meeting with the initiated masters, Christian Rosenkreutz pointed to the great danger that in the future humanity might develop into two groups that would be unable to have any contact or mutual understanding of each other. On the one hand, there would be those who would through materialistic thinking and ingenuity control the earthly world in an outer sense and submerge themselves in practical life, but entertain completely illusory thoughts regarding the spiritual reality of the world. Facing these would be people who would lead a spiritual life in their own inner world like St. Francis, but would no longer have a connection with the practical aspects of earthly existence. On earth there would exist no way of preventing the development of these two groups, because people would bring the tendency to think like Copernicus already with them from life before birth.

Between death in the previous, and birth in the subsequent incarnation, the human soul goes through the spiritual spheres of the planets and absorbs important forces and impulses from them. Since the beginning of the sixteenth century forces reigned in the sphere of the planet Mars—emanating from spiritual beings of course—that in its passage through this sphere the human soul was impregnated, as it were, with vehement luciferic impulses that led to illusory ideas about the cosmos.

In the Mars sphere, from which human beings absorbed very positive forces in prior times, a demonization had set in, which was comparable to the condition of the earth shortly before the Mystery of Golgotha. To reverse this degeneration in the sphere of Mars, a similar deed would have to take place as was accomplished by Christ in the physical sphere of the earth. In the circle of leaders of humanity Christian Rosenkreutz now announced that the spiritual being who had worked as Buddha on earth would move his activity to the planet Mars.

The Buddha being was thus sent to Mars by Christian Rosenkreutz, and there he performed a sacrificial deed comparable to the death of Christ on earth. This occurred in 1604. In this way the great teacher of compassion and peace brought his blissful influence into the sphere of unbridled aggressiveness, fighting, and demonic war, in order that in their passage through the Mars sphere between death and rebirth, human souls can take in positive forces again from this cosmic area.

The result of this was that the fatal split between two groups of human souls on earth was counteracted. What would have led to a one-sided group of Buddhist-Franciscan monk souls on earth, has from the early seventeenth century on been absorbed as a healing, anti-materialistic force by all human beings in their pre-birth existence. The materialistic impulses that were unleashed by the negative Mars effects were of course not fully eliminated by Buddha's sacrificial deed, but a certain condition of balance was created.

These deeds by Christian Rosenkreutz and Buddha, which were of such salutary importance for the cosmos and the earth, took place in service of the highest leader of mankind, Christ, in the continuing stream of His revelations. It is therefore not surprising that in the beginning of the seventeenth century an opening was made on earth to allow an esoteric element to flow into world history. The publication of a number of Rosicrucian writings in Germany, and the foundation of Rosicrucian societies in several European countries, may just have been preparations that, in certain respects, were of a hybrid character, but their unprecedentedly positive effects, as well as the fierce resistance and repression they evoked, indicate that it was not a 'trial balloon', but a serious attempt to integrate the Rosicrucian principle into European culture.

Only a few years apart, the writings of Johann Valentin Andreae appeared in Germany, of which the most important are *The Chymical Wedding of Christian Rosenkreutz* (1616), the *Fama Fraternitatis* (1614), and the *Confessio Fraternitatis* (1614). Remarkably, Andreae who, in view of the content of these works, certainly stood under the direct inspiration of Christian Rosenkreutz, denied at a later age what must surely have been a serious matter to him as a young man.

However, the movement that came into being all over Europe out of Andreae's writings had great attraction for the enlightened spirits of the time, such as philosophers, artist, poets and natural researchers. Although the 'secret league of brothers' who strove for a great reformation of spiritual and political life, of which the *Fama* and the *Confessio* spoke, was never discovered by those who assiduously tried to find these wise men, the influence of the Rosicrucian principles was great, especially in Protestant countries. What were these principles?

First of all, to foster a science of nature that was not detached from the spirit. Also, to take up battle against 'Rome' and 'Mohammed', in other words, to oppose the one-sided, authoritarian principle of the Roman Church, as well as the Arabic influence in science. Directly connected with this: to oppose the so-called double truth—one of the most important points. In scholasticism, the nominalists (Roger Bacon and others) had developed the position that there exist truths of faith and truths of philosophy and science, and that the two could contradict each other. They had accepted the fact that faith and intellect each went their separate ways. The Rosicrucians wanted to eliminate this fatal gap in the search for truth, or rather, wanted to bridge the gap.

Finally, they strove for the reformation of social-political life that was already mentioned before. What this reformation was to consist of may have been clear only to the truly initiated brothers, but we may safely presume that the ideas that were later, in the eighteenth century, the germinal forces of the great revolution, were prepared in the seventeenth century in many brotherhoods, societies, Lodges and leagues that were in one way or another connected with the Rosicrucian inspiration.

Of course, all of this evoked strong reactionary forces. These expressed themselves in part in the form of direct opposition, in part through lack of understanding, tendencies toward outer expressions, illusionism, and all kinds of inner and outer confusion. In Germany the movement succumbed in the Thirty Years War (1618-1648). In England Francis Bacon changed the inspiration into its opposite, and Cromwell banished every form of esoteric Christianity. In Holland the movement ran aground on the narrow-mindedness of the Calvinist preachers and the materialism of the scholars in the new university of Leiden. The Counter-Reformation, which the Church of Rome had launched with great determination, turned sharply against the Rosicrucians, and the Jesuits played the most important role in this.

In the foreground of the theatre of world history many things were happening: wars on land and at sea, peace treaties, successions to thrones, revolutions, conquests of gigantic territories, progress in science and technology, flourishing culture in cities and in courts and salons, slow decline of feudal conditions, and the rise of mature burghers as the carriers of the new natural-scientific and economic tendency—but behind these phenomena, which a historian can recognize as symptoms of a deeper reality, the spiritual leadership of the current age was both concealed and revealed.

Christian Rosenkreutz shed his anonymity in the eighteenth century and worked as the Count of St. Germain in the turbulent world of the European culture. It is extremely difficult to get a clear picture of this enigmatic figure, who probably also worked under different names. And to make things even more confusing, his name, *Comte de St. Germain*, was also appropriated by charlatans and impostors.

In a certain respect, he was the preparer of the great social and political revolution that took place at the end of the century. On the other hand however, he did all he could by his personal influence with the kings and rulers of the European countries to guide this revolution on a gradual and non-violent path. He was not successful. The revolution happened like a volcanic eruption of emotion and violence. The great ideals of liberty, equality and fraternity were heard, but not understood.

4. Liberty, Equality and Fraternity

For a historian who bases himself only on external documents to try and form a picture of how the French Revolution arose, it is impossible to indicate where and when the great threefold ideal for humanity of liberty, equality and fraternity was first pronounced. The only thing certain in this regard is that prominent Freemasons do not hesitate to credit Freemasonry with them. When we know the role that Freemasons' Lodges played in the preparation of the great revolution of 1789, we need have no doubt as to the veracity of this assertion. The only remaining question is whether the three ideals were comprehended in their deeper spiritual significance within the circles of the Lodges, or had even then become an outer phrase and were no longer understood in the right way.

One thing is certain, from the moment the three ideals began to make history, they had already become phantom-like illusions that set off the most terrible negative effects. On the one hand, in the name of liberty, equality and fraternity unbridled passions and emotions were called forth that led to a bloody Terror; on the other hand, these concepts were seized by a dead, abstract kind of thinking that degraded them into a mere slogan.

And yet, this triad of ideals which, in its threefoldness, is related to the very essence of the human being, continues to bear in it the most important impulses for the future. When we go into this more deeply it will prove to be a central motif of our subject of the *Temple and the Grail*. I am referring here to the book by Karl Heyer mentioned in the previous section.

At first sight, the three ideals seem to contradict each other. Freedom appears to eliminate equality, and it can also conflict with brotherhood. But brotherhood is in a certain regard compatible with equality. We might think of the disposition that was present among the first Christians in their original congregations, or of the ideals of socialist communes. The combination of brotherhood and equality could quite justifiably be called love. Then, however, it right away becomes clear that the third ideal, freedom, does not contradict the other two at all, but is even a prerequisite for them. Love is only given in freedom, at any rate when a spiritual activity of the human being is meant, and not an instinctive inclination out of passion. And the reverse is also true: freedom cannot exist without love when it wants to bring about fruitful effects in human society.

Therefore, although freedom and love (with its components of equality and brotherhood) essentially belong together, we can observe two streams in cultural history, a freedom stream and a love stream, which have a polar relationship to each other.

In order to get a good picture of the freedom stream it is necessary to realize what freedom really is. Freedom is in the first instance not experienced by human beings in their deeds, but in their thinking. A free deed only comes into being when we let a free insight become the motive for the will. Insight is the result of a cognition process, also when it has an intuitive character. The Tree of Knowledge stands at the origin of the freedom stream. All striving for wisdom, knowledge and insight was originally a gift from Lucifer. Luciferic spirits who, in a very ancient period of the development of the earth, began to exert influence on humanity, were the instigators of the will to be independent, free. In itself this was not evil, but it created the potential of evil.

Viewed positively, the luciferic freedom stream was the stream of wisdom and knowledge. Kings were the bearers of this stream. They wore crowns on their heads, that were the expression of the striving for insight through thinking. One may therefore also call this stream the royal stream of humanity. We might consider as its most important representative in pre-Christian times the founder of the Persian mystery religion, Zarathustra. He came indeed from a royal family, and we imagine that he was a mighty royal figure, a wise teacher of mankind, whose knowledge of heavenly and earthly things had made him free. His teaching was not only about good and evil, but we can view all wisdom that can be found in the Avesta (the holy book of the Zoroastrians) as a revelation of the spirit of truth, the Holy Spirit, which in Iranian is called *Spenta Mainyu*. This is the Spirit who makes *free* ('and the truth shall make you free'—John.8:32).

The other stream points to the paradisial origin of the human being, where the forces of the Tree of Life still work in their fullness. The human being is there still embedded in divine light and warmth like a slumbering child. On earth this becomes the mood of loving care, mercy and compassion of the shepherd-like person. We find the highest pre-Christian representative of this stream in Gautama Buddha. Here we do not witness a striving for truth that creates freedom, but for finding a way back to the pure, paradisial existence of brotherliness and equality. The people who belong to this shepherd-like stream are not the bold thinkers. Rather, they will be simple people who experience enlightenment *in their hearts* as warm compassion and solidarity with the creatures of the earth.

In the stories about the birth of Jesus according to Matthew and Luke we find the two streams represented. The freedom stream lives in the royal child of the line of David's son Solomon, to whom the Wise Men from the East come with their gifts; and the love stream lives in the child from the Nathan line of descent, who is worshipped by the simple shepherds when they had heard the message of the angels in the fields outside Bethlehem.

As was mentioned in Chapter 2, Anthroposophy points out the most interesting fact that in the revelation of the angels in the *Gloria in excelsis Deo*, the *nirmanakaya*, i.e. the spiritual being of the Buddha, was working. Out of the being of Buddha streamed the proclamation of 'peace on earth to all people of good will'—peace on earth when people make their equality before God and their brotherliness as creatures on the physical earth into a practical ideal.

In Jesus of Nazareth the two streams are connected by the amalgamation of the royal I of the Solomon boy with the soul and body of the Nathan boy, who is filled with the Buddha spirit. One might say: *Jesus is the Grail Being in whom liberty, equality and fraternity are united.* But it is only through the indwelling of Christ that this union becomes a creative principle for the future.

In another connection we have also seen that pre-Christian streams, which achieve their completion in the Christ mystery, nevertheless continue in metamorphosed forms after Christ's appearance on earth. But the fundamental connection made by Christ, through which all that has gone separate ways can come together again on a higher level, still has to be brought to realization in a long developmental process by humanity.

We see the contrast between the freedom stream and the stream of love very clearly in the two great monastic orders of the Dominicans and Franciscans in the Middle Ages. The relationship between St. Francis and Buddha has already been mentioned; we are all familiar with the impulse of brotherhood and equality that was put in practice by Francis and his monks, and which has had an immensely profound effect in the world.

When we think of the Dominicans as representatives of the freedom stream, it looks as if we might embarrass ourselves because of the

Inquisition, which was a Dominican affair, and of which it is hard to maintain that it had anything to do with freedom. Yet, an historical symptom like the Inquisition belongs as paradoxical phenomenon to the striving for freedom. The manner in which this striving was handled was of course extremely problematic. The fact that evil can deeply infiltrate the freedom stream is understandable because of the origin of this stream. The wonderful picture of the *Grand Inquisitor* in Dostoyevsky's novel *The Brothers Karamazov* speaks eloquently about this problem. The Inquisitor tells Christ that He wrongly gave freedom to humanity. Human beings cannot bear freedom; for that reason, the Church of Rome takes this freedom away from people. Only the Inquisitors have the painful freedom of those who know, and they use it to give to the people what they consider to be a salutary unfreedom!

From the same Dominican Order, however, also came the highest and most noble forms of striving for 'the truth that makes free', particularly in the works of Thomas Aquinas and Albertus Magnus.

In modern times the 'royal' freedom stream was metamorphosed into the stream of astronomical-mathematical science. That this sharp, abstract thinking in modern times has been the most important factor leading to the emancipation of the free personality needs no argument. And we find the 'shepherd' stream in the loving observers of nature, of which Goethe and Haeckel are impressive examples.

In the previous section it was pointed out that the astronomical-mathematical way of thinking that made its entry into world history with Copernicus, had its cosmic origin in a luciferic deterioration of the Mars sphere. It was described that the great leader of humanity, Christian Rosenkreutz, was facing the necessity of countering a danger that threatened to split humanity into two groups. One group would consist of Buddhist-Franciscan monk souls without any relationship with earthly practical life; the other of earthly oriented people who would, however, have a totally luciferic-illusory picture of the world, the Copernican-Newtonian world view. One could also say: a split was threatening to develop between a freedom stream that would become ever more entrapped in illusory-materialistic one-sidedness, and a stream of love that would lose all relationship with earthly-material reality. A definitive separation, therefore, of two streams into irreconcilable extremes which, ultimately, would no longer comprise either freedom or love.

The response of the spiritual guidance of mankind to this danger was the sacrificial deed of Buddha in the Mars sphere. This opened the possibility on earth to launch the three concepts of liberty, equality and fraternity as social ideals in their inherent threefoldness. There can be no doubt that Christian Rosenkreutz, as Count of St. Germain, let this social triad stream into Europe at a time when the old feudalism and absolutism was dying and a new order needed to be born. Only, he was not able to prevent that even in the most enlightened individuals of the pre-revolutionary period these ideals were corrupted by the already all-powerful materialism in human souls.

Equality, fraternity, liberty—what do these words mean, considered not historically, but from the point of view of human nature? Equality cannot refer to the physical bodies of people; those are not equal. In the physical world equality would mean uniformity, but that is exactly the realm where we see endless variation.

Are human souls equal to each other? On the contrary, the differences between souls are even greater than between bodies. Equality can only signify—at least, as regards the individual human being—equality before God. Our human spirit, our I, is still so young, so much the baby among the other parts of our being, which came into existence in prior cosmic phases, that we can say: just as equality strikes us in very small children, who all still have something angelic, our I-spirits are all equal before God. Equality applies to the spirit. When in our individual soul we penetrate to insight, to truth, we bear this in us as a spiritual property that is the same for all people. Through our I-spirit the individual becomes universally human. Because of that we can understand each other as human beings. The spirit is the leveller in a higher sense; it connects the human being with humanity.

Fraternity has to refer to our physical existence. As we have to live as physical creatures on a physical earth, have to feed and clothe ourselves, have to find shelter and work, fraternity is required. Without fraternity, brotherliness, wellbeing on earth is impossible.

Liberty, however, cannot be true for physical bodies; it belongs to the soul. Where the forces of a higher spiritual world and a lower earthly world have to be kept in balance, freedom unfolds in the soul. There the true creative powers of the human being are living. Freedom is creativity; creativity is freedom. Freedom as a socially active power can rest only on interest in the other soul, which also experiences its own freedom.

Every time the ideal of freedom begins to work without profound interest, love for our fellow human being, it brings disaster. In our time we witness this in countless movements of emancipation and freedom. When the slaves in the colonies and the serfs in Russia were liberated without any real interest in these individuals, but exclusively out of an abstract idea of freedom, insoluble problems developed. 'Liberation of people of colour' as a political slogan without real love for these fellow human beings has increased racial hatred rather than diminished it.

In the eighteenth century the enlightened spirits who prepared the French Revolution had already lost sight of the differences between freedom for the soul, equality for the spirit, and brotherliness for the body. They were no longer aware of the human being in his threefold-ness of body, soul and spirit, because the spirit had been abolished by the Church in 869. When one applies all of the three concepts to the physical body, which happened more or less unconsciously because of the general materialistic orientation, the three ideals are turned into distorted caricatures.

In social life people made the mistake of wanting to place the three ideals equally in the form of government. In lieu of replacing the unitary state, which had become a monster under absolute rulers, by a threefold constitution in which the three ideals could work like the three elements of body, soul and spirit in the human being—to some extent autonomously, but harmoniously interwoven—the effort was made to organize the state as a republic with the three ideals as leading principles. In 1791 *liberté, égalité, fraternité* was proposed as the revolutionary platform. During the Reign of Terror of 1792 one added: *ou la mort*: liberty, equality, fraternity or death!

But in 1791 Duport had already prophesied that freedom would rest on the egoistic individuality, and equality on a continuing process of downward levelling. Later, in the nineteenth century, the caricature of brotherhood was added to this in the form of the Communism of Marx and Engels, the class war due to the exclusive brotherhood of the working class. Once again the powers of evil triumphed that want to keep humanity from building the invisible Temple.

The attack on the Grail impulse of the Templars had a twofold result. On the one hand, the sacrifice of the tortured and executed knights could be brought into the stream of spiritual development as inspirations in the souls of human beings who wanted to serve the continuing Christianization of humanity. On the other hand, humanity had to fall more deeply into materialism because due to the torture, which had caused the knights to make untrue confessions, Ahriman had succeeded in channelling an ongoing stream of *untruth* into the culture.

It always looks as if the countermeasures of the good powers don't have enough effect. But it is just as with a good therapy: the sick person himself has to want to be healed, and even then the remedy often only works in the long run.

Buddha's deed in the Mars sphere was a healing deed. Buddha's being is connected with the sphere of the planet Mercury, from which emanate 'softening' cosmic influences, as opposed to the 'hardening' tendencies of the planet Mars. Christian Rosenkreutz and Gautama Buddha work on the transformation of Mars impulses into Mercury impulses; this is the esoteric Christian task for the present and future.

The French Revolution could have had a softening effect for Europe and humanity in general, if the ideals of liberty, equality and fraternity had been comprehended and applied in the right manner. This did not happen. And the consequence was an extreme martial impulse: Napoleon and the unitary state continued to the extreme. Disappointed idealists learned to abhor the slogan of 1791. In subsequent revolutions, both in France and elsewhere, the social-political impulses of Christian Rosenkreutz were less and less recognizable.

In the same years when in France the great revolution was prepared and erupted, in central Europe another revolutionary development took place which, despite its completely peaceful nature, was no less spectacular and influential than what was happening in France. In Lessing, Herder, Goethe, Schiller and Novalis, in Hegel, Fichte and Schelling and in many others, which certainly also include the great classical composers, we find not only germs, but also ripe fruits of a renewed Christian culture that is carried by the spirit. These great thinkers and researchers of nature, poets and artists show unmistakable traces of direct or indirect Rosicrucian inspirations.

This is most clearly the case in Goethe's unfinished poem *Die Geheimnisse* (*The Mysteries*), in his *Fairytale of the Green Snake and the Beautiful Lily*, in his *Faust*, and in several other works.

But this too was overwhelmed by the materialism of the nineteenth century. The works of these and many other authors and artists were either completely forgotten or raised up as a kind of monument, as a result of which they remained unproductive for the future. The great composers got off mostly unscathed thanks to Romanticism, because the Romantics who often fought materialism or tried to escape it, kept the music of their great predecessors in high honour, and therefore alive.

Did the impulse of Temple and Grail completely succumb to the rise of nineteenth century materialism that became all-powerful after 1840? It looks that way, but backstage behind world events, behind the ever less spiritual culture, behind the much-vaunted 'progress', a gigantic battle took place between the powers of light and those of darkness.

The spiritual guidance of humanity does not work as the instrument of God's omnipotence. The leading Masters have to respect the freedom of the human being, they have to work within given circumstances; they have to open possibilities that human beings must then recognize and try to make use of. Most of all, they have to wait patiently for a critical moment when humanity becomes responsive to an inspiration or impulse.

In the following section we will highlight efforts that were made in the nineteenth century to bring spiritual influences into the culture. However, the full strength of a renewed Grail impulse could only become effective when a certain hour had sounded in the world. This was at the transition from the nineteenth to the twentieth century.

5. The Task of the Middle

In the course of the nineteenth century we can begin to see the contours of the age-old contrast between East and West developing in such a way that 'in the shadows of yesterday' the crystal clear problems of today can already be distinguished. Even though during this entire century the history of humanity is in fact still made in Europe, we witness to the West of it, across the Atlantic Ocean, the American continent rising up with its unlimited potential oriented on the future, while to the East ancient mother Asia begins to stir in a new way, reviving forces from the past.

It is clear that the European West with its 'American annex'—in the twentieth century the roles are reversed—obtains its world power both by its faultless handling of natural science and technology and by its command of the economy. And of course, the power of capital adds to this. Out of this position of power, which rests on the principle of usefulness and economic instincts, through which humanity on earth is promised progress, prosperity and happiness, the rest of the world is manipulated and, if at all possible, exploited with an inexorable and implacable business mentality that will not shrink from ruining entire countries and peoples.

As an example of this, just take a look at the Opium Wars (1839-1842 and 1856-1860). These wars were waged by Britain, later supported by France, against the Chinese Empire in order to break the ports of that country open for the highly profitable opium trade. The Chinese government wanted to block the opium import for the protection of the people, but the British and French won out. The ports were opened for western traders, and the insidious opium poison could begin its work among the millions of Chinese people. A century later the West was facing the consequences in the form of drug addictions that ruined millions of Western people.

Of course, the dark aspect of Western world power is but one side of the picture. In a positive sense, one could point to the great advantages that were brought to all of mankind in the form of the progress in science and technology. The expansion in the means of travel and communication, for instance, has given all people a much stronger awareness of the planet as a whole than ever before. Freedom and personal maturity of the individual are positive factors offsetting the negatives of loss of religious feeling, reverence and spirituality. And let me just keep silent about atom bombs and dying forests.

In the East, it seems as if in the nineteenth century the age-old wisdom of the subcontinent of India was waking up in a certain sense. Several great teachers appeared who heralded a renewal of Hindu culture, which was also a signal of a political independence movement against the British rulers. This struggle was crowned with success in 1947 with the declaration of India's independence by the Labour government of Clement Attlee—according to Winston Churchill 'the most un-English deed ever committed by an Englishman'.

Up to that time, yoga, Buddhism and a few other streams from the East had some little influence in Europe and America, but the great invasion of guru wisdom only started gaining traction in the second half of the twentieth century. Interestingly, many of these oriental movements did and do not shirk from using outright Western capitalist financial dealings and methods.

In other areas of Asia the emancipation seemed to take place purely in the field of politics, for example in China and Vietnam, but it only looks that way. The political ideas of Communism became a new *religion*. The same thing happened in Soviet Russia. A system that was imported from the West, that certainly does not belie its Western-materialistic character, and promulgates a view of life completely from an economic vantage point, became a state religion in the hands of oriental despots, steeped in a kind of sacramentalism that equals, or even exceeds, other forms of this kind.

Thus in broad outline, the West (Europe and America) developed a culture of the *body*, oriented toward outer prosperity, outer wellbeing, bereft of spirituality and true religious consciousness. What still exists in the way of a puritanical spirit in the American West turned into a culture-mummy a long time ago, and now it is more and more falling apart under the attacks of unbridled passion. We witness here the 'curse of gold', the greed and egotism that much of the time become the driving forces behind people's actions. Freedom and equality (democracy) are greatly praised, but not out of an idealistic view of society—for idealism is ideology and therefore impractical—but for their usefulness. After all, it is easier for a free citizen in a democratic state to do business than for a subject of a totalitarian system.

In such a general characterization we don't do justice to single individuals whose life and strivings may of course deviate considerably from the general picture. Similarly, the more deeply hidden spiritual forces of the American West are neglected.

The Orient, which strongly begins to resist the West, preserves a culture of the *spirit*, but it is an old, and therefore no longer living spirituality (India). In very large areas of Asia, atheistic Marxism has become the state religion. Islam also keeps millions of souls shackled by its simplistic, lofty content and strict sacramental forms. For the oriental human being, fraternity, brotherliness, is a primary factor in life, as is a capacity to accept suffering that is incomprehensible to Western souls. The physical existence of an individual soul does not seem to count.

In Japan we find a remarkable variant of oriental culture. The Japanese have perfectly imitated and often improved on Western technology, but despite their high level of industrialization and technical expertise they have remained true to their age-old spirituality, full of mystery and wisdom.

In this way East and West face each other in virtually irreconcilable opposition, which reveals itself with exceptional vehemence in the conflict around the State of Israel. One wonders whether there is not a middle that can reconcile the inimical brothers and sisters of East and West. The famous phrase of Rudyard Kipling, 'East is East and West is West, and never the twain shall meet,' is usually quoted incomplete and therefore distorted into its opposite.[118] Kipling felt that the encounter of the two is absolutely possible if certain conditions are met. This potential to meet could be viewed as the task of the middle.

And indeed, in the transition from the eighteenth to the nineteenth century, central Europe developed a culture that could have made a bridge between the one-sided tendencies that began to show in East and West. Over against the West a science of nature had to come into existence that was not materialistic and utilitarian; a science that could recognize the spirit in nature by a fundamentally different attitude regarding reality than that adopted by Western humanity.

Goethe especially was the one who inaugurated and developed this kind of science of nature. He was inspired by Christian Rosenkreutz.[119] If natural science had developed following Goethe's findings and ideas, technology would probably have adopted a different form than it has. One might suspect that a connection would have arisen between art and technology, because of which forces in technology that now have an enslaving effect on the human being could have been neutralized.

We should not be surprised that in Rudolf Steiner's work we find statements that clearly indicate that Goethe was also inspired out of the spiritual world by the Templars who were executed early in the fourteenth century.[120] Regarding his unfinished poem *Die Geheimnisse* (*The Mysteries*), in which the symbol of the cross with roses appears, Goethe himself said that he had wanted to take the reader through a kind of ideal Montserrat. With that he meant a *Grail experience*. The connection of the twelve world religions or world views, represented by twelve individuals standing around a thirteenth named *Humanus*, in order jointly to prepare the future, was Goethe's high human ideal. And we also find the picture of the bridge in his Fairytale, where the green snake sacrifices itself in order to permanently unite the spirit realm of the Lily and the realm of earthly reality.

To face the East something more was required to build the bridge of the middle. In Friedrich Schiller's *Letters upon the Aesthetic Education of Man* we find a more philosophically formulated reconciliation of the polar forces that Schiller discovered both in culture in general and in the human being himself, namely a bond with the spiritual and a bond with the earthly. Between these two works a creative power that enables the human being to be a creative being. This is the power of *freedom*, a function of the middle that not only enables the two one-sided forces to work together harmoniously, but also makes them healthy so that they are freed from the evil aspects of their one-sidedness.[121]

Western humanity needs to be delivered from its glorification of matter; Eastern humanity from its contempt of matter. Western humanity has to reconsider its contempt of spirit, and Eastern humanity has to make its glorification of spirit real, by freeing it from the power of Lucifer that chains it to the past. Freedom in the central European sense is not the pragmatic freedom in the economy, but *the creative power in the individual human soul.*

Schiller was another person who was open to the Templars' inspiration; witness his intended drama *Die Malteser.* The play was never written beyond a brief fragment of the first scene. But from his notes we know that in this play he wanted to show the deeper impulses of the Templars in a particular way.

Remarkably, not only were *Die Geheimnisse* by Goethe and *Die Malteser* by Schiller never finished, but those of their works, and of the works of contemporary kindred spirits, that were completed, never grew into an impulse of the middle in the nineteenth century. The Germans themselves were not really conscious of this, their task. They fell for the Mammon of Western materialism and left Eastern humanity, which was perhaps unconsciously asking for a renewal of its ancient spirituality, out in the cold.

We see the tragedy of central Europe in the touching history of Kaspar Hauser, an individuality who, according to spiritual insight, came to earth with a high mission, namely to make what was achieved in the time of Goethe and Schiller fruitful in a social sense. But first, unknown powers pulled him out of his task for humanity in diabolical ways, and when it was feared that he could perhaps realize his task anyway, he was murdered.

With the year of Goethe's death (1832) and that of Kaspar Hauser (1833), Germany lost the Grail impulse of the middle. One hundred years later it was even turned into its absolute opposite by the National Socialism of Adolf Hitler and his henchmen. However, we should not think that the spiritual guidance of humanity did not make efforts in the nineteenth century to let other impulses stream in to create at least a counterweight against the ever more drastic influence of materialism.

The spiritualism that arose in America from 1848 and actually had the character of a cultural stream may be regarded as such an effort. This movement did indeed cause thousands of people in America and Europe to believe in ghosts, which is of course not at all the same as insight into spiritual realities. As a counterweight against an overly aggressive materialism, spiritualism had a positive effect. However it got caught almost right away in a materialistic rut because the 'spirits' only made themselves known through material phenomena.

A second effort from occult sources were the inspirations that led to the spiritual revelations of Helena Petrovna Blavatsky, the founder of the Theosophical Society in 1875. Initially, this remarkable woman, who possessed exceptional spiritual gifts, received her inspirations from Christian Rosenkreutz.[122] Besides her gifts, however, she also had exceptional weaknesses, which caused her to become the victim of less noble occult powers from the West that succeeded in manoeuvring the

Theosophical movement into a one-sided direction. Noteworthy in this regard was the tendency toward India that became progressively stronger in Theosophy, particularly after Annie Besant succeeded H. P. Blavatsky.

We do indeed see a connection between East and West in this case, but without a true middle. The Christian element was totally lacking, as was the aesthetic element that is so characteristic for central Europe, in the sense of Schiller's use of the word.[123]

When Rudolf Steiner connected himself with the theosophical movement from a completely different viewpoint, namely that of Goethe and Schiller, he was hoping to be able to add this lacking element of the middle. His Anthroposophy did not originate in the Theosophy of Blavatsky, as is often asserted, but is a metamorphosis of the original Johannine-Christian impulse that was placed in the channel of Theosophy with its strong oriental orientation. Steiner knew that Blavatsky was originally inspired by Christian Rosenkreutz, and therefore what he did was to lead Theosophy back into its original direction by turning it to Rosicrucianism—one could also say by connecting it with Goethe. The leaders of the Theosophical Society, however, identified themselves already too much with Britain and America, and had also become politically tainted—witness their strongly anti-German statements shortly before World War I—to appreciate and follow Steiner's turn to the impulse of the middle. From 1913, Theosophy and Anthroposophy went their separate ways; the majority of the German members followed Rudolf Steiner.

Finally, in this connection we should take note of the work and especially the intentions of Richard Wagner. This composer, reviled as often as revered, tried more or less all by himself to create a new mystery culture out of the source of the middle. Initially he built on the old Germanic sagas of the *Nibelungen* and, in so doing, exposed the origin of the 'curse of gold'. But from the beginning, he also clearly pointed to the Christian motif of redemption in *The Flying Dutchman*, in *Tannhäuser* and in *Lohengrin*, culminating in his *Parsifal*.

An interesting aspect of Wagner's works is the appearance of oriental motifs. His great love and admiration of Buddhism led him to the motif of *compassion*. The motif of *reincarnation*, which connects the Ahasverus saga with Herodias-Kundry in a moving manner, probably also comes from his interest in the Orient, although it may have arisen in his soul as a spontaneous insight. He viewed the combination of drama and music as the mystery art *par excellence*, that can contribute to the redemption of the soul from the power of evil. Wagner inspired important precursors of Rudolf Steiner, such as the Frenchman Edouard Schuré and Friedrich Nietzsche before his derangement.

Between the murder of Kaspar Hauser and the rise of Adolf Hitler lies an interval of exactly 100 years. For the adversary powers time is not a factor; they are patient, efficient and mercilessly consistent. Nevertheless, between these two events lay a turning point that opened the potential of addressing the question of the middle with much more thoroughness and depth than was possible in and after Goethe's time. This turning point arose from the fact that two important developments in the evolution of humanity coincided quite closely.

The first development occurred in the year 1899 that marked the end of a five thousand-year epoch—called Kali Yuga in the Indian tradition—during which humanity had lost more and more of the old wisdom and had become estranged from the light world of the spirit. At the end of this period of darkness, materialism, the world view of darkness, had reached its apex. After 1899 it has become possible to make a renewed, modern connection with the light realm of the spirit, for which the fruit of those 5000 years of darkness, human freedom of consciousness, has to be utilized.

The door to this modern connection with the spiritual world opens when two things are accomplished on earth. First, a foundation has to be laid *within the normal day-consciousness of the human being* so that we can find the door. In philosophical terms, there has to be a basis in a theory of cognition, through which freedom in thinking can be experienced as a creative activity, which is the first form of a real relationship to the spirit realm. Second, a sufficient amount of occult wisdom has to be revealed so that human soul life can be strengthened by it, and find the courage to venture into the unknown land of the spirit. In other words, an initiation science has to come into being that will begin to work as a factor in culture. Both these things were accomplished by Rudolf Steiner, the first one by his *Philosophy of Freedom*,[124] and the second by his Anthroposophy.

The second development in human evolution has to do with the beginning of the so-called Michael Age in 1879. Occult science not only speaks of cultural epochs of 2160 years, but also distinguishes shorter historical periods of 354 years in which the seven archangels of the seven classical planets, each in turn, work as Time Spirits. Michael is the archangel of the Sun, the cosmic Christ Knight. He took up his function again in 1879, as a result of which the new light forces that have begun to work in the human soul after the end of Kali Yuga, can connect themselves in the right way with the being of Christ.

However, Michael has to respect the freedom of the human being. If people do not want to take up the new revelations that are related to Michael's working, the powers of darkness have free play. These powers have not disappeared with the end of the age of darkness. On the contrary, as human beings come closer to the threshold of the light realm, the spirits of evil will become more and more energetic in their activity, since it is their objective to derail the proper development of humanity at any price.

We should understand the task of the middle, which one can also view in the picture of the scale, as a Michaelic task, a specific task for our current epoch. This task is the culmination for today and the near future of that which in this book has been called the Grail stream. All the impulses we have considered in the previous chapters—the Johannine-Pauline stream, Platonism and Aristotelianism as esoteric Christianity, the Grail stream with its metamorphoses in the Templars and the Brotherhood of the Rose Cross, with Manichaeism in the background—all of this comes together in the mighty Michael stream of Anthroposophy with its branches in social life, art, and religion.

Rudolf Steiner indicated many times, sometimes with considerable emphasis, that it is the great mission of central Europe to create the bridge between East and West that has been mentioned before. European history in the twentieth century has made this extremely difficult. However, the need for this bridge is more urgent than ever, and subsequent social and political developments in Europe may give hope that it is becoming better understood. In addition, however, the function of the middle should now also be taken up by individuals and groups of people who, spread over the entire world, are becoming conscious of their Michaelic responsibility.

6. Michaelic Christianity

The life and work of Rudolf Steiner can be contemplated in many different ways, but every manner of looking at it only acquires meaning 'in the light of the Holy Grail', particularly against the background of the developments sketched in this book. In 1924 Steiner himself wrote in a notebook certain years that were of special importance in his life, and reading this it will strike us that he makes a direct connection between his destiny and the Council of Constantinople of 869, in which the spirit was abolished.[125] A thousand years after this Council, in 1869, we see the eight-year-old Rudolf Steiner stand before an extremely important moment in his life. The Steiner family had moved to Neudörfl, Austria, where little Rudolf went to grade school. There an assistant teacher brought him into contact with geometry, and the village priest with the astronomical world picture of Copernicus, which this worthy cleric explained to the older pupils of the village school with great enthusiasm. Little Rudolf was allowed to be there.

Geometry brought the boy, who was clairvoyant, the greatest joy because in it he discovered an area which, although lying within the normal field of human consciousness, is to be regarded as pure spirit and, as such, meant a justification of his trust in his own spiritual observations. He said the following about this in his book *The Course of My Life*:

> In my relation to geometry I must perceive the first budding forth of a conception which later gradually evolved within me. This lived within me more or less unconsciously during my childhood, and about my twentieth year took a definite and fully conscious form.
>
> I said to myself: 'The objects and occurrences which the senses perceive are in space. But, just as this space is outside man, so there exists within man a sort of soul-space which is the scene of action of spiritual beings and occurrences.' I could not look upon thoughts as something like images which the human being forms of things; on the contrary, I saw in them revelations of a spiritual world on this field of action in the soul. Geometry seemed to me to be a knowledge which appears to be produced by man, but which, nevertheless, has a significance quite independent of him. Naturally, I did not as a child say this to myself distinctly, but I felt that one must carry knowledge of the spiritual world within oneself after the manner of geometry.
>
> For the reality of the spiritual world was to me as certain as that of the physical. I felt the need, however, for a sort of justification of this assumption. I wished to be able to say to myself that the experience of the spiritual world is just as little an illusion as that of the physical world. With regard to geometry, I said to myself: 'Here one is *permitted* to know something which the mind alone through its own power experiences.' In this feeling I found the justification for speaking of the spiritual world that I experienced just as of the physical. And I spoke of it in that way.

The reality of the spirit was experienced by the young Rudolf Steiner as an objective given, while he of course also knew that this reality inwardly revealed itself on the stage of his subjective soul. He did not fall into the error of the dogma of Constantinople that described the spirit as a quality of the soul, and therefore abrogated it as an objective reality. Because of this inner victory over the 1000-year-old deceit by Ahriman— for the resolution of the Council of 869 was a result of the ahrimanic attack from Gondishapur (see section 1 of this chapter)—Steiner was able to build the bridge from the sensory to the spiritual realm.

Noteworthy is the fact that, almost at the same time as his joy about the justification of his spiritual experiences because of geometry, he had the greatest enthusiasm for the 'spiritless' Copernican vision of the world that he learned from a Catholic priest.

In 1879 he went to the technical university in Vienna to study mathematics and natural science. In the same year, through the intermediary of an herb gatherer, a most original, somewhat eccentric man full of wisdom of nature with whom he became friends, he met an initiated master whose identity he later never disclosed. At the beginning of the new Michael Age the student Steiner joined battle with the 'dragon' of materialism, but following instructions of the unknown master he did this by 'creeping into the skin of the dragon'. He did not combat materialism from the outside; he plunged into it, even to the extent that he became a fiery defender of Ernst Haeckel when Haeckel was attacked by the Church, by scientists and philosophers. All these people recoiled before the courageous writings of Haeckel. And similarly he defended the 'anti-Christian' Friedrich Nietzsche.

His systematically thought-through materialistic way of considering things led him to a *science of the spirit*. This must not be built on renunciation of the world and oriental detachment, but has to rest on the will to redeem the hardening world principle, to bring what is fossilized into movement, to awake the living from the dead. This is only possible if we take up the fossilized world picture of materialism with fiery enthusiasm, something to which Steiner was already inclined as a child; witness his reaction to the Copernican world picture.

In 1899, at the end of Kali Yuga, Rudolf Steiner was ready to give the inner battle with the power of Ahriman that had taken place in the privacy of his soul, a decisive turn to the outer world. He decided to make the occult insights he had acquired public, thus entering into open conflict with all 'established' powers that manipulate public opinion: religion, science, state and media, as well as all those people who are averse to what they themselves call fantasms, vagueness, mystical blabber.

In 1902 appeared his book *Christianity as Mystical Fact*, in which he revealed the mystery of Lazarus-John. This publication about Christianity and the mysteries of antiquity is to be considered as the point of departure of a renewed Christian-Johannine stream of revelation that can be followed throughout Steiner's entire further work. He summarized the initiation knowledge he thus placed before the floodlights of publicity with the term 'the Fifth Gospel'. He called this, side by side with the other Gospels, the Gospel of *Erkenntnis*, of knowing insight. He gave critical importance here to the revelation of the 'second coming of Christ in the etheric sphere', which was happening in the course of the twentieth century.

In 1909, Steiner wrote *An Outline of Occult Science*, the book about the evolution of humanity and the earth. In this book we find clearly expressed that this 'occult science'—the word *occult* refers to the supersensible aspect of reality—may be called *Grail science*. In the chapter 'The Present and Future of Cosmic and Human Evolution', he says about Christian initiates:

> A knowledge thus arose among these new initiates that included everything that was the subject of ancient initiation, but in the center of this knowledge there radiated the higher wisdom of the mysteries of the Christ event. ... Then the dawn of the new age broke, which is to be designated as the fifth cultural period. Its nature consists in the advance of the evolution of the intellectual faculties, which have unfolded to an exuberant blossoming and will unfold still further in the present and into the future. ... But in its place there developed what may be called an increasingly stronger influx into human souls of the knowledge gained through modern supersensible consciousness. The 'hidden knowledge' flows, although quite unnoticed at the beginning, into the mode of thinking of the men of this period. ... The 'hidden knowledge' which takes hold of mankind now and will take hold of it more and more in the future, may be called symbolically 'the wisdom of the Grail.' If this symbol, as it is given in legend and myth, is understood in its deeper meaning, we shall find that it is a magnificent image of the nature of what has been spoken of above as the knowledge of the new initiation, with the Christ mystery at its center. The modern initiates may, therefore, also be called 'initiates of the Grail.' The way into the supersensible worlds, the first stages of which have been described in this book, leads to the 'science of the Grail.' This knowledge has the peculiarity that *research* into its facts can be made only if one has acquired the necessary means that have been described in this book. If, however, such research has been made, these facts can then be understood through the soul forces developed in the fifth cultural period. ... We move now in an age in which this knowledge ought to be received more abundantly into general consciousness...

Seven years later, in 1916, Rudolf Steiner gave the great lectures about the Order of the Templars.[126] In the lecture of October 2 the theme of liberty, equality and fraternity is discussed in direct connection with the Templars and the adversarial forces that were attacking them. The years that followed were completely dedicated to the activities that were related to a movement of social renewal, the movement for *social threefolding*, that unfolded from 1917 to 1922, but which Steiner had to stop due to opposition from political and religious sides, which even led to acts of violence.

This period ended with the burning of the first Goetheanum, a building that could be considered as a modern Grail temple. It was a free school for spiritual science, but simultaneously the kind of all-encompassing work of art that Richard Wagner already aspired to, in which all arts, musical as well as visual, were united, each in a completely new style. As Goethe once famously said, in the combination of science and art religion is also included. The building burned down on New Year's Eve 1922; the fire was set by 'enemies of the Grail'.

By the destruction of the Threefold movement and the Goetheanum the impulse of the middle was seriously disabled. In the all-encompassing work of art of the building in Dornach (Switzerland), the West, on the one hand, would have had in outer, visible form a creation that bore testimony to the spirit in forms and colours that enveloped movement and word; on the other hand, in a social order that did not rest on power and spiritual unfreedom, the East would have developed an inwardly experienced trust in the white peoples which it currently regards with distrust.

It was not to be. 'But the work must go on,' said Rudolf Steiner. In the year 1923 he created the new form of the General Anthroposophical Society and the School of Spiritual Science. The Goetheanum found its resurrection in this new form, which rests on the Foundation Stone, a mantric formula that expresses in words the mystery of the threefold human being as image of the divine Trinity.

After the Christmas Conference of 1923, when this new configuration of the Anthroposophical Society was created, Rudolf Steiner only lived another 15 months. Until the end of September 1924 he unfolded a superhuman activity in lectures, courses, conversations, and new initiatives such as curative eurythmy and biodynamic agriculture and gardening.

During the last six months of his life he was bedridden and could communicate with people only in writing. His weekly letters to the members of the Society that were included in the newsletter are often called the Michael letters, because Michael is the prominent theme.[127] Rudolf Steiner's work began in Vienna in the sign of the new Time Spirit; it ended with the most profound revelations regarding the being and the task of this heavenly warrior.

In the previous section the task of the middle was discussed, and the need to recognize that between the threatening one-sidedness of both East and West a Michaelic culture of balance has to grow. However, that is only possible if humanity also develops a vertical connection, in other words, that we create a new connection with the supersensible world. This means not only a relationship with the world of the deceased, but also with the unborn—which is in essence the same world. Following the human I after death into the realm of the spirit, hoping for a continued existence and perhaps even to receive signals from the world of the dead—this was possible even during the epitome of materialism because human egoism can easily make a connection with such thoughts about an existence after death. But the idea of a pre-birth existence of the human I precludes all egoism.

For this reason, even ignoring its objective truth, this idea has a therapeutic nature. Egoism is the most deeply rooted illness of the human race. Its great therapy is the doctrine of reincarnation and karma, provided that it is not handled in a superficial and dilettantish manner. Knowledge of re-embodiment, which implies the continued existence of the individual I, as well as awareness of the laws of human destiny (karma) as taught by Steiner's Anthroposophy, shed a completely new light on the social relationships among people.

In addition, concrete points of view are needed that bring movement into society when time after time things run aground and get stuck in fixed patterns. Thinking in models and structures, and acting accordingly, should be replaced by the creation of, and living in, *processes*. Concrete points of view for a renewal of the structure of society around the end of World War I could specifically be found in the Steiner's Social Threefolding. He advocated relative independence for each of the three main elements of society, the economic life, legal-political life, and cultural life. In the modern state these are intertwined with each other in an unhealthy way in the sense that one of the three dominates the other two. In the West economic life exercises compulsion and control over politics and culture.

Steiner outlined three basic principles for the independence of the three above-mentioned realms in society. The economy needs to be regulated by associations of producers, distributors and consumers in order that the interests of all parties are taken into account; this reflects brotherhood, fraternity. The life and organization of the state, in a narrow sense, which includes contracts, agreements and all kinds of legal rules, requires the principle of equality, and the cultural life that of liberty, freedom. However, these basic principles can never be handled as 'models'; they indicate different processes that have their own particular character in each of the three social realms.

Today's conditions in central Europe are of course different from those at the end of World War I, but the conflicts that Steiner already then pointed to have only become worse. And the need for a middle has therefore grown correspondingly more acute.

Social threefolding should have been adopted by Germany and Austria in 1919 in response to Wilson's ill-fated Fourteen Points and Lenin's Bolshevism. This could have prevented World War II with its tens of millions of casualties. Given current conditions it is probably impossible to introduce threefolding in its entirety anywhere in the world. As was mentioned before, the function of the middle must be provided for all over the world, and should be put in practice wherever possible, even if partially. In this regard, I believe that the Waldorf Schools, also called Rudolf Steiner Schools, which can be found all over the world, have an important task. The first Waldorf School came out of the impulse to social renewal by threefolding.

Now, in view of the title of this section, the question may be posed of what threefolding has to do with Christianity. When we consider threefolding as the social dimension of Grail science the connection is not so hard to find. Threefolding is often viewed as the direct continuation of the impulse of the Templars, but this is probably a little too simplistic. Certain aspects of threefolding, however, can be brought into relation to the striving of the Templars, which helps make the answer to the question more concrete.

The Templars did not yet know freedom, equality and brotherhood in the sense outlined by Rudolf Steiner for social life. At that time everything was still one, in a certain sense. They had detached themselves from State and Church, but their supra-national organization and religious life were closely connected because of the unity of the Order. Their economic activities were still fully based on landed property. The administration of justice and their spiritual life were in their own hands but, apart from the initiation knowledge possessed by the knights, there was no difference with the world outside the Order. Brotherhood did not exist in the form of associations of producers, distributors and consumers, because such associations did not yet exist. Brotherliness and equality were given through the monastic vow and the rules of the Order. Their intensive prayer life did connect the Templars directly with the divine world, but freedom as a creative capacity of the soul was not yet developed. To that extent their social-economic activity in European countries did not differ in principle from that of the medieval monastic Orders such as Cluny and Citeaux.

There was, however, a profound difference caused by the fact that these monks were also knights, that they built more fortresses than churches, but that in social life they transformed this *martial power* into *mercurial movement*. This determined the way they handled money, which was different from the usual way of the time, and also from the way it is done in our current world of banking. The money they possessed in gold and silver in unheard-of quantities, as well as an immeasurable wealth of personal and landed property—everything belonged to the Order and not to individuals. The Order stood in the service of Christ, just as each member personally stood in His service by the *offering of his blood*.

They regulated the circulation of money in such a way that it could flow like a nourishing bloodstream through the economic, cultural, and even political life, but governed by the intention of their principle: without any self-seeking motives. Also, the supra-national character of their organization originated in the complete surrender of the Order as a whole and of the members as individuals to the Christ Being as *the representative of humanity in its entirety*, not in outer sacramentalism, but in inner truth and self-worth.

The Templars could therefore be considered as precursors of threefolding in regard to the way they worked with money. In Rudolf Steiner's threefolding, money also has to play a completely different role than in a capitalistic or communist (state-capitalistic) system. Handling money unselfishly in the sense of a nourishing process in a macro-social context, and not as a way to accumulate power, is a prerequisite for the concept of threefolding.

This is precisely the crucial point: a social practice that rests on service to the Christ Being, separation of money from self-interest—that is what the Templars have given us as an example, and that is indeed the genuine foundation of Steiner's social impulse. It is not so much in its structure, as it is in the functional aspect of threefolding that the methodology of the Templars can serve us as an example, and thus we may speak with a certain cautiousness of a continuation of the task of the Templars.

But the Christian principle of unconditional service to the Redeemer is not really within reach for the modern human being. In the Middle Ages people could evoke this through their feeling life. We have to go another way, the way of insight. Through the truth of spiritual content we find the connection with Christ. It is the way of freedom. To give unconditional service to Christ and at the same time make unconditional freedom real is Michaelic Christianity.

One of the essays Rudolf Steiner wrote for the periodical *Luzifer* in 1905 contains what is called his fundamental social law:[128]

> In a community of human beings working together, the well-being of the community will be the greater, the less the individual claims for himself the proceeds of the work he has himself done; i.e., the more of these proceeds he makes over to his fellow workers, and the more his own requirements are satisfied, not out of his own work done, but out of the work done by others.

Not only must the Christian unselfishness Steiner expressed in this law grow through insight into a feeling, a social instinct; also the idea of a threefold social order is a Christian truth that must be thought through as a 'gospel of knowing insight' before it can become operative. Social threefolding is humanity's invisible temple of the future, because it is the image and sheath of the threefold human being. Both conceptions belong together and flow out of the source of the 'hidden knowing' that is irradiated by the central Christ mystery.

The overwhelming force of evil that has turned against this is involuntary testimony of the truth of the above.

7. World Future

In 1911 Rudolf Steiner spoke in a lecture about the working of the Christ Being on earth since the Mystery of Golgotha as an upbuilding force of renewal, whereas we can characterize the opposite forces of destruction, in which demonic beings work, as anti-Christian.[129] From this lecture one has the impression that the upward movement of development, which is identical to the progressive working of Christ—an etherization, a spiritualization of matter that will liberate humanity and the earth from the density and fetters of physical-material existence—signifies at the same time a fall for the cosmic forces that are still lying *under* today's physical-material nature.

Although we certainly have to view this sub-nature as the sphere of evil, we are compelled to use the forces of destruction in order that the earth will go under as a material 'thing' in a process of spiritualization: '... in order that man may become free of the earth and that the earth's body may fall away'. Steiner distinguishes three regions of sub-nature in which different kinds of forces work, namely, electricity, magnetism, and 'a third force that will affect civilization in a still more miraculous way'. In the question-and-answer session following the lecture he said about this third power:

> ... an even more terrible force—which it will not be possible to keep hidden very much longer—is generated. It can only be hoped that when this force comes to be known—a force we must conceive as far, far stronger than the most violent electrical discharge—it can only be hoped that before some inventor gives this force into the hands of humankind, human beings will no longer have left anything immoral in them.

We may assume that this third force has in the meantime been given to mankind in the form of nuclear energy, and we know that Steiner's wish regarding the morality of human beings has remained unfulfilled. Humanity has therefore fallen into the ambivalent situation that, on the one hand, we are forced to build up, or preserve, our culture with destructive powers and, on the other hand, before having developed the necessary moral maturity we are forced to deal prematurely with the kinds of forces that can lead to total annihilation of the earth and humanity. Add to this the fact that these destructive forces are in the hands of people who are completely governed by national considerations, which by definition virtually precludes all morality.

The attack against humanity that began in Gondishapur in the seventh century, and was continued early in the fourteenth century, developed in the twentieth century a third wave which, without a doubt, has a decisive character. We may presume that the premature invention of the 'third force', before a sufficient level of moral balance had evolved in humanity, forms part of this third wave.

The destructive power of the third sub-earthly sphere is the realm of the Asuras, evil beings that far exceed the luciferic and ahrimanic hosts in violence and evil intentions.[130] Compared with the 'triple alliance' of the powers of evil, which are now unfolding their activity, the good and positive human element looks like a mere piece of straw that will be washed away in a churning stream. There are many people who feel called to try and build dams to contain this churning stream of violence and destruction, for instance, through external actions such as protests, demonstrations, petitions, et cetera. These are often impressive acts. They show that many thousands of people all over the world are of good will, but they are mostly inspired by fear and disgust, by an elementary feeling of 'I don't want to perish in this way' or 'I want my children to live in a peaceful world.' Will they have any effect, when in opposition to the calculations of the evil powers there are no free deeds of people who have developed an inner force of altruism and creative morality that can stand up to the frightful power of evil?

And does humanity stand all alone in this gigantic battle, or may we expect help of the good spiritual powers? In Chapter 6 it was pointed out that the Mystery of Golgotha took place 333 years earlier than was planned by the divine world. This occurred to meet the attack of Gondishapur with a divine prophylaxis: by the sacrificial deed of Christ the human soul became less closely bound to the perishable body and more strongly to the imperishable spirit.

When in the beginning of the fourteenth century the power of evil culminated for the second time in the impulse that is indicated with the number 666, it seems as if no comparable prophylaxis took place. Yet, there certainly was a preventive influence. Esoteric Christianity, the Grail stream, everything that based itself on the Mystery of Golgotha, exerted a spiritualizing influence on mankind throughout the Middle Ages and, in so doing, acted as a kind of defence against the second attack. But as we saw in the case of the Templars, this spiritualization always ran the danger of being infiltrated by Lucifer, who tries to estrange us human beings from our true destiny on earth.

Currently, in 2020, we are in the third wave that began toward the end of the twentieth century. Was there nothing that preceded this wave that formed a counterforce against evil? There certainly was. What preceded it was the most important event in the twentieth century, namely the Second Coming of Christ in the etheric world, not in a physical appearance such as once in Palestine, but in the form in which He appeared to Paul before Damascus—an etheric figure radiating light, who reveals Himself not only visually, but also through words.

Rudolf Steiner described this Second Coming of Christ for the first time in his Mystery Drama *The Portal of Initiation*, in which the seer Theodora beholds the etheric appearance of Christ and relates to the persons around her the words this appearance spoke.[131] Subsequently, Steiner discussed it in many lectures and he named a year as the beginning of the time when the etheric Christ would begin to reveal Himself on earth, first to a few people, then gradually to more and more in the course of the coming centuries.[132] The year he named was 1933, the same year that Adolf Hitler came to power in Germany marking the prelude to the third attack of evil.

The appearance of the etheric Christ awakes in human beings the germ of a new clairvoyance that will in time replace the current intellectual consciousness. In Rudolf Steiner's statements about this subject we also find an emphasis on the comforting, helping force that emanates from the etheric Christ. How many people have had an encounter with the etheric Christ since 1933 is very hard to know, because such experiences are not usually written down or published. But in the work of the French author Simone Weil (1909-1944) we can find a very clear description of such an encounter with Christ.[133] Also the experience of George Ritchie can probably be counted among such Damascus revelations.[134] And in the 1970s a book appeared in Sweden reporting that more than a hundred people had seen Christ.[135]

The new possibility to meet the Christ Being leads to an experience that initially is bestowed on just an occasional person as a blessing. Of course, this blessing has a profound significance for these people, but in most cases they are likely to relate this significance only to their own personal development. However, to realize that in these intimate personal experiences *world future* wants to germinate, and in order to enable the counterweight against the powers of evil that is given with the Second Coming of Christ in the etheric to work as a moral-spiritual force in human society, something more is needed.

What is needed is insight, clarity of consciousness that is at the same time a fathoming of the depths of our own human essence. Many people are eager to come into action and immediately do something to counter evil in the world. But we actually see only a little sector of the total circle of reality. We have to expand our knowing to the hidden sectors of the circle, because the driving forces of what happens in the world lie there, in that hidden part.

A new Grail quest is needed, and in our time it has to take the form of knowledge. The knowledge of the Grail that has appeared in the form of Anthroposophy is inextricably connected with the mystery of the Second Coming of Christ. But this knowledge does not just 'happen' to anyone; it has to be sought and, in a certain respect, has to be conquered through intensive thinking. Although this thinking does take place in our normal consciousness, it has a somewhat different character than conventional intellectual thinking. The latter is bound to the organ of the brain; one might also say, to falling matter. For it is known that our nervous system is subject to a continual death process. For this reason, the kind of thinking that only makes use of the nervous matter of the brain can understand nothing but the falling, material side of the world.

Thinking that wants to grasp upward development has to loosen itself from the brain, just as a master violinist is able to let the music sound out of the space and not out of the little box of his instrument. This 'body-free' thinking engages the will much more than conventional thinking usually does, which has a more reflective function and is therefore more passive. It may seem as if this 'will-filled' thinking would be subjective and therefore not exact, but that is only so when viewed from the point of view of the materialistic thinker.

The experience of impotence, which the intellect necessarily has to have when it comes to the boundary where the sensory-rational and the supersensible are separated from each other, continually pushes the intellect back into its own illusions, of which this purported objectivity is one of the most deceptive. This experience of the boundary is actually a phenomenon of fear. But there is no reason why thinking that has the courage to cross the consciousness barrier in order to take in revelations about the spiritual side of the world, would have to sacrifice exactness and objectivity. Only, it is less 'physically determined'; it develops the character of a capacity to perceive spiritual realities.

In Goethe we can see how this kind of thinking, which he called 'perceptive power of discernment', is developed, namely by careful sensory observation, not only of details, but especially of the whole, and by strongly holding back our rational, analytical thinking. In other words, we need to hold back all forms of theorizing. In lieu of a theorizing nature, thinking then has a more meditative character. Because of this, together with their sensory appearance, phenomena also begin to reveal their spiritual essence. Goethe said: 'Everything in the realm of facts is already theory.'

In this activity, which becomes considerably more intense in pure meditation, thinking slowly loosens itself from the falling matter of the brain. The mobility that thinking thus acquires makes a very first step possible, an extremely modest, but also extremely important beginning of a new form of clairvoyance which, in contrast with the old dreamlike clairvoyance of ancient humanity, will lead to free, clearly conscious imaginations.

The question may be raised of whether modern Grail science presents itself exclusively in the form of Steiner's Anthroposophy. By nature, Anthroposophy will not answer this question in a dogmatic way. The Time Spirit, Michael, also inspires people who don't know spiritual science in its anthroposophical form. Besides this form, other forms are conceivable, and the new Damascus experience is certainly not reserved for people with an anthroposophical outlook—witness the examples given above. However, so far I have not become aware of a philosopher or spiritual leader in our time whose work comes close to Steiner's Anthroposophy in universality, depth, and exactitude. Compared with the truth and reality of these spiritual insights the question is ultimately not an essential one. Most of the time the problem is only raised to evade or entrap Anthroposophy.

Just as with all essential things, the point here is not what people think or what their views are, but the reality of the spirit. The intellect always demands proof, but the living spirit does not let itself be proven by the intellect; it wants to be recognized and experienced in its working and reality.

When we review the pre-Christian and Christian times that we have contemplated in this book as the history of the Temple and the Grail—and today we are witnesses of an apocalyptic crisis such as so far has not happened in post-Atlantean times—we have to pose the weighty question of what is really needed so that the future of the world can form itself in a positive sense? In the section about *The Invisible Temple* in Chapter 3, and also elsewhere in this book, we spoke about the future in relation to the evolution of the human being. The question can only be satisfactorily answered if we know what the human being is. I don't mean that we need to formulate a definition of the human being, but that in our consciousness we can form a true picture, and not a illusory one, of what it is to be human, as well as of the possible meaning of being human in the world as a whole.

To arrive at this we could put together a compendium of all philosophical views of the human being, which would give us a wide variety of ideas and scientific points of view. We would probably have to come to the conclusion that it is impossible to solve the riddle of the human being in this way. Do we then acquiesce in this conclusion, which also implies that we cannot come to know what kind of future is needed for the world? Or do we have the courage to realize that such a scientific compendium is completely irrelevant and the method therefore useless?

I think that is indeed what we have to do.

When we then call in the help of Grail science, which was of course lacking in the compendium, we first have to view the phenomenon of the human being in a relatively simple manner. Without adhering to any pre-set theory we see then that human beings relate to the world in three ways. We have to do with a world 'below' us, the three realms of nature; we have to do with our fellow humans, a world around us; and with a world 'above' us, a divine world. Even when we deny the third one as a reality, we reveal through this very denial a relationship with that world, albeit a negative one. In addition, we have to do with ourselves, and between the relationship human beings have with themselves and with the world there exists a profound connection.

Now, it is not difficult to recognize that today's so-called civilized person suffers from dysfunction in all three relationships. We are in the process of destroying nature, which is 'below' us and nourishes us, by exploiting it. It takes the greatest effort to curb our egoism in our relationships with our fellow human beings; most of the time we don't succeed in this anymore. And finally, there is a profound disturbance in our relationship with a higher, divine world.

Just as we often do not realize what health really is until we are ill, behind this threefold break in relationships we could conjecture what true being-human is like in the world. And then we come to the certainty that restoring the threefold relations with the world is only possible if we trace the cause of the break.

This cause is without any doubt to be found in the emancipation of self-consciousness at the cost of a spiritual conception of the world. This emancipation has been developing since the beginning of the fifteenth century. Human beings increased the spiritual power of their consciousness by energetically denying the spirit in the cosmos, in the human being, and in nature. This denial of the spirit has to be overcome by the conscious I. Why? The threefold break with the world turns out to be accompanied not so much by a loss of moral awareness, but mostly by a paralysis of moral action. It was pointed out in section 1 of this chapter that the 'third attack' is directed against the human will, just as in the fourteenth century the target was the feeling life, and in the seventh century a pernicious acceleration of intellectual thinking.

The denial of the spirit in 869 was a result of the attack on humanity; the evil powers aim at the soul, at the thinking, feeling and willing soul. By cutting the soul off from the spirit and binding it too closely to the material body, one also cuts it off from its source of nourishment, the divine-spiritual world from which all moral influences permeate the human being like a nourishing, up-building stream. This cannot be proven by natural-scientific means for the simple reason that since the beginning of our epoch natural science has emphatically turned away from the spiritual-moral side of the world.

The soul that has sold itself more or less to materialistic natural science—which not only reigns justifiably in its appropriate field of knowledge, but also unjustifiably in virtually all other fields—is at the mercy of the forces of death and decline. This may sound theatrical, but it is a truth that is proven by unprejudiced observation of the world. Even if there is no nuclear war, Western civilization will perish unless a sufficient number of people overcome the denial of the spirit, and I don't mean 'perish' in the sense of a physical annihilation, but a falling more and more into barbarism by growing demonic influences.

When the French economist and historian Jean Gimpel predicted the demise of Western civilization,[136] mainly based on economic insights, he pointed to a number of symptoms that indicate that we are in a dying phase of our culture. One of these symptoms is the great increase in mysticism and occultism. He is reminded of the cultures of Egypt and Rome, which in the phase of their decadence showed a similar development of all kinds of sects as are now inundating our Western culture.

The forms of occultism of that time were degenerations of old wisdom that was cultivated in the ancient mysteries. During the time of the Roman Empire the demonized mysteries were defeated by Christianity. But in a certain sense, Christianity was the most occult of all occultisms. The Mystery of Golgotha was the fulfilment of the old mysteries, and all those who wanted to hold on to the old without a willingness to experience rejuvenation through the Christ impulse necessarily had to fall into decadence and demonic influences.

What presents itself in today's Western culture as mysticism and occultism is in most cases similarly a degeneration of Eastern wisdom that has its roots in ancient oriental mysteries. Just as at the end of Roman times, a rejuvenating, renewing force is only to be expected from the Christ impulse. However, if what flows out of the source of this impulse—a renewed mystery awareness, a renewed occultism, an exact occult science, and not a mystically hidden science—is viewed as a morbid peripheral phenomenon that is one of the many symptoms of downfall, this would be a tragic mistake with far-reaching consequences.

The anti-Christian powers are not only hoping that humanity will make this mistake, they deploy all their forces to prevent human beings from entering into a relationship with Christ. For this reason, they will certainly create their own mysteries on earth that will lead large groups of human beings to develop a new clairvoyance much too early. Once human beings have delegated all thinking activity to computers, their hollowed-out souls will have a strong need for clairvoyance. This will be given them from some source, without effort, as a spontaneous 'initiation' that makes the laborious path of thinking guided by the will and moral development superfluous. And the way to a future in a positive sense will then be cut off or, at least, be strewn with the most difficult obstacles.

To the question of what is really needed so that the future of the world can have a positive form, the only answer is the old mystery word that has never lost its admonishing force: Man, know yourself. No self-knowledge in a trivial sense, but the deepest fathoming of the essence of the human being.

This is not some miracle of political détente in which rulers of West and East shake hands and solemnly declare never to shoot cruise missiles or other nasty weapons at each other. For even if such a miracle happened, development in a positive sense would not be guaranteed. It will never happen through external intervention, because it has to be an inner turnabout that only the free human being can achieve in himself. No peace miracle will really disturb the intentions of the evil powers in their third attack, which threatens to pull humanity out of its 'middle' course but, most of all, clear human thinking about the hidden sectors of the 'circle of reality'. For example, we need to realize that what happens in the world is no coincidence or blind natural mechanism, but *karma*, meaning that everything that happens is governed by the cosmic law of cause and effect in a spiritual sense. And in addition, human individuals need to have true freedom so that out of free insights they can come to constructive deeds of renewal in the middle of a world of violence and downfall.

AFTERWORD

In former times people made pilgrimages to places where famous saints were buried, such as the grave of St. James in Santiago de Compostela, the grave of St. Peter in Rome, or the grave of Jesus Christ in Jerusalem. Remarkably, the fact that this latter grave was empty did not always lead people to the realization that we should not be seeking the dead Christ but the living Christ, who is not far away but very near us.

The medieval pilgrims usually did not travel to the grave of St. John in Ephesus. It soon fell into the hands of the Muslims, but this circumstance is but an external cause for the fact that it did not attract the pilgrims. We may consider it as a symptom, however, as a fact of inner significance, that there is no grave-cult connected with St. John.

Johannine Christianity, the stream of Temple and Grail, is resurrection Christianity. The raising of Lazarus was the sign Christ performed to end the old mysteries and to open the new mysteries in the light of His Resurrection.

Johannine Christianity is Christianity of the future. This future has begun.

To bear testimony to this is the purpose of this book.

NOTES

1 W. J. Stein, *The Ninth Century. World History in the Light of the Holy Grail*, Temple Lodge 1991.

2 W. J. Stein, *England as the Nucleus of the Foundation of Commercial Towns. The Origin of the Lohengrin Saga Traced According to English History*; in: *Present Age*, Vol. I No. 3, London 1936.

3 In Waldorf Schools the principal subjects are taught in so-called blocks. The first two lesson periods of the day are devoted to the same subject for about three to six weeks.

4 Rudolf Steiner wrote four Mystery Dramas that were performed under his direction in Munich in the summer months of 1910 through 1913. See *Four Mystery Dramas*, CW 14, SteinerBooks 2007. The same characters appear in all four dramas, people of Steiner's time who go through a development that leads to spiritual experiences. These dramas continue to be performed regularly in Dornach, Switzerland and elsewhere.

5 Burgenland is an area in Austria south of Wiener Neustadt, bordering on Hungary. Rudolf Steiner spent his childhood years there in Pottschach and Neudörfl.

6 In the vicinity of Eisenstadt (Burgenland) there is an antimony mine, situated between two castles, Schloss Bernstein and Schloss Lockenhaus. See Ita Wegman, *An die Freunde*, Natura Verlag, Switzerland.

7 Manichaeism was a Gnostic movement, founded by Manes, or Mani, (215-276 AD) in which the old mystery wisdom of the East, especially ancient Persia, was connected with Christianity. Of key importance in Mani's teaching is the victory over evil by its redemption. The teaching spread throughout the New-Persian Empire, and from there into China, as well as across North Africa. Another Manichaean stream moved into southern Europe and became known as the Cathars.

8 Rudolf Steiner called a cultural epoch a period that lasts 2160 years, which time span is connected with the precession of the equinox, the position of the sun on March 21, that moves slowly through the zodiac. The equinox is currently in Pisces; before this it was in Aries, before that in Taurus, etc. Rudolf Steiner spoke of seven post-Atlantean epochs occurring after the deluge that destroyed the continent of Atlantis. They are the following:

  1. Ancient Indian epoch—equinox in Cancer, app. 7200-5100 BC
  2. Ancient Persian epoch—equinox in Gemini, app. 5100-2900 BC
  3. Egypto-Chaldean epoch—equinox in Taurus, app. 2900-750 BC
  4. Greco-Roman epoch, including the Middle Ages—equinox in Aries, app. 750 BC-1400 AD

5. Fifth (European?) cultural epoch—equinox in Pisces, app. 1400-3600 AD

6. Slavic epoch—equinox in Aquarius, app. 3600-5700 AD

7. American epoch—equinox in Capricorn, app. 5700-7900 AD.

[9]   Rudolf Steiner, *Macrocosm and Microcosm*, CW 119, and *According to Matthew*, CW 123.

[10] See for instance *An Outline of Esoteric Science*, CW 13.

[11] Rudolf Steiner, *Mystery Knowledge and Mystery Centres*, CW 232; and *World History in the Light of Anthroposophy*, CW 233.

[12] Translator's note: According to a note by the author, the Dionysian mystery cult and the Mithras cult that is related to it are the ritual forms underlying the Christian Mass. He refers to Robert Spörri's book, *Vom Geiste des Urchristentum*. However, Spörri refers to a statement by Rudolf Steiner that the Mass is an 'imitation' of the four phases of the mystery initiations. Rudolf Steiner said in his lecture of March 17, 1905 (*The Christian Mystery*, CW 97, lecture 1) that the Mass originated in the Persian and Egyptian mysteries; later, on April 24, 1917 (*Building Stones for an Understanding of the Mystery of Golgotha*, CW 175, lecture 8): 'The Mass and all that is related to it is a continuation and development of the Mithras mysteries, blended to some extent with the Eleusinian mysteries.'

[13] Rudolf Steiner, *Christianity as Mystical Fact*, CW 8, chapter 8.

[14] Rudolf Steiner, *An Esoteric Cosmology*, CW 94, chapter 7.

[15] Rudolf Steiner, *The Theosophy of the Rosicrucians*, CW 99, chapter 14.

[16] The last sentence is usually translated as 'And from that hour the disciple took her to his own home'. However, it really means 'into his own being'. The Greek phrase used here, *eis ta idia*, means 'into his own'.

[17] Rudolf Steiner spoke about the mystery of the threefold sun in connection with the Palladium in *Cosmosophy*, Vol. II, CW 208, lecture of November 6, 1921.

[18] Rudolf Steiner spoke often about this subject. I only mention here *Building Stones for an Understanding of the Mystery of Golgotha*, CW 175.

[19] In 529 Justinian closed the 'pagan' schools of philosophy in Athens, including the Academy of Plato that had existed for close to a thousand years.

[20] Rudolf Steiner, *According to Luke*, CW 114, Anthroposophic Press 2001.

[21] Emil Bock, *The Three Years*, Floris Books.

[22] Comparing the two genealogies of Jesus given by Matthew and Luke one clearly sees that the messianic line splits into two branches, one via David's son Solomon (the lineage given by Matthew) and the other via David's son Nathan (a lesser known, priestly figure). Luke gives the latter lineage in his Gospel.

[23] Emil Bock, *The Childhood of Jesus*, Floris Books 1997.

[24] Rudolf Steiner, *Esoteric Christianity and the Mission of Christian Rosenkreutz*, CW 130, Rudolf Steiner Press 1984.

[25] See Christine Gruwez, *Mani & Rudolf Steiner*, SteinerBooks 2014.

26 Jacques de Voragine, *The Golden Legend*, Princeton University Press 2012.

27 Rudolf Steiner, *The Spiritual Foundation of Morality*, CW 155, lecture of May 29, 1912.

28 Rudolf Steiner, *Building Stones for an Understanding of the Mystery of Golgotha*, CW 175, lecture 1.

29 Rudolf Steiner, *Mystery Knowledge and Mystery Centres*, CW 232, lecture 10.

30 H. H. Schoeffler, *The Academy of Gondishapur*, Mercury Press 1995.

31 The *Fama Fraternitatis* by Valentin Andreae appeared in Germany in 1615. Together with the *Chymical Wedding of Christian Rosenkreutz* it is the most important written document about the original Rosicrucian movement. The *Fama* describes the life of Christian Rosenkreutz.

32 Rudolf Steiner, *Karmic Relationships*, Vol. I, CW 235, Rudolf Steiner Press, lecture of March 16, 1924.

33 Osman was Emir in Turkey and founded the Ottoman Empire about 1300, which encompassed the former Greek areas of the eastern Roman Empire. Timur, also called Tamerlane (1336-1405), a Mongolian despot, conquered a gigantic empire in Asia. Both men were fanatical Muslims.

34 Rudolf Steiner, *The Philosophy of Thomas Aquinas*, and *The Redemption of Thinking*, CW 74.

35 Rudolf Steiner, *Cosmic Memory*, CW 11.

36 Rudolf Meyer, *Nordische Apokalypse*, Stuttgart 1967.

37 See Hans Gsänger, *Die Externsteine*, Freiburg 1964.

38 Hans Gsänger, *Das heidnische Irland*, Freiburg 1969.

39 Around 500 BC the Brythonic-speaking Celts came to the British Isles; the Welsh and Cornish dialects go back to their language. The Goidelic-speaking Celts came about 1000 years earlier; their language developed into Irish and Scottish Gaelic.

40 Hans Gsänger, *Das christliche Irland*, Freiburg 1970.

41 Rudolf Steiner, *The Mission of the Individual Folk Souls*, CW 121, Rudolf Steiner Press 1970.

42 Rudolf Steiner, *Where and How Does One Find the Spirit?*, CW 57, lecture of May 6, 1909.

43 Rudolf Steiner, *According to Luke*, CW 114, Anthroposophic Press 2001.

44 Rudolf Steiner, *The East in the Light of the West*, CW 113, Garber 1986, lecture of August 31, 1909.

45 Baigent, Leigh & Lincoln, *The Holy Blood and the Holy Grail*, London 1982.

46 Louis Charpentier, *Les Mystères Templiers* and *The Mysteries of Chartres Cathedral*.

47 These yearbooks were published by the Natural-Scientific Section of the School of Spiritual Science in Dornach.

48 Rudolf Steiner, *Approaching the Mystery of Golgotha*, CW 152, SteinerBooks 2006.

49 Wolfram von Eschenbach, *Parsifal*, IX, 469, translated by H. M. Mustard & C. E. Passage, Vintage Books 1961.

50   Robert de Boron, *Joseph of Arimathea*, Rudolf Steiner Press 1995.

51   Sigismund von Gleich, *Marksteine der Kulturgeschichte II*, Stuttgart 1963.

52   Rudolf Steiner, *Christ and the Spiritual World. The Search for the Holy Grail*, CW 149, Rudolf Steiner Press 1963.

53   Cadmus, who was a Phoenician, later brought the mysteries of Hebron to Greece which, as the mysteries of the Kabiri on the island of Samothrace, had a profound influence in the Greek world, particularly on Aristotle.

54   Rudolf Steiner, *From Jesus to Christ*, CW 131, Rudolf Steiner Press 1973, lecture VIII, p. 138 and 140.

55   Rudolf Steiner, *According to Matthew*, CW 123, Anthroposophic Press 2002.

56   Ephraim the Syrian, *The Book of the Cave of Treasures*, English translation, London 1927.

57   Rudolf Steiner, *The Temple Legend*, CW 93, Rudolf Steiner Press 1985, lecture of May 22, 1905.

58   Rudolf Steiner, *Mythen und Sagen. Okkulte Zeichen und Symbole*, CW 101, Dornach 1992, lecture of December 28, 1907.

59   Op. cit. note 57.

60   Ibid.

61   Emil Bock, *Genesis*, Floris Books 183, p. 49.

62   Op. cit. note 57.

63   Ibid.

64   Heinrich Schliemann (1822-1890) not only excavated Troy in northwestern Turkey, but also Mycenae and Tiryns on the Peloponnese. His achievements proved that Homer's epics are grounded in historical truth.

65   Rudolf Meyer, *Zum Raum wird hier die Zeit*, Stuttgart 1980.

66   Rudolf Steiner, *Ideas for a New Europe*, CW 194, Rudolf Steiner Press 1992, lecture 2, p. 16.

67   Lars-Ivar Ringbom, *Graltempel und Paradies*, Stockholm 1980.

68   Rudolf Steiner, *The Mystery of the Trinity and the Mystery of the Spirit*, CW 214, Anthroposophic Press 1991.

69   Rudolf Steiner, *The Principle of Spiritual Economy in Connection with Questions of Reincarnation*, CW 109, Anthroposophic Press 1986.

70   Hans Jantzen, *High Gothic*, Princeton University Press 1984.

71   *The New Testament, A Rendering by Jon Madsen*, Floris Books 1994.

72   Wolfram indicates that Herzeleide, Parsifal's mother, lived 11 generations before his time around 1200. Deducting 11 generations of about 30 years each from 1200, the approximate date of Wolfram's epic,we arrive in the ninth century.

73   Rudolf Steiner, *Supersensible Influences in the History of Mankind*, CW 216, Rudolf Steiner Publishing Co. 1956, lecture 6.

74   See note 39.

75   Hans Gsänger, *Irland, Insel des Abel. Das heidnische Irland*, Freiburg 1969.

76   Rudolf Steiner, *Foundations of Esotericism*, CW 93a, Rudolf Steiner Press 1983, lecture 3; and Ernst Märti, *The Four Ethers*, Schaumburg Publications 1984.

77   Peronnik is a character in Breton folklore whose story parallels that of the Welsh Peredur and the Arthurian Percevel. Peronnik is a poor country orphan who, after many knights have failed, enters the castle Kerglas of the wicked magician Rogéar in order to retrieve the stolen lance and cup. When he restores the purloined treasures to the rightful king, peace and prosperity return to the kingdom. Source: oxfordreference.com.

78   See note 73.

79   Rudolf Steiner, *Karmic Relationships*, Vol. VI, CW 240, Rudolf Steiner Press 1975, lecture 6

80   The Order of St. James, also called Order of Santiago, was approved by Pope Alexander III in 1175. It protected the pilgrims on their way to and from Santiago de Compostela from attacks by Spanish Moors.

81   The three articles are: *The Revival of the Arthurian Legend in the Fifteenth Century* (1934), *Basilius Valentinus in the Context of Arthurian Legend* (1935), and *Portugal as the Preparer of the British Mission* (1936). They can be found in: *The Death of Merlin*, a selection made by Thomas Meyer of articles and lectures by Walter Johannes Stein, Floris Books 2008.

82   Ibid., *Basilius Valentinus in the Context of Arthurian Legend*.

83   See Johannes Tautz, *W. J. Stein, A Biography*, Temple Lodge Press 1990.

84   Ibid.

85   Ibid.

86   *The Revival of the Arthurian Legend in the Fifteenth Century*. See note 81.

87   W. J. Stein, *Tristan and Isolde against the Background of Greek Mythology*, in: *The Death of Merlin*, Floris Books 2008.

88   In the first few centuries of Christianity people who wanted to convert to Christianity went through a kind of preparation to be 'instructed in the Word'.

89   Bernard de Clairvaux, *In Praise of the New Knighthood*, Cistercian Publications 2000.

90   Rudolf Steiner, *Inner Impulses of Evolution*, CW 171, Anthroposophic Press 1984.

91   Rudolf Steiner, *Rosicrucian Wisdom*, CW 99, and *The Gospel of St. John*, CW 103, and others.

92   Rudolf Steiner, *The Course of My Life*, CW 28, Anthroposophic Press 1951.

93   Veltman's note: I suspect an error here. Such a *tempietto* does not exist in Santiago but in Tomar, Portugal.

94   Op. cit. note 57, lecture of May 22, 1905.

95   Jean Gimpel, *The Cathedral Builders*, Perennial 1992.

96   Rudolf Steiner, *Art History*, CW 292, SteinerBooks 2016, lecture of October 22, 1917.

97   Op. cit. note 57.

98   René Guénon, *The Esotericism of Dante*, Sophia Perennis 2004.

99   J. H. Probst-Biraben, *Les Mystères des Templiers*, Nice 1947.

[100] Dante Alighieri, *The Divine Comedy*, transl. by John Ciardi, New American Library 2003.

[101] Op. cit. note 57.

[102] Op. cit. note 26.

[103] Op. cit. note 57, lecture of May 29, 1905.

[104] Rudolf Steiner, *Die Mission der neuen Geistesoffenbarung*, CW 127.

[105] The apocalyptic events affecting the Order of the Templars took place a few years earlier, but we should not be looking for an exact match in the rhythm of 666 years.

[106] Op. cit. note 1.

[107] Rudolf Steiner, *Spiritual Guidance of Man and Humanity*, CW 15, Anthroposophic Press 1950, chapter 2.

[108] Rudolf Steiner, *Esoteric Christianity and the Mission of Christian Rosenkreutz*, CW 130, Rudolf Steiner Press 2005, lecture of September 27, 1911.

[109] Ibid.

[110] Ibid.

[111] Rudolf Steiner, *Correspondence and Documents 1905-1925*, CW 262, Rudolf Steiner Press 1988, p. 16.

[112] Ibid.

[113] For the inspiration of Lessing, see Rudolf Steiner, *Karmic Relationships*, Vol. I, CW 235.

[114] A. Wertheim-Aymès, *Hieronymus Bosch*, Amsterdam, Van Ditmar 1957.

[115] Rudolf Steiner, *Gegenwärtiges und Vergangenes im Menschengeiste*, CW 167.

[116] Karl Heyer, *Geschichtsimpulse des Rosenkreuzertums*, Kressbronn 1959.

[117] Op. cit. note 108, lecture of December 18, 1912.30

[118] The complete quotation from *The Ballad of East and West* is as follows:
> Oh, East is East and West is West, and never the twain shall meet
> Till Earth and Sky stand presently at God's great judgment seat;
> But there is neither East nor West, Border nor Breed, nor Birth,
> When two strong men stand face to face, though they come from the ends of the earth!

[119] Op. cit. note 15.

[120] Op. cit. note 90.

[121] Friedrich Schiller, *Letters upon the Aesthetic Education of Man*, Kessinger Publishing 2004.

[122] Rudolf Steiner, *The Occult Movement in the Nineteenth Century and its Relation to Modern Culture*. CW 254, Rudolf Steiner Press 1973.

[123] Op. cit. note 121.

[124] Rudolf Steiner, *Intuitive Thinking as a Spiritual Path*, CW 4, Anthroposophic Press 1995.

[125] See Rudolf Grosse, *The Christmas Foundation; the Beginning of a New Cosmic Age*, Steiner Book Centre 1984, p. 95.

[126] Op. cit. note 90.

[127] Rudolf Steiner, *Anthroposophical Leading Thoughts*, CW 26.

128 Rudolf Steiner, *Anthroposophy and the Social Question*, CW 34, Anthroposophic Press 1958.

129 Rudolf Steiner, *Esoteric Christianity and the Mission of Christian Rosenkreutz*, CW 130, Rudolf Steiner Press 2005, lecture of October 1, 1911.

130 Rudolf Steiner, *The Being of Man and His Future Evolution*, CW 107, Steiner Book Centre 1981.

131 Rudolf Steiner, *The Portal of Initiation*, in: *Four Mystery Dramas*, CW 14, SteinerBooks 2007.

132 Rudolf Steiner, *The Reappearance of Christ in the Etheric*, a collection ed. by Gilbert Church and Alice Wulsin, SteinerBooks 2003.

133 Simone Weil, *Waiting for God*, Harper 2009.

134 George Ritchie, *Return from Tomorrow*, Revell 1996.

135 G. Hillerdal & Berndt Gustafsson, *We Experienced Christ*, Temple Lodge 2016; or. title: *He näkivät Jeesuksen*.

136 Jean Gimpel, *Ultime rapport sur le destin de l'occident*, Paris 1988.

A note from the publisher

For more than a quarter of a century, **Temple Lodge Publishing** has made available new thought, ideas and research in the field of spiritual science.

Anthroposophy, as founded by Rudolf Steiner (1861-1925), is commonly known today through its practical applications, principally in education (Steiner-Waldorf schools) and agriculture (biodynamic food and wine). But behind this outer activity stands the core discipline of spiritual science, which continues to be developed and updated. True science can never be static and anthroposophy is living knowledge.

Our list features some of the best contemporary spiritual-scientific work available today, as well as introductory titles. So, visit us online at **www.templelodge.com** and join our emailing list for news on new titles.

If you feel like supporting our work, you can do so by buying our books or making a direct donation (we are a non-profit/charitable organisation).

office@templelodge.com

TEMPLE LODGE

For the finest books of Science and Spirit